Chosen among Women

Chosen among Women

Mary and Fatima

in Medieval Christianity

and Shi`ite Islam

Mary F. Thurlkill

University of Notre Dame Press

Notre Dame, Indiana

Library of Congress Cataloging-in-Publication Data
Thurlkill, Mary F., 1969–
Chosen among women : Mary and Fatima in medieval Christianity
and Shi`ite Islam / Mary F. Thurlkill.
p. cm.
Includes bibliographical references (p.   ) and index.
ISBN-13: 978-0-268-04231-8 (pbk. : alk. paper)
ISBN-10: 0-268-04231-4 (pbk. : alk. paper)
1. Mary, Blessed Virgin, Saint—History of doctrines—Middle Ages, 600–1500.
2. Fatimah, d. 632 or 3. 3. Shi`ah—Doctrines—History. I. Title
BT612.T48   2007
232.91—dc22
2007033025

For Edmund and Geraldine Thurlkill

And for
my students,
who always challenge and inspire

Contents

Acknowledgments

When time for writing these acknowledgments approached, I noticed a sharp increase in my propensity for procrastination. I have lived with Mary and Fatima for so long, providing the final touches to the manuscript feels like a death of sorts, not only the end of a research project, but also the loss of a part of myself. I first met medieval Mary and Fatima when I was an undergraduate at the University of Arkansas; they followed me to Indiana University for my graduate work and to Southern Arkansas University for my first academic post. They remain close by, now at the University of Mississippi, as I begin the tenure process. The Blessed Virgin and Fatima al-Zahra have remained my constants as I moved across various state lines, making new friends and leaving old ones and learning to face the challenges of life in academia. It is with profound humility and sadness that I now complete my time spent with their lives and legacies and introduce them to my readers.

Because this study has consumed me for so many years, there are many people to thank for their continued support and encouragement. First, however, I should like to recognize the generosity of Southern Arkansas University and Ole Miss; both institutions provided summer research funds that allowed me time to write. Various colleagues and friends also made this book possible: Paul Babbitt, who counted my paradigm shifts; David Brakke and Dyan Elliot, who read early drafts; Jan and Bonnie Duke; Chris and Maren Foley; Ben Johnson; the Rasmussen clan, who protected my sanity; William Tucker; Mary Jo Weaver; and James Willis.

I especially want to thank two mentors and friends, Lynda Coon and Scott Alexander. I met Lynda when I was an undergraduate, and she challenged my notions of history, religion, and gender. During her classes, I reexamined everything I thought I knew about myself and the world around me. She continued to offer advice—and sometimes threats—throughout my graduate career; and she provided a critical reading of the manuscript in its final stages. Her comments revealed her stunningly sophisticated insights that compelled me to rewrite and revise in imitation of her own scholarship (though not always success-fully). Scott Alexander, my mentor at Indiana University, introduced me to the mysteries of the Arabic language and guided me with ques-tions and comments during hours of conversation about Shi`ism, the holy family, and comparative religion. I remain in awe of his breadth of knowledge, generous spirit, and masterful teaching. In view of Lynda and Scott's constant encouragement, it seems disingenuous to present this work as wholly my own—I can hear their comments, opinions, and critiques blending with my analysis in conversation (and sometimes dis-agreement) about medieval hagiography, holiness, and gender. Without their voices, this book would not exist.

Preliminary Notes

Translations

The Latin and Arabic transliterations for all extensive quotations are provided in the notes. Modern translations that I consulted are identified following the appropriate citation.

I have attempted to render all important Latin and Arabic terms into English. I have retained two Arabic designations that, because of their mystical bent, escape a literal translation: *nur*, or light, is the preexistent form of Muhammad and the Imams who resided on Allah's throne in paradise; *ahl al-bayt*, or people of the house, refers to Muhammad's family. According to Shi'ite theology, Allah awards the Prophet's family, the *ahl al-bayt*, special authority and status among humanity. The appendix includes a glossary of Arabic terms for nonspecialists.

Transliteration

I have standardized as many Arabic transliterations as possible, so I do not use the macron or underdot in the body of the text. I do include all diacritical marks in the notes, following the transliteration guide adhered to by the *International Journal of Middle East Studies*. I do not include diacritics for common words and names; for example, the *ahl al-bayt*'s names are rendered as Muhammad, Fatima, `Ali, Hasan, and Husayn throughout the text and notes.

Dates

The standard Gregorian dating system is employed throughout the work. Therefore, all Islamic dates (AH) are converted to common era (CE).

Introduction

Greetings, favored one! The Lord is with you. . . . Do not be afraid, Mary, for you have found favor with God. (Luke 1.28–30)

Allah has chosen you and purified you and chosen you above women of all peoples. (Qur'an 3.42)

According to both Christianity and Islam, the angel Gabriel delivered the above pronouncements to Mary, informing her that she would give birth to a son even though she was a virgin. Mary obeyed God's will and bore the Christians' God-Man and the Muslims' great prophet, `Isa/Jesus. Shi`ite tradition relates that Gabriel repeated the same Qur'anic pronouncement to another favored woman, Fatima, the prophet Muhammad's daughter, also known as *Maryam al-kubra*, or Mary the Greater.[1] For Shi`ites God chose both women for a sublime purpose, mothers of an exalted progeny; yet Fatima, as *Maryam al-kubra*, surpasses Mary in both purity and divine favor.

Mary and Fatima afford scholars of medieval Christianity, Islam, and gender studies an opportunity to examine feminine imagery in sacred traditions. Christian authors elevated Mary as Christ's mother, and Shi`ite authors recognized Fatima's offspring as their community's infallible

1

leaders (called Imams). Both religions asserted the holy women's wondrous bodies and deeds without compromising their more conservative feminine ideals. As Mary and Fatima performed miracles, rewarded the pious, and punished the heretical, they also remained submissive, chaste, and immaculate.

Mary and Fatima provided more than just models for feminine compliance, however; these female exemplars also betray complex political, social, and religious agendas. Late antique and early medieval Christian authors (c. 200–750 CE) identified Mary with the church and labeled those outside as heretics. Early medieval Shi`ite authors (c. 700–1000 CE) explained that Fatima led her supporters to paradise and consigned her enemies to the hellfire. Hagiographers and theologians alike imbued Mary and Fatima with symbolic markers of political, theological, and communal identity as they redefined their societies.

In late antiquity and the early Middle Ages, church fathers and hagiographers transformed Mary into a symbol of sectarian identity. The fifth-century theologians Augustine and Ambrose assimilated Mary to the Christian church: both remained pure and spotless, yet fecund with converts. Mary symbolized an emerging orthodoxy (or, right theology); those labeled heterodox remained outside her maternal care.

The early Merovingian Kingdom (c. 400–750 CE) also employed Mary as a symbol of unity and orthodoxy. The Merovingians revolutionized the late Roman Empire in Gaul. They were a Frankish tribe that both supplanted and assimilated Roman rule, Gallo-Roman cultural patterns, and Rome's state religion.[2] When the Franks converted to orthodox Christianity, they infiltrated the church's ruling structures as bishops and further stabilized their sovereignty. As an orthodox Christian kingdom, they separated themselves from their barbarian competitors, the Arian Huns and the Goths.[3] Fourth-century church fathers and theologians had pronounced Arianism a heresy that denied Christ's full divinity; the Merovingians thus became orthodox Christians among a sea of Arian enemies.

Frankish authors proclaimed their unique Christian identity by adopting several Gallo-Roman saints (e.g., Saint Martin of Tours, a fourth-century holy man from Gaul) as well as more ecumenical holy figures (e.g., the Virgin Mary). In their sacred histories and hagiographies Frankish authors also assimilated their holy women to Marian prototypes. Just as the

Virgin Mary nurtured and sustained Christians, Merovingian queens and abbesses mothered their emerging communities and congregations. Some Merovingian bishops and priests even advertised their authority with Marian relics.[4] Marian imagery in the early Middle Ages, prolific yet often subtle, reflected the Franks' Christianization and orthodoxy in the midst of both God and the Merovingians' heretical enemies. By affiliating themselves with Mary, Frankish authors managed to sharpen their communal boundaries without seriously threatening traditional gender expectations.

The proliferation of Fatima imagery also signaled religious and political shifts in the Islamic community by the eighth and ninth centuries. Shi`ite scholars began to outline their basic theological assumptions and tenets, which firmly identified their orthodoxy against other Shi`i groups as well as their Sunni competitors.[5] The Shi`ites acknowledged `Ali, Muhammad's cousin and son-in-law, as the Prophet's chosen successor; they also recognized `Ali's offspring as the true religious authority regardless of any other political ruler. The Shi`a soon disagreed, however, as to who the Imams actually were: some designated five, some seven, and others twelve different figures. They all accepted the Imam as infallible and pure; there was disagreement as to several of the Imams' identities.

As the Shi`ite community honed its sectarian theology regarding the Imamate, it emphasized Fatima's miraculous motherhood. Theologians outlined her attributes to explain the Imams' status: they existed before created time; they were infallible; they possessed divine wisdom. Fatima, the only female among Muhammad's miraculous holy family (the *ahl al-bayt*), supplied the Prophet's sublime progeny and then welcomed others into the group as extended kin. Yet, as in Christianity, male authors simultaneously praised Fatima's virtues while extolling the holy family's masculine dominance. Fatima's presence among the *ahl al-bayt* ultimately depended on her role as Muhammad's daughter, `Ali's wife, and the Imams' mother.

The majority Sunni Muslims, on the other hand, elected the Prophet's friend and companion, Abu Bakr, as the rightful legatee after Muhammad's death. These supporters of Muhammad's companions, instead of his family, eventually founded the Umayyad caliphate (661–750 CE). In the largely Sunni Muslim empire, most Shi`ites openly heeded caliphal rule while they credited the Imams (`Ali and Fatima's descendants) as their true spiritual guides.

Locating Mary and Fatima within these early Christian and Muslim milieus is a difficult task for many reasons. First, a successful comparison brings together sources from two disparate cultures at times of critical shifts in communal and religious identity. There is no historical or geographic symmetry. In the Christian context, Marian imagery appears in the earliest theological treatises and continues into Merovingian circles in western Europe (c. 200–750 CE). In the Muslim context, Fatima imagery becomes particularly prevalent during the ʿAbbasid caliphate (750–1258 CE) and proliferates throughout Shiʿite dynasties in Egypt, Persia, and Yemen. While dissimilar in space and time, both Christian and Muslim audiences struggled to define themselves in a rapidly changing world.

Second, comparing Mary and Fatima depends on vastly different types of sources. Late antiquity and the early medieval period yield a number of ecclesiastical treatises and hagiographies referring to the Virgin. From these texts scholars can glimpse the elite, theological descriptions of Mary alongside the more approachable miracle texts and ritual descriptions. Theologians clearly rely on Mary's miraculous body as they define their Christology; hagiographers subtly elevate Mary as a model for holy women to imitate. Merovingian authors even present many of their queens and abbesses as sublime virgins, styled in Mary's image.

Shiʿite sources that extol Fatima are more difficult to categorize. An ideal cross-cultural comparison would correlate Fatima images in theology and hagiography with their Christian counterparts; unfortunately, no easy parallel exists. Shiʿite theologians and hagiographers alike relied on the transmission of hadith (sayings about the Prophet and his family) to define the Imams' miraculous nature. Hadith collections, often anonymous, reveal the emerging beliefs and teachings esteemed by the early Shiʿa. They provide a theology as well as hagiographic accounts of the Imams' miraculous deeds.

Like their Merovingian counterparts, Shiʿite hagiographers assimilated powerful queens to their idealized Holy Woman. Unlike the Merovingians, who ruled in Gaul, however, Shiʿites lived and ruled throughout the Middle East. Scholars have yet to examine systematically the gendered rhetoric employed by specific Shiʿite communities, particularly how they imagined Fatima. The Ismaʿili queen ʿArwa (d. 1138) ruled Yemen, for example, and she assumed many of Fatima's characteristics.

The Safavid dynasty, founded in sixteenth-century Iran, also styled many of its queens as new Fatimas, with epithets similar to their namesake's. These appellations included *al-zahra* (the radiant), *tahira* (pure), and *ma`suma* (infallible).[6] This study explores the more general Shi`ite beliefs regarding Fatima transmitted through common collections of hadith. It provides a foundation for future, more discrete works that might analyze how and to what purpose specific dynastic leaders chose to transform pious women into their own "Fatima of the age."[7]

The third difficulty of comparing Mary and Fatima within their respective traditions is that male authors often described them with conflicting and paradoxical images.[8] Mary and Fatima were both idealized yet inimitable, chaste yet fecund, intercessors yet submissive handmaids. Such bewildering imagery leaves the historian questioning how Christian and Islamic communities actually viewed women and gender roles.

According to theologians, for example, God elevated Mary and Fatima as venerable mothers and exceptional women. Yet they were aberrations among their sex: part of their charismatic authority stemmed from the fact that God transformed them into pure vessels (a miracle in itself). For Christians Mary held God-made-flesh within her chaste womb and, according to early church fathers, eschewed public activities by confining herself within domestic boundaries.[9] Scholars promoted Mary as the perfect model for all young virgins to imitate: be chaste and stay at home.[10] At the same time, Christian scholars labeled women in late antique and early medieval Christianity as the spiritually depraved daughters of Eve. Women symbolized the sinful flesh finally conquered by Christ's redemptive act. No greater miracle could occur in late antiquity than the transformation of a female into a holy figure. Such a salvific event only emphasized the abundance of God's mercy as such a lowly female sinner received grace.[11]

Islamic theology placed women in an equally precarious role. Classical texts included women among *shayatin* (devilish) forces sent to delude and confuse male Muslims.[12] Islamic rhetoric also equated the female with the base soul (*nafs*) that tempted humanity to sin.[13] Yet Shi`ite scholars also praised Fatima, the prophet Muhammad's daughter, as the mother of the Shi`ite Imams.[14] As matriarch Fatima shared the Imams' privileged status and miraculous gifts; she, uniquely among women, remained ritually pure and divinely inspired.

Both Christian and Muslim theological systems condemned the female body in its impurity and taint while extolling Mary and Fatima as holy vessels for sublime offspring. Hagiographers transformed the two holy women into pristine containers of God's presence, presenting multivalent images of the womb. Early church fathers encouraged believers, both male and female, to become pregnant with God's seed (faith) and produce children (good works) just as Mary conceived Christ in her womb.[15] According to Shi'ite cosmology, Fatima's womb held the *nur* (light) of the Imamate; her purity protected this radiant "semen," and she gave birth to Hasan and Husayn, God's chosen Imams.

Political and sectarian discourse reveals equally contradictory versions of Mary and Fatima in theological texts.[16] Male authors manipulated their holy women's lives and miracles to reflect shifting social and political identities. Nascent Christian and Shi'ite communities associated themselves with these feminine figures and celebrated their miraculous powers. In doing so, these communities formulated and advertised new political boundaries and sectarian divisions.

Mary and Fatima as mothers, quickly synonymous with orthodox (right) doctrine, effectively weaned their communities from hellfire. One medieval exegete associated Fatima's name with the root meaning, ف-ط-م (*f-t-m*), which can mean "to wean."[17] Fatima has the authority to intercede for her family (i.e., the Shi'a) on judgment day and condemn her enemies to eternal hellfire. Hagiographers express that authority through her domestic station as the holy family's sublime matriarch: she cares for her family's earthly needs, cleans the home, feeds her family and neighbors (often through miraculous intervention), and provides wise counsel to her children and husband. Christian Marian imagery also describes a powerful heavenly matriarch, seated at her Son's right hand, ready to intercede for the church and dismiss the heterodox. She gained that position, however, by submitting to God's will as his holy handmaid. Male authors encourage Christian women, including abbesses and secular queens, to imitate that submissive quality. In both cases, the male householder never yields his ultimate authority: the father and sons rule within the *ahl al-bayt*, and the male priest presides over the church.

These theologies and ideologies regarding Mary and Fatima appear not only in sacred narratives but also in material culture.[18] Mary's and Fatima's textual bodies literally assumed built form while appealing more widely to believers' imaginations. Early Christian catacombs and churches displayed images of Mary, glorified as virgin, mother, and bride. Mosque lamps and prayer niches could easily be interpreted as symbolizing Fatima's radiant presence along with the Imams'. Shi`ite amulets shaped as the human hand effectively evoked the *ahl al-bayt*'s intercessory authority. Medieval artists and architects transformed their theological, social, and political symbols into visual form.

This work concentrates on feminine imagery in political, cultural, and theological rhetoric as well as material culture during periods of transformation and conversion. This approach reflects current trends among gender historians to correlate structures of power and authority with the literary and rhetorical nature of feminine imagery. As poststructuralist theory dictates, cultural systems often modify gender categories to accentuate changes in political and social conventions.[19] For scholars of Christianity and Islam, for example, the early medieval shift of Mary and Fatima imagery signals dramatic social, political, and even religious transitions. Male authors employed Mary and Fatima as rhetorical tools in a complex discourse of identity and orthodoxy; they were more than models for women to emulate.

This approach is in sharp contrast to earlier feminist theory and modes of historical inquiry. During the 1970s, feminist historians of early Christianity read late antique and early medieval authors as patriarchal proof texts. Feminist theologians rejected early church writings as misogynistic and oppressive.[20] In the 1980s, more moderate revisionist historians sought to reclaim the church's secret history by revealing the actual lives of pious women. Although women were largely absent from the texts, feminists sought to re-create women's considerable contributions to the early Christian movement.[21]

A feminist hermeneutic concerning women in Islam is more difficult to trace. Works available to Western audiences confine women to apologetic argument, descriptive historiography, or modern political rhetoric.[22] Modern feminists reimagine early Islamic women in an attempt to discourage veiling, segregation, and patriarchal leadership in Muslim societies. Scholars generally ignore the abundant gender imagery and the rhetorical nature of miracle accounts to focus on their own political agendas.

More recent historical methodology attuned to literary criticism and poststructuralist examinations of gender and culture allows for a review of feminine imagery in general and Mary and Fatima in particular. Most Marian scholars, for example, largely neglect the fourth through eighth centuries and focus on the Marian cult's rapid proliferation during the high and late Middle Ages. Scholars of Islam include brief surveys that recount Fatima's exalted position within Shi`ite Islam, yet none move beyond detailed narratives to offer feminist interpretation. Scholars still argue over Fatima's historicity and generally ignore the social and gender implications of Fatima texts.[23]

This study, in contrast, focuses on late antique and early medieval Christianity, particularly in Gaul, as well as medieval Shi`ism. The presence of Marian imagery in Merovingian Gaul is certainly not an exception among the barbarian kingdoms. It is clear, for example, that Mary's cult flourished in Anglo-Saxon England well before the Norman invasion.[24] Bede explains that the earliest missionaries such as Augustine and Mellitus sent by Pope Gregory the Great in the late sixth and early seventh century brought Marian relics such as her hair along with them.[25] Early lives of the Irish Saint Brigid also mention the Virgin Mary: hagiographers recommend that female saints participate in Christ's divine motherhood along with Mary herself.[26] Historians would benefit from future explorations of Marian imagery in these western empires with an eye toward political and sectarian motivation, in the same way that this work concentrates on Gaul.

Although this study limits its investigation of Christian Marian imagery to late antiquity and early medieval Gaul, it approaches Shi`ite accounts of Fatima more universally because of the nature of the sources. Tracing and confining Shi`ite traditions to their specific geographic roots is almost impossible (and would constitute another book in itself). This study examines Shi`ite theologians and hagiographers who generally lauded the Imams' lives and miracles while exploring the community's connection as a whole to a pristine past. As already noted, future studies might well reveal the many ways that specific Shi`ite dynasties assimilated their royal women to a Fatima prototype.

By exploring the various conventions of Christian and Shi`ite sanctity, I offer a comparison of cross-cultural hagiography, a complex symbolic literature that assumes divergent forms in each cultural milieu. Hagiographies are contentious texts for scholars of both religions, yet male authors employed this literary genre to promote Mary and Fatima effectively as feminine exempla. Read skillfully, hagiographies provide historians and feminists alike with not only sacred models meant to transcend time and space but also reflections of contemporary political and social debates. Such texts reveal distinct cultural contexts wherein male authors construct feminine images for a variety of audiences and purposes.

Chapter One

Holy Women in Context

Hagiographers certainly embellished Mary and Fatima's roles in Christianity and Shī'ite Islam for rhetorical purpose. Throughout sacred texts these women perform various miracles such as healing the (pious) sick and punishing the (heretical) evildoers with righteous anger. Historians, on the other hand, have struggled to locate Mary and Fatima chronologically, in their sociopolitical contexts. Although their historical personae might be forever shrouded in sacred memory, scholars can identify some of the pivotal moments in theological debates and dynastic lineages when Mary's and Fatima's veneration proliferated most fervently.

Late antique Christian theologians, for example, invoked the Virgin Mary as an image of orthodoxy; Mary's body displayed the church's purity and incorruptibility. Battling theologians, arguing most ardently over Christ's nature, articulated their ideas by describing Mary's nature. Early medieval dynasties depended on the same didactic technique. Families such as the Merovingians aligned themselves with the Blessed Virgin and orthodox Christianity against their barbarian counterparts (who adhered mostly to Arian Christianity; i.e., those Christians who denied that Jesus was cosubstantial with the Father).

In a similar fashion, the evolving *shi'at 'Ali* (party of 'Ali) came to define themselves through their connection with Fatima. While all Muslims esteemed Fatima as the Prophet's daughter, she uniquely symbolized the reverence for and status of the Prophet's family among the early Shi`a. Shi`ite theologians developed a distinctive notion of authority that they believed passed from the Prophet to `Ali and his descendants (the Imams) through Fatima. Fatima's maternity became increasingly important as Shi`i scholars defined her miraculous, pure, and intercessory capacities to strengthen a definition of power imbued with spiritual significance and unique to `Ali's patriline and Fatima's matriline. As Fatima's descendants became more privileged, various Shi`ite groupings emerged, sometimes arguing over the Imams' true identity and then forging separate dynastic claims.

The historical personae of both Mary and Fatima thus may be hidden within layers of hagiographic formulas and sacred memory, but the sociopolitical contexts from which they emerge can be reconstructed to some degree. Hagiographers and theologians, Christians and Shi`ites, retold and reformulated the women's lives to reflect and refine emerging notions of sanctity, community, and dynastic authority. Mary and Fatima, shaped and reshaped through time, demonstrate the importance of women in constructing a sense of historical anamnesis and identity.[1]

Mary, the Church, and the Merovingians

Mary's greatest contribution to Christian theology is perhaps that she literally conferred flesh upon Jesus, the Christ. Yet early Christian sects considered this seemingly basic point the most controversial; many groups argued over the exact nature of Jesus well into the fourth and fifth centuries. Gnostic groups questioned whether Divinity could be encapsulated in flesh; Arian Christians suggested Jesus was created in time and thus was unlike God the Father. Only by the fifth century did an emerging Christian orthodoxy firmly claim that Christ, fully divine and equal to the Father, bore a human body composed of flesh and blood that suffered and died at Calvary. Theologians made such assertions by designating Mary Theotokos, or God-bearer, to prove Christ's unique composition.[2] Nestorian Christians quickly countered this claim and forced the church to finally, and very distinctly, define the God-Man's nature and birth.

The church confirmed Mary as Theotokos at the Council of Ephesus in 431 CE (although the title had appeared throughout theological discourse since the time of Origen, d. 254 CE). The council acted after a heated dispute developed between two important church leaders. Nestorius, patriarch of Constantinople, considered the title Theotokos an infringement on the God-Man's divinity.[3] The appellation, he feared, implied that the deity required a natural birth, a mundane gestation; to suggest that Mary contained God within her womb bordered on paganism. Cyril, bishop of Alexandria, insisted that Mary as Theotokos verified the unity of Christ. The Marian appellation showed clearly, he believed, that Christ was God and Man simultaneously. At the hastily convened council, church leaders sanctioned Cyril's position, condemned Nestorius, and presented Mary's new title to a boisterous crowd.

The Council of Ephesus generated Marian devotion almost as a by-product of Christological explanation. Popular piety had already revealed a vibrant Marian devotion evidenced in prolific tales of her infancy and childhood, yet theologians also harnessed the image and popularity of Mary in their emerging orthodoxy regarding both Christ and his church. Mary functioned as a proof text for Christ's unique nature as well as a metaphor for the church itself. Both Mary and the *ecclesia* evoke the image of a spotless, pure virgin and a fecund mother producing Christian offspring.

Church officials' use of Mary to craft a Christian orthodoxy corresponded with the Roman Empire's political transformation. During the fifth and sixth centuries, Germanic kingdoms replaced the (once) more ecumenical Roman administration with local kings, bishops, and priests who wielded substantial local power. Holy men, in particular, served as theologians as well as political figures because the church easily appropriated local vestiges of Roman authority.[4] Theological resolutions and even political might came to reside more in the church than traditional political offices. These church officials appeared particularly powerful as they defended their communities not against external, foreign enemies but against the internal abominations of heresy.

By the late fifth and early sixth century, for example, the Gallo-Roman population no longer feared barbarian onslaughts, ethnic contamination,[5] or usurpation by Germanic overlords; in fact, Gregory of Tours considered most freemen of Gaul as Franks, even if they descended from the indigenous Gallo-Roman population.[6] If they felt secure in some ways, however, they were not free from perceived threats of spiritual contamination. Church leaders viewed Arianism and Judaism as threats to Christian theology and life itself. The general Frankish population of Gaul identified their barbaric enemies not only in terms of ethnic or linguistic otherness but also as threats to Catholic orthodoxy.[7]

It is important to remember, too, that theological orthodoxy was not considered part of an elite culture accessible only to a literate scholarly class.[8] Theologians and laypersons alike debated many issues. While it would be difficult to find a sixth-century theologian of Augustine's or Ambrose's caliber, Christian orthodoxy was nonetheless felt and lived in every social stratum partly by way of the cult of saints, devotions promoted by the clergy and taken up avidly by the laity. Ideas about orthodoxy were not located primarily in theological treatises or formulaic accounts of Trinitarian disputes. They were found in complex diatribes against heresy, which, in turn, were embedded in a variety of popular devotions, many of which centered on the figure of Mary.[9]

Orthodox Christianity, unlike its heretical counterparts, necessitated the union of humanity and divinity in the God-Man, Jesus. Judaism denied Jesus as the Messiah, and Arianism questioned the full divinity of Christ, thinking him a creature and therefore not on the order of the Creator. Both refused the Christian claim that in Jesus the human and divine were united in one person and thus denied that the vast chasm between God and humanity could be bridged.

Orthodox (or "right") Christianity, in contrast, maintained that Christ could and did breach the abyss separating heaven and earth. Christ was not only a divine person capable of uniting humanity and divinity within himself; he afforded a model for others to follow. Accordingly, saints, by imitating Christ, could themselves transcend the human condition after death by taking on immortality in an eternal paradise. The power of the Jesus story and those of the saints animated the landscape of medieval Gaul. In the experiences of ordinary people, the divine touched their lives every day, every moment, through miraculous healings, exorcisms, and intercession.[10] Catholic orthodoxy and its prolific hagiography confirmed miraculous displays of divine power and effectively denounced Arianism and Judaism.

Such imagery was not unexpected as Merovingian (and later Caro-lingian) historians assimilated their past to a biblical framework and re-named themselves the "new Israel."[11] Gregory of Tours recognized the Frankish struggle to establish its kingdom and spread Christianity as one ordained by God.[12] The Franks' eventual triumph was simply a matter of divine providence as they banished heresy (i.e., Arianism instead of the Israelites' Canaanite enemies) and preached orthodox Catholicism. In his *Ten Books of Histories*, Gregory recasts Merovingian kings in the guise of Old Testament heroes. As Frankish warriors struggled against Goths and unruly offspring, they became new Davids braving the Philistine threat.[13]

Within the Merovingians' early alignment with Israel, Mary takes on the role of Eve's righteous counterpart. Extant Merovingian mis-sals (books describing the liturgy of the mass), for example, emphasize perfected Christianity as compared to imperfect Judaism.[14] The Bobbio Missal and the *Missale Gothicum* rely on temple ritual language to dem-onstrate the superiority of Christ, the sacrificial lamb, who completes the Old Covenant and initiates the New. In this system of salvation, the missals juxtapose the sinful Eve to the redemptive Mary while also af-firming Mary's perpetual virginity.[15] Mary's obedience to God's will and miraculous parturition provide the mode of Christ's birth, proof of his unique nature, and the foundation of Merovingian orthodoxy.

Merovingian devotion to Mary is manifest in a number of other ways. First, Frankish Christians celebrated at least two masses dedicated to Mary, one being the Feast of the Assumption, during the liturgical calendar.[16] This feast recognized Mary's bodily assumption into heaven without physical death, a theological point that became official doctrine only in 1950. Second, Merovingian holy men gained prestige through the procurement and possession of Mary's relics. As the Franks accepted Mary's bodily ascension, these relics probably related to her clothing or physical remains such as hair or breast milk.

The cult of relics in general signified the church's power on earth; miracles, exorcisms, and divine displays ratified God's presence and provided a framework for Frankish communities to make sense of their world.[17] Merovingian royalty and aristocrats certainly understood the im-portance of relics as symbols of both authority and heavenly mandate. By the sixth century, aristocratic families also sought prominent bishoprics throughout Gaul. Local authority, now centralized in the church offices instead of senatorial clout or ancestral prestige, provided a substantial source of sociopolitical ascendency.[18] The ownership or even the discovery of saintly relics only added to aristocratic fame in the competition for episcopal title.[19]

Saint cults and relics also enhanced royal authority in Gaul. The two Merovingian queens Brunhild and Balthild consolidated their position at court not only by supervising the appointment of bishops but also by managing local saint cults.[20] Brunhild sponsored Saint Martin's local clique, and Balthild procured several different saints' relics for her monasteries.[21] Merovingian kings and queens rendered themselves conduits of heavenly power by (ideally) appointing bishops sympathetic to their royal agendas and proving themselves appointees of the saints. These early medieval saint cults, in comparison with those of the later period, remained mostly localized and regional while at the same time the belief and rituals surrounding the living dead provided a kind of unity. Gregory of Tours could discuss northern Gaul's practices and saint figures with a sense of familiarity because of his experiences in central and southern Gaul. Some cults transcended local boundaries and proliferated through all the Gallic provinces. Relics of Saint Martin of Tours, for example, spread throughout Gaul and attracted cultic practices from many towns (this, of course, required some clever stories about his travels and adventures to account for how his relics ended up in so many different areas).

Gregory of Tours also suggests that most Franks adored other common saintly figures identified in the Scriptures, such as Peter, John the Baptist, and Paul. He even boasts of Marian relics, although he is vague in identifying exactly what type of relics he owned. Gregory is usually noted as the first Western hagiographer to describe Mary's corporal assumption into heaven just before her death, so it is doubtful that he would refer to her dead body parts as he might refer to John the Baptist's head or Saint Denis's arm.[22] He does describe, however, the miracles performed by her relics both in Jerusalem and in Gaul.

When Gregory begins his discussion of various Marian miracles, he includes Saint Mary's church in Jerusalem as a place-relic. He explains that the emperor Constantine had commissioned the edifice, but the building required supernatural facilitation. According to Gregory, the architects and workmen proved unable to move the massive columns intended for the church's support. Mary, as a sublime engineer, appeared to the architect in a dream and explained how he should construct appropriate pulleys and scaffolding to aid in the job. The next day the architect followed Mary's instructions. He summoned three boys from a nearby school (instead of the grown men previously employed), and they raised the columns without incident.[23] Gregory establishes Jerusalem as one of the first focal points of Marian piety.

Gregory then explains how many Marian relics found their way into Gaul. In one narrative, Johannes, a pious pilgrim, traveled to Jerusalem to be healed of his leprosy. While in the Holy Land he received the Virgin's relics and then proceeded home via Rome. On his journey highwaymen ambushed him and stole his money and reliquary. After they beat Johannes, they discovered that the reliquary contained nothing of value (such as gold) and tossed it into a fire. Johannes later retrieved the relics, miraculously preserved in their linen cloth, and advanced safely to Gaul where the relics continue to work miracles.[24]

Gregory himself boasted of owning Marian relics and carrying them in a gold cross (around his neck) along with relics of Saint Martin and the holy apostles. These relics, in fact, once saved a poor man's house from burning. Gregory explained, "Lifting the cross from my chest I held it up against the fire; soon, in the presence of the holy relics the entire fire stopped so [suddenly], as if there had been no blaze."[25] While the poor man's family had been unable to quench the flames that would consume his home, the simple presence of the bishop's relics brought relief.

Gregory's attestation to the presence and power of Marian relics not only boosts his own authority, but also the authority of Gaul as a locus of religious piety. He introduces Marian miracles at Jerusalem and then follows the transmission of her relics to his own land. In this way, Gregory is transforming Gaul into a biblical Jerusalem, comparing Mary's miracles and cures in the Holy Land to her current residence in Gaul.[26] Instead of traveling to Jerusalem on a holy pilgrimage, the pious could simply tour Mary's relics at Clermont. Gregory proclaims Gaul as a spiritual center equal to Jerusalem and the Holy Land, operating freely from the constraints of Rome.[27]

Gregory, like his late antique and Merovingian counterparts, transformed the Virgin Mary—a woman barely mentioned in the Christian canon—into a champion of orthodoxy and even prestige. Patristic authors constructed their evolving Mariology to bolster the church's evolving Christology. Merovingian theologians, bishops, and kings relied on the saints, including Mary, to warrant their expanding spiritual (and political) authority.

Fatima, the Holy Family, and Shiʿite Dynasties

Just as Christianity transformed the Virgin Mary, Shiʿite hagiographers and theologians transformed Fatima into a symbol of orthodoxy and dynastic mandate. Fatima's authorization of the Imamate enables the designation of those within the *shiʿat ʾAli* and the other. As with the Virgin Mary also, exposing the exact historical persona of the Prophet's daughter proves elusive. Shiʿa date their emergence to the moment of Muhammad's death (632) when some of the community allied themselves with Abu Bakr instead of the Prophet's chosen successor and son-in-law, ʿAli, Fatima's husband.

Historically, ʿAli's party certainly emerged at a specific moment, usually identified as 656, when ʿAli became the fourth caliph. This precipitated the first civil war in the Islamic community as ʿAli defended himself against his predecessor ʿUthman's kin and those who generally rejected his election. Yet those who endorsed ʿAli as the community's leader, and subsequently distinguished Fatima as the mother of the Shiʿite Imams, hardly composed a monolithic group.

The earliest *shiʿat ʾAli* were certainly political; that is, they supported ʿAli as the community's leader. After the death of ʿAli and his son Husayn, however, the party began to assume religious implications. A member of the Kharijites, an early ʿAlid (pro-ʿAli) sect, assassinated ʿAli in 661 because the group disagreed with his arbitration with those who opposed him.[28] After ʿAli's death, Muʿawiya (ʿUthman's kinsman) declared himself caliph and ushered in the Umayyad caliphate. ʿAlids turned first to his son Hasan for leadership; Hasan refused to rebel against Muʿawiya's forces and instead retired from public life.[29] After Hasan's death in 669, ʿAli's supporters (and the Umayyad's opponents) turned to ʿAli's second son, Husayn, for guidance. Husayn finally decided to make a public bid for power against Muʿawiya's successor-son, Yazid, after hearing rumors of tyranny and receiving pledges of support.

In 680 pious Muslims in Kufa (present-day Iraq) appealed to Husayn to lead their community against the caliph Yazid. Husayn agreed after thousands of Kufans professed their loyalty; he set out from Mecca to meet them. Before he arrived the caliph tamed any threat of revolt through terror tactics and bribery. When Husayn and his party (numbering seventy-two armed men plus women and children, including his own family) reached the plain of Karbala outside Kufa, they met a detachment assembled by `Ubaydullah ibn Ziyad, the commander sent by the caliph.

On the tenth day of Muharram, 680 CE, after several days of siege in desert terrain, Husayn and his companions fell to the Umayyad forces. Husayn was decapitated and his head returned to Kufa where `Ubaydullah publicly struck the lips of the Prophet's own grandson. Husayn's martyrdom became a central point in Shi`ite theology representing suffering, penance, and redemption: Shi`ites continue to re-create the martyrdom at annual ta`ziya ceremonies, demonstrate repentance for deserting Husayn, and finally gain redemption through symbolic participation in Husayn's sufferings.

After Husayn's death, leadership of the shi`at `Ali became much more complex. `Alids disagreed over who inherited the Prophet's son-in-law's position of authority and exactly what type of authority was involved. The Shi`a then began to craft their own kind of orthodoxy wherein Fatima's maternity proved particularly important. In the midst of a blatant patrilineal system of descent, Shi`ite theologians uniquely transformed Fatima's motherhood into the cornerstone of the Imamate, the system of Shi`ite authority. The Shi`ites argued, over time, that Fatima transcends the importance of her mother, Khadija (the Prophet's first wife); Maryam, the mother of Jesus (or `Isa); and `A'isha, the Prophet's beloved wife. They effectively placed Fatima in a singular position as the mother of the Imams.

Unfortunately it is almost impossible to discover the exact historical evolution of such traditions and theologies. Some historians date Fatima traditions and the importance of her bloodline to the earliest community, apparent during the Prophet's own lifetime (d. 632). A second group situates Fatima's popularity and evolving Shi`ite identity in the period surrounding the `Abbasid revolution (750) and subsequent consolidation of `Abbasid authority that usurped the Umayyad caliphate.[30] A third group of historians describes the proliferation of Fatima traditions as slowly evolving throughout the first several centuries of Islam as a rejoinder to extremist (*ghuluww*) doctrine.

The first theory, favored by most pious Shi`ite Muslims, accepts traditions that limit the *ahl al-bayt* to Fatima's children (which, in turn, emphasizes Fatima's unique status) and that allegedly date to the Prophet's own lifetime and certainly to the time of Husayn's martyrdom (i.e., seventh century).[31] One such tradition defined Muhammad, `Ali, Fatima, Hasan, and Husayn as the specific "people of the cloak," or *ahl al-kisa´*.[32]

According to the "cloak" hadith, Muhammad met a group of Christians at Narjan, a town located on the Yemeni trade route, and attempted to convert them. After some debate, the Christians agreed that Jesus foretold the Paraclete, or Comforter, whose son would succeed him. They agreed that since Muhammad had no son he could not be the fulfillment of such a prophecy. The Christians also consulted a collection of prophetic traditions titled *al-Jami`*, which referred to one of Adam's visions wherein he encountered one bright light surrounded by four smaller lights. God revealed to Adam that these were his five beloved descendants.

Although the Christians rejected Muhammad at Narjan, they were nonetheless intrigued by his message and later sent a delegation of scholars to Medina to question the Prophet further and engage in *mubahala* (mutual cursing).[33] When Muhammad arrived, he had `Ali, Fatima, Hasan, and Husayn with him wrapped in a cloak. The Christians identified the family with the prophetic chapter of *al-Jami`* and quickly withdrew from the contest.

Various Shi`ite traditions directly relate the people of the cloak to the *ahl al-bayt* and say that Muhammad repeated the Qur'anic verse 33.33 as he wrapped the holy family in his mantle: "Allah only wishes to remove all abomination from you, members of the family, and to make you pure and spotless." This asserts the (eventual) Shi`ite notion of the Imams' infallibility and ultimate ritual purity.

The traditions attesting to the holy family's supremacy encountered some resistance. A set of countertraditions, usually transmitted by prominent Umayyads, erupted that placed others under the cloak with Fatima's family such as the Prophet's servant, Wathila b. al-Asqa`, and wife, Umm Salama.[34] These traditions denying the exclusivity of the *ahl al-bayt* allegedly predate the `Abbasid revolution and at the least recognize the controversy surrounding the meaning of the *ahl al-bayt*. This challenges, then, the second theory of Fatima tradition that places her sublime status (as well as her family's) as only an `Alid rejoinder to `Abbasid denigrations.

This second theory, favored by most historians, emphasizes the propaganda potential of Fatima imagery when employed by sectarian leaders. The early `Abbasid movement, so this argument holds, merged forces with the Hashimiyyah, a Shi`ite sect originating with Mukhtar ibn Abu `Ubayd al-Thaqafi (d. c. 686) as it prepared to usurp the ruling Umayyad dynasty. Mukhtar had arrived in Kufa around 680, just after Husayn's tragic martyrdom under Caliph Yazid. Mukhtar, acting as a prophet of sorts, proclaimed Muhammad ibn al-Hanafiyya, Imam `Ali's third son by a woman of the Hanifa tribe (and *not* Fatima) as the Mahdi (anointed one). As Mahdi, Muhammad ibn al-Hanafiyya would restore peace and order to the Kufan community and relieve Umayyad oppression. After both Mukhtar and Muhammad ibn al-Hanafiyya died, a group of supporters called the Kaysaniyya continued their adoration by proclaiming that the Mahdi had entered occultation (*ghayba*), a type of hiding or sublime stasis, instead of truly dying.[35]

The Kaysaniyya was not a monolithic sect. After Muhammad ibn al-Hanafiyya entered occultation, the group split into separate branches. One of these branches, the Hashimiyya, taught that Muhammad ibn al-Hanafiyya did indeed die after relegating his authority and divine knowledge to his son, Abu Hashim. The `Abbasids later asserted that Abu Hashim conferred his Imamate on Muhammad ibn `Ali (the great-grandson of al-`Abbas, the Prophet's uncle) and, thereby, the descendants of al-`Abbas (with no bloodline through Fatima). The `Abbasids identified themselves with the Hashimiyya and, by association, the "party of `Ali" because `Ali was Abu Hashim's grandfather through the Hanafite woman. The `Abbasids advanced their revolution by harnessing the discontent of the early *shi`at `Ali* against the ruling Umayyad dynasty.

After the `Abbasids firmly established their own caliphate, however, their propaganda machine disassociated themselves from the Hashimiyya and the `Alids (and also persecuted the Shi`a who refused to recognize their authority). By al-Mansur's caliphate (c. 754–775), the `Abbasids stressed their relation to Muhammad's uncle al-`Abbas instead of their connection to `Ali and the Banu Hashim. They argued that Allah favored the male relative, in this case the paternal uncle, over inheritance through a female (implying, of course, Muhammad's daughter, Fatima). Court clerks circulated Mansur's declarations against the `Alids:

> As for your assertion that you are direct descendants of the Prophet, God has already declared in His Book, "Muhammad was not the father of any of your men" (33.30); but even though you be descended from the Prophet's daughter, which is indeed a close kinship, this still does not give you the right of inheritance.[36]

`Ali and Fatima's family, according to the `Abbasids, held no esteemed position among the community.

The `Abbasids also questioned the very meaning of the *ahl al-bayt* and its association with `Ali and Fatima's progeny. Caliph Mahdi (d. 785), Mansur's son, circulated various hadith and poetic verses promulgating a distinctively anti-Shi`a interpretation of the people of the cloak.[37] According to these traditions, the people of the cloak instead included Muhammad's uncle `Abbas and his descendants:

> The Prophet came to `Abbas and his sons and said: "Come nearer to me." They all pushed against each other. He then wrapped them in his robe and said: "O, Allah, this is my uncle and the brother of my father, these are my family; shelter them from the fire in the same manner that I shelter them with my robe."[38]

This understanding of the *ahl al-bayt* promoted the house of `Abbas while challenging the notion of the infallible Imamate as well as Fatima's unique status.[39]

The `Alids responded to these `Abbasid claims, first, by pointing out that `Abbas was only Muhammad's half uncle and that Abu Talib, `Ali's father, was Muhammad's full uncle. `Ali's relationship as the Prophet's cousin therefore outweighed any claims of `Abbas.[40] Second, the `Alids punctuated their direct descent through Fatima. A proliferation of traditions proclaiming the predestined status of Fatima and the *ahl al-bayt* ensued.[41] Historians then might view Fatima hagiographies as the `Alids' political rejoinder to `Abbasid claims of ascendancy.

A third group of historians consider Fatima traditions and the *ahl al-bayt*'s glorification as a response to extremist theologies (or *ghulat* sects) within the Shi`a instead of an overtly political move.[42] Many `Alid scholars advertised mystical traditions that promoted divinely inspired reason (`*aql*) instead of logical rationality, the esoteric (*batin*) above the exoteric (*zahir*), and cosmogonic links between the Imams and humanity.[43] Shi`ite theology that evolved during the ninth and tenth centuries represents a process of mitigating, negotiating, and eventually integrating some of these mystical views.

The emerging orthodox traditions, for example, define the Imams as the divine light (*nur*) and Fatima as the Confluence of the Two Lights (*majma` al-nurayn*; i.e., her husband's and her father's light). Fatima resides as the nexus between Muhammad (exoteric knowledge) and `Ali (esoteric knowledge), where the sublime meets the human. In a sense Fatima manages to bridge the great chasm between Allah and humanity just as the Christian saints and Mary do; she exists as part of Allah's light (divine *nur*), yet she is the attending mother, flesh and blood, beckoning her extended (and spiritual) family to her care. Fatima traditions display Shi`ite scholars' careful incorporation of esoteric cosmology in an evolving, rational theology. These traditions directly deny some of the *ghulat*'s more extreme assertions that the Imams themselves (such as the sixth Imam, Ja`far al-Sadiq) were incarnations of Divinity.

Whatever the genesis of Fatima traditions, whether in political discourse or in esoteric theology, Fatima remains a signal throughout for the orthodox (right) community. Sometimes that might be interpreted as the `Alid claims against the `Abbasids, as the Banu Hashim against the Umayyads, and perhaps even the Shi`ite theologians against extremist sects. From a more general perspective, Fatima always symbolizes Shi`ism against the other. Beginning in the late ninth century (and the solidification of an Imami orthodoxy, or rightness), Fatima's image provided a powerful proof for theologians as well as future dynastic leaders.

As Shi`ite theologians eventually came to recognize `Ali and Fatima as the Imamate's progenitors and bestowed spiritual potencies on the Imams themselves, they disagreed as to the Imam's designation process. These disagreements continue to distinguish Shi`ite sects today: many Shi`a recognize five initial Imams (Zaydis); some, seven (Isma`ilis); and others, the majority of the Shi`ite world, twelve (*Ithna-Ashariyya*, or

Twelvers). The different groups accepted different descendants of `Ali and Fatima as Imams. According to Twelver Shi`ite traditions, the fifth and sixth Imams (Muhammad al-Baqir [d. 731] and Ja`far al-Sadiq [d. 765]) addressed the problem by carefully articulating the theory of *nass*, the process by which the current Imam designates his son (the Prophet's bloodline) and bestows on him `*ilm* (authoritative knowledge). The problem lies, however, in which son the community recognizes as having received *nass*.

By the mid-tenth century, most of these Shi`ite groups had control of substantial geographic regions. The Buyid dynasty (Twelvers) controlled much of Iraq and Iran, although they allowed the `Abbasid caliph to reign as a figurehead; the Isma`ilis established the Fatimid dynasty in North Africa and founded Cairo; and the Zaydis controlled areas of northern Iran and Yemen.[44] By the tenth century there is a true flowering of Fatima traditions in Shi`ite theological texts. As Buyids came into power, they had to articulate what distinguished them from their Isma`ili competitors. Zaydi Shi`ites explained their unique view of the Imamate: the Imam must be descended from `Ali and Fatima, but he must also make a public claim for power and oppose illegitimate rulers. As Shi`ite dynasties seized leadership throughout the Middle East, Shi`ite identity became increasingly distinct from Sunni Islam.

Fatima proved important to theologians of all these Shi`ite groupings because she gave birth to the Imams; through this Mother, the Imamate's authority flowed from husband/`Ali and father/Muhammad. For the majority of Shi`ite Muslims (Twelvers), that authority ended with the twelfth Imam's great occultation in 941 CE. Until his return at the end of time, Shi`ite clerics and theologians speak in his stead, drawing on the traditions of the *ahl al-bayt* and the Imams for guidance.

Mary and Fatima, as they appear in late antique and early medieval sources, must be placed in the historical contexts from which they emerge. Theological disputes, dynastic authority, and shifting lines of community certainly affected the interpretive tradition that perpetuated their legacies. Whether through the writings of patriarchs or bishops, Twelvers or Isma`ilis, Mary's and Fatima's lives helped to shape historical memory and communal identity. Their stories are told most fully not only in theological tracts and historical chronicles but also in hagiography. Hagiographers fully defined Mary's and Fatima's status in their respective communities by assessing their miraculous and intercessory powers. Comparative hagiography provides a glimpse at the various and contrasting ways these male authors refashioned their holy women to fit their rhetorical strategies.

C h a p t e r   T w o

Holy Women in Holy Texts

One of the most important goals of comparative religion is not simply to detail historical similarities and differences in religious systems but to discover new ways of understanding them.[1] To that end scholars often assign categories or topical classifications to specific cultural elements, for example, ritual, myth, or mysticism.[2] Hagiography and gender also serve as comparative categories, although they pose a set of unique problems.

Employing hagiography as a comparative tool is difficult first and foremost because of the debate over how to define this genre, as well as use it as source material. Hagiography in its broadest sense is symbolic literature that presents the holy (Greek, *hagios*) to both popular and elite audiences in a variety of forms.[3] Medieval hagiographies were read aloud, memorized, proliferated by scholars, and displayed in pictorial or symbolic compositions for the illiterate population.[4] In written, oral, and visual form, hagiographies praised the virtues and damned the vices of heroic persons set forth as didactic exempla; yet these texts reviewed the miraculous happenings involving more than just holy people. Hagiography celebrated sacred locales, architectural structures, and holy objects: early Christian hagiographers, for example, popularized Jerusalem as a holy site, the Holy Sepulcher as a holy structure, and bits of the true cross as holy relics.[5] Jerusalem was not unique in this respect; almost every Christian town publicized its local saint's site. Shi`ite communities likewise celebrated the Imams' lives by recounting their miracles and visiting their shrines.[6] Holiness in one form or another permeated the learning and the physical landscape of medieval life for both Christians and Shi`ite Muslims.

As literature intended to depict cultural ideals symbolically, hagiography is a complex genre in terms of both substance and agenda. On the surface hagiography appears biographical and descriptive; it speaks of life and death, joy and suffering. However, it was not intended primarily to preserve and communicate a historical kernel of truth or recount an objective chronicle of events. Gregory of Tours opted to name his hagiographic collection "Life *[Vita]* of the Fathers" rather than "Lives *[Vitae]* of the Fathers." Gregory explained that "there is a diversity of merits and virtues among [the saints], but the one life of the body sustains them all in this world."[7] In Gregory's compendium the saints' differences and distinctions disappear as he reveals the underlying holiness that unites them all.

Hagiography is thus fundamentally didactic: it edifies through exemplary displays of piety and holiness; it promulgates sacred narratives and then explains the moral and theological imperatives embedded in them; and it models proper modes of ritual and other cultic practices. Hagiographic discourse aims to resurrect and then reconstruct for its audience examples of holiness or ideal modes of being intended for pious imitation. With this functionalist definition of hagiography in mind, scholars should expect that any hagiographic tradition would be radically determined by the canon of values, beliefs, and authoritative texts particular to the cultural context from which it emerges. This certainly holds true for early Christian and Islamic hagiographic texts, which reflect their (sometimes) radically different ideals of the holy.

Hagiography also includes idealizations of masculine and feminine piety that modern readers might find distressingly misogynistic. Literate men mostly constructed these gender paradigms as very few texts by women exist. These male-authored texts provide the only substantive view of women (and expectations of women) in early Christian and Shi`ite religious communities. By using gender as a point of comparison, it becomes clear that theologians and hagiographers in both traditions limit holy women's miraculous actions and proscribe holy women's miraculous bodies to the domestic sphere.

Medieval and Modern Audiences: Christianity

Late antique and early medieval Christian hagiographers transformed their saintly characters and sacred landscapes in accordance with Greco-Roman and biblical formulas.[8] Some of the most influential early Christian hagiographies sprang from Syria and Egypt during the fourth and fifth centuries.[9] These texts applauded the efforts of holy men and women who surrendered mundane existence for a higher, angelic life. The era of Christian martyrs had all but ended as Roman emperors legalized Christianity throughout the empire. As martyrs became increasingly unnecessary, ascetics supplied another model of Christian heroism: they mortified their bodies and sought to transcend the problems of the flesh as they struggled against their spiritual enemy, Satan, and his demonic forces.[10]

Bishop Athanasius of Alexandria (d. 373) constructed one of the most important Christian hagiographies in his *Life of Anthony*, an Egyptian recluse who haunted nearby deserts and caves.[11] Athanasius describes a vicarious martyr, guarding the periphery of human existence against evil while struggling against his interior lusts and desires. In the end Anthony provides his audience with a new Christ figure who prays in the desert, casts out demons, heals the sick, and raises the dead.[12] Anthony's hagiographer produces a hero-hermit much like the biblical Elijah, reconstructed in the fourth century, intended to model the miracles and grace of Christ. Indeed, one of the greatest signs of sanctity was *imitatio Christi* (the imitation of Christ) wherein holy men and women performed Christ's miracles after symbolically sharing in his suffering by means of ascetic feats.

As Christianity expanded from the Syrian and Greek East to the Gallo-Roman/Latin West, hagiographers encountered a new audience.[13] It proved difficult if not impossible to transform urban Gaul into a physical wasteland of caves and demon-inhabited deserts. Western hagiographers thus created a spiritual desert and challenged the Roman elite and Mediterranean nobility to convert to Christianity and to live as Christ through renunciation of wealth and status. Women proved particularly important in this newly imagined desert as the viable patrons of the church who gladly distributed their Roman patrimony among ecclesiastical authorities.[14] Hagiographers in Gaul expressed innovative ideals of holiness for a new constituency of sinners.

The fourth-century author Sulpicius Severus created perhaps the most influential hagiography in early medieval Gaul. His *Life of Martin of Tours* transformed a Roman soldier known for his valor into an Old Testament prophet, traveling and preaching throughout Gaul, who only reluctantly accepted the bishop's office of Tours.[15] Martin's life became the hallmark of Western hagiography: the loyal Roman citizen forsakes his mundane wealth to serve his heavenly king. Martin, in typical fashion, healed the sick, exorcised the demon possessed, and practiced profound charity and kindness. At the same time, he assumed the bishop's mantle and dutifully acknowledged the church's authority. The hagiographer modified his wandering holy man at first reminiscent of the eastern Anthony into a stable bishop ever mindful of his parish and his flock. A pious Christian but also a good Roman, Martin embodied the ideals of hierarchy and structure.[16]

Merovingian hagiographers inherited the model of Martin and effectively blended their new bishops with this very Roman ideal: Frankish clergy promoted order and hierarchy within both church and state. Merovingian hagiographers were aware also of the saint cults that proliferated throughout Gaul as they addressed popular audiences who increasingly committed themselves to local saints, both living and dead. Merovingian hagiography thus served a pastoral purpose, aimed directly at teaching and educating a general constituency about the developing protocols for the veneration of saints.

Linguists in particular first recognized the pastoral function of Merovingian texts by their distinctive Latin vocabulary: the language is both colloquial and active.[17] Merovingian hagiographers focused on how to venerate local holy figures and what miraculous results might be expected. They provided models instructing pious petitioners to gather remnants from the cells of saints such as ash, candle wax, or oil; through these contact relics, miraculous healing followed and the saints' fame spread.[18] These instructive texts compare dramatically with the later Carolingian hagiographies intended for monastic use; Carolingian Latin indicates more interior action such as meditation and prayer.[19] In contrast, Merovingian hagiography speaks to a nonmonastic audience, defining innovative notions of holiness associated with the spread of saint veneration.

There is considerable disagreement among modern scholars of medieval Christianity as to what to do with hagiography as a source. European intellectuals generally scoffed at Christian hagiographic sources during the Enlightenment period. Scholars of the ancient world such as David Hume and Edward Gibbon dismissed hagiography as an irrational literature confined to the lower classes that recounted fanciful miracle stories and fantastic displays of a misnamed polytheism.[20] Beginning only in the 1930s, scholars and theologians began to mine hagiography for details about life, society, and intellectual history. Hippolyte Delehaye and the Bollandists, a group of Jesuit priests dedicated to recovering and categorizing hagiographies, led this movement, although much of their work still attempted to separate the factual from the spurious, the believable from the unbelievable.[21]

During the past two decades, hagiologers have generally disregarded the fact or fiction debate and gleaned information about cultural milieus and gender roles from holy texts.[22] Most scholars now agree that hagiography was not just a literature intended for a lay, mostly illiterate population; instead, wealthy and poor audiences alike shared a hagiographic corpus that greatly defined their experiences. This literature provided the system of cultural symbols that united western Christendom.

Medieval and Modern Audiences: Islam

Early Shi`ite hagiography reveals an equally dynamic symbolic system at least during the late eighth and ninth century. Shi`ite notions of power and authority increasingly considered `Ali and Fatima's descendants Imams responsible for their community's spiritual guidance. Hagiographies explained the Imams' miraculous births, their infallible lives, and their sublime wisdom. These models of holiness inspired ritual activities surrounding the Imams' tombs and shrines. Shi`ite hagiographers, for example, encouraged devotees to visit holy places on pilgrimages (ziyara).[23] Most Shi`ites turned their attention to the shrine of Husayn, `Ali and Fatima's son who died a martyr's death at Karbala. Husayn's body was interred at Karbala, but tradition also placed his head at Karbala, Damascus, Najaf, and Cairo.[24] All these locales remain important pilgrimage sites where Shi`ites venerate their third Imam.

Locating the mainstream notion of sanctity is more difficult in Islam than in early Christianity. Many Muslim theologians avoid the elevated designation of sainthood, stressing instead that every individual maintains direct access to Allah, thus disallowing the need for a saintly intercessor.[25] Qur'an 39.44 declares, "To Allah belongs exclusively the right to grant intercession. To Him belongs the dominion of the heavens and the earth: in the end, it is to Him that you shall be brought back." Thus in Islam no centralized clergy propagates and authorizes a genre of literature akin to Christianity's saints' lives. Saintly canonization is almost completely within the province of hagiographers and reader response to their products (both oral and written).

Medieval Muslims nonetheless maintained a definite notion of holiness (*wilaya*) and disseminated those sacred ideals through their own, distinct forms of hagiography. These sacred collections included biographies of the Prophet, battlefield accounts, or, for Shi`ites, descriptions of the Imams and their miraculous powers. The earliest known biography of the Prophet, for example, resembled early Christian tales of desert saints.[26] Bedouin tribes on the edges of the Arabian peninsula certainly were familiar with Christian veneration of desert holy men and their miracles: historical records indicate that they shared the same deserts and caves as Christian hermits, witnessed their fame, and heard about their miraculous powers. The Prophet's biographer cast him as a functioning holy man to his community: Muhammad healed the sick, provided righteous judgments, and multiplied food.[27] Many of the Prophet's friends and family described in the biographical materials also served as pious models intended for emulation and edification.

While Muslim hagiography might vary in intent and audience—for example, some collections, *qisas al-anbiya*, or "Tales of the Prophets," featured miracle stories of the same prophets shared by Jews, Christians, and Muslims—most of it has the same format. Accounts of holiness are usually recorded as hadith, one of two genres of sacred texts in Islam, the other being the Qur'an.

Like Christianity, Islam is a religion of the book and reveres a sacred and revealed scripture. The Qur'an confers the direct revelation of Allah through his final messenger, Muhammad. The holy text describes humanity's virtues and vices, directs the actions of the community (*umma*), and offers a glimpse of an impending apocalypse.[28] It also presents a series of prophets and holy men and women for pious Muslims to imitate.[29]

The hadith collections advance their own notions of holiness. Hadith (used here as a collective noun; the proper plural is *ahadith*) are traditions that relate back to the Prophet Muhammad's own lifetime, describing his actions and utterances as well as those of his friends, family, and other contemporaries.[30] The hadith literature functions as hagiography when read as a means of resurrecting a pristine past and endowing Muslims with models of holiness and virtue. Read in this way, hadith literature allows scholars and others to eavesdrop on the earliest Muslim community: the Prophet's lifestyle and the faithfulness of his friends and family (and the perfidy of his enemies), and directives and patterns outside the Qur'anic framework. Taken together the Qur'an and hadith (the "trodden path," or *sunna*), provide models for emulation; scholarly exegesis (*tafsir*) then attempts to explain and contextualize the *sunna* so that pious Muslims may follow them.

Islamicists approach hadith literature as carefully as medievalists approach Christian hagiography, and this is not a recent methodological problem. Medieval Muslims themselves devoted an entire science to proving or disproving hadith authenticity. To do this they focused most strenuously on the chain of transmitters, or *isnad*. The hadith consists of two parts: the tradition itself (*matn*) and a detailed list of individuals who observed or transmitted the Prophet's advice or actions (*isnad*). Scholars and linguists identified the transmitters, reconciled their death dates with times of transmission, and located the hadith in an elaborate spectrum of categories ranging from sound (*sahih*) to weak (*da'if*), from precious (*'aziz*) to forged (*mawdu'*).

Medieval hadith collections contributed more than personal models of piety and words of wisdom from the Prophet. The central role of hadith was to lay the foundation of Islamic law: Islamic jurisprudence (*fiqh*) carefully reasoned what was obligatory (*fard*), recommended (*mandub*), neutral (*mubah*), reprehensible (*makruh*), and forbidden (*haram*). By the late ninth and early tenth century, Islamic scholars generally accepted as canonical the six rigorously scrutinized compendia composed by separate hadith critics: al-Bukhari, Muslim, Ibn Da'ud, al-Tirmidhi, al-Nisa'i, and Ibn Hanbal. Other scholars compiled their own hadith collections, but these six became the pillars of Sunni piety and law.

Shi'ite Muslims, on the other hand, esteem additional hadith collections as authoritative.[31] The Shi'ites value above all the traditions that

relate back to the Prophet's family. For Twelver Shi`ites, this includes the
twelve Imams, among them `Ali himself. Since the Shi`a regarded `Ali and
the Imams as Muhammad's rightful successors, they gathered accounts of
the Imams' deeds and sayings for both political and spiritual guidance.[32]
Shi`ites maintain that `Ali and Fatima's descendants, beginning with their
sons Hasan and Husayn, became the sources of true spiritual sustenance
to the Islamic community. According to one tradition, Husayn (quoted by
Ja`far al-Sadiq, the sixth Imam) proclaimed:

> "God created His servants solely that they might know Him, for
> when they know Him they worship Him and thus free themselves
> from the worship of anything that is not Him." Someone then asked:
> "What is knowledge of God?" "It is, for the people of each age,
> knowledge of the Imam to whom they owe obeisance."[33]

For Shi`ites recognition of and dependence on the Imams equaled
knowledge of God himself. It was irrelevant if the ruling Umayyad or
`Abbasid dynasty acknowledged the Imams as the community's rightful
leaders. Allah required the Shi`a itself to identify the Imam and maintain
his sublime teachings through its collective memories and records.

Many Shi`ite hadith collections function, therefore, as a form of po-
litical and spiritual rhetoric explaining the cosmological link between
the Prophet's beloved family and the community.[34] These hadith demonstrate the Shi`a's sublime authority in heaven even if it is not always
recognized on earth.[35] They also offer adoptive membership into the *ahl
al-bayt* for those who recognize the Imam's authority. The hadith function as hagiography because they outline a mode of holiness (acceptance
into the family), reveal moral and theological imperatives (allegiance to
the family), and supply holy models to imitate (the prophets, Imams,
and early community members). Like Merovingian hagiography, hadith
reconstruct a sacred past in their own dynamically changing context to
promote a new identity, namely, the identification of the Imams and an
evolving Shi`ism as it distinguished itself from Sunni Islam.

As in Christian hagiography, there exist equally contentious debates
about how to use hadith as hagiography. Many Muslims view the Prophet
Muhammad with esteem and adoration and therefore strive to achieve
a real view of him and his community. Hadith accepted as authentic are

windows into that reality and afford a genuine depiction of the Prophet. Many Muslim scholars maintain the historicity of hadith transmission and argue that the earliest community assured hadith veracity. These scholars admit that hadith evolved from an oral to a written genre, but they also insist that skilled, literate scholars held the transmissions to high standards of authentication.[36]

The question of veracity has plagued non-Muslim and secular scholars as well. Since the early twentieth century some Islamicists have recognized that formally written hadith compilations only circulated in the late eighth century. They have argued that these hadith reveal more about eighth-century life than about Muhammad's own community.[37] This approach fundamentally questions the hadith's reliability as a historical source for the earliest Islamic period; and, for Muslims, this critique challenges hadith as an authoritative source of sublime direction and models of piety. Other Islamicists have forged a middle ground: hadith reflect the Prophet's own lifetime, but the standardized method of transmission and compilation must be dated much later. According to this argument, it remains impossible to demonstrate absolutely the hadith's historicity.[38]

I avoid the question of hadith veracity altogether; instead of expecting the hadith to betray an objective historical reality, I see them as revealing important cultural symbols and notions of holiness relevant to their medieval audiences.[39] If hadith were deemed important enough to copy, memorize, and scrutinize, then they must disclose valuable clues about the community that treasured them. Even the more obscure, "weak" hadith that "sound" compendia often fail to include are important; they help to recapture the evolutionary nature of Muslim identity by revealing the developing hagiographic tradition. As in Christianity, theology and religious identity evolved over the centuries as leaders, theologians, and scholars formulated and answered questions important for their nascent communities. Even those hadith that were later rejected or considered spurious by Shi`ite scholars reflect the stages of that evolutionary process.

Classical Shi`ite sources are especially difficult to date and ascribe to specific compilers. Although the hadith format provides lists of transmitters, the editors themselves sometimes evade designation. Some extant compendia do give the names of editor and author, such as the tenth-century *Kitab al-Irshad* (Book of Guidance into the Lives of the Twelve

Imams) by Shaykh al-Mufid. Other hadith survive only in later compilations such as that of the seventeenth-century Safavid scholar Muhammad Baqir al-Majlisi, *Bihar al-anwar* (Sea of Lights). Although this collection is rather late, it is indispensable to scholars of Shi`ite Islam.

With the help of scholars such as al-Majlisi, the seventeenth-century Safavids of Persia launched a prolific religious campaign against Sunni and Sufi piety.[40] Al-Majlisi's job as a member of the `ulama´ was to collect and distribute hadith that illustrated Shi`ite identity and the holy family's election since before created time. He intended his collections to serve as a type of propaganda, popularizing a legalistic form of Twelver Shi`ism while disavowing Sunnism and some Sufi orders. He was the first scholar to translate a large number of hadith collections, theologies, and histories into Persian for greater availability to a general audience.

Al-Majlisi's collection is important for another reason: it includes both the widely accepted, sound hadith and the potentially spurious (or weak) traditions. For example, al-Majlisi repeated many of the earliest Shi`ite sources from al-Kulayni and Ibn Babawayh, renowned tenth-century Shi`ite scholars,[41] some of which are extant only through his encyclopedic collection. But he also chose hadith that were not included in ordinary compilations of Shi`ite texts. Because of this broad inclusiveness, some scholars doubt its historical veracity. (One colleague referred to the *Bihar al-anwar* as the "great trash heap of Shi`ite traditions.")[42] Because al-Majlisi cast such a wide net in collecting his hadith, he provides scholars with an opportunity to view Shi`ism as it developed and blossomed throughout the classical and medieval periods.

Al-Majlisi quite naturally focused on the Prophet's family and particularly his daughter Fatima to prove Shi`ite Islam's superiority over Sunnism and Sufism. The traditions range from those of the most mystical bent (which define the holy family in terms of pure light with absolute knowledge)[43] to those of more practical application (which define the twelfth Imam as the source of all spiritual authority).

This grand collection of hadith also certainly added authority to al-Majlisi's own position. According to Twelver doctrine, the twelfth Imam, Muhammad al-Mahdi, did not die but went into a sublime hiding, or occultation. During this period of hiddenness, the Shi`ite community relies on the scholars to discern the Imam's justice. Al-Majlisi was just such a scholar who implicitly designated himself as one of the twelfth Imam's spokesmen until the final, apocalyptic return. Through his hadith compilations, al-Majlisi justified his own political station while constructing a hagiographic edifice praising the holy family's spiritual status.[44]

Sources and Gender

As Merovingian Christians and Shi`ite Muslims sought to make sense of their world and to delineate their place in it, they devised and articulated dynamic notions of holiness. For the people of Gaul, the changes in their world involved the political transition from late Roman to Merovingian rule and the spiritual acculturation to a new, unifying Christendom. Shi`ite communities, in many cases bereft of political ascendancy because of a Sunni majority (except for a brief interim in the mid-tenth century), articulated their unique cosmology and loyalties to the Imam and the holy family. In both these cases, discussions of sanctity in hagiographic sources betray both theological and political agendas. On closer examination it becomes clear that gender expectations and the introduction of feminine ideals signaled radical changes in society as well. Both Christian and Muslim cultures supported and preserved the literary products of a male elite, which constructed paradigms of community and holiness via women, in particular Mary and Fatima.

Most extant Christian texts from late antiquity originate from the ecclesiastical sphere. Theologians such as Ambrose, Augustine, and Jerome charted the twists and turns Christian theology would take in terms of asceticism, ideals of marriage, the Trinitarian debate, and the path of Christ's church (*ecclesia*).[45] Late antique authors both reflected and refuted beliefs about the Virgin Mary popularized by anonymous, apocryphal texts. They absorbed, for example, the precept of Mary's perpetual virginity (both before, during, and after Christ's birth), yet some cautioned against Mary's Immaculate Conception, or birth free from sin.[46] Marian theology, and Christian theology in general, was only slowly evolving.

The early Middle Ages yield a wider variety of sources, although most still come from the ecclesiastical sphere: church councils left records of decisions and debate; bishops wrote histories of their bishoprics (which were more like family trees); priests and popes wrote hagiographies;[47] and holy men crafted monastic rules for female religious to follow. One of the most prolific authors of Merovingian Gaul was Gregory of Tours; he provided a veritable who's who among Merovingian bishops in his *Ten Books of History* and numerous hagiographies of male and female saints.[48] In early Christian hagiography, few texts written by women survive, and only one of those has a self-identified female author (Baudonivia, who wrote her saint's life only to complement an earlier redaction by a man, Fortunatus).[49] Scholars suspect other works might be written by women, especially nuns who had firsthand knowledge of their saint-abbesses.[50] In most cases male clergy wrote about women.

A similar case arises in classical Islam. Women may have lent considerable time, faith, and even wealth to their respective traditions, but they remained largely silent in the sources. Muslim women's social expectations depended largely on the geographic locale and ruling elite; yet in most cases women played a sizable role in the establishment of schools and the transmission of knowledge. Like female patrons of Christianity, wealthy wives and mothers commissioned schools and donated land for educational institutions, and with those same sources of wealth, many women acquired personal tutors and received competitive educations.[51] Also as with Christianity, tradition largely circumscribed women's practical role in the public classroom as teachers or students; modes of formal education, including Qur'anic studies, remained confined to males.[52] Any formal training or introduction to Islamic jurisprudence and hadith studies also remained a mostly masculine domain.

Although Muslim scholars restricted women from formal educations, they did not release them from the burden of learning and studying the hadith and models of holiness. Theoretically, women bore the same responsibility as men to understand and follow Islamic teaching. Hadith scholars even recognized several women of the early community as worthy transmitters. Many of these women, such as `A'isha, the Prophet's youngest wife, lived with Muhammad and had intimate dealings with him. These women like none other could transmit information about the Prophet's actions, words, and directives because of their association in the domestic sphere.[53] Women's official roles largely ended in the domestic sphere, however; while many women acted as hadith transmitters, there are no extant compilations by female scholars and no information about them. Thus our medieval sources are once again written by men about women.

In these male-authored medieval texts about women, gender, and holiness, hagiographers and theologians transformed Mary and Fatima into champions for their pious agenda. Mary marked the boundaries between Christianity and heresy; Fatima led her family to paradise and consigned her enemies to hell. Both communities fashioned a view of piety, politics, and family by manipulating traditional gender roles while still assigning their heroines to the domestic sphere as miraculous mothers and virgins. Today's readers might be tempted to dismiss much of the hagiographers' works as too proscriptive if not blatantly misogynistic, but closer examination reveals a more complex agenda.

Chapter Three

Virgins and Wombs

In her work *Purity and Danger*, the anthropologist Mary Douglas explains that concerns for the physical body—its intactness, purity, and integrity—reflect concerns held by the body politic.[1] Douglas sees purity and pollution rituals relating to the body as symbols for society and social boundaries. The Israelites' halakhic (legal) preoccupation with bodily issues and orifices, for example, ultimately reveals their political and cultural apprehension about unity and security as a minority group.[2] In effect, legalistic obsessions with menstruation and ejaculation might tell the historian more about how Jews distinguished themselves from their Gentile neighbors than about how they viewed women's and men's bodies.

Gender historians of early Christianity have recently expanded Douglas's approach to reevaluate the early church fathers' admonitions against the female form. From this perspective, patristic texts and hagiography offer more than misogynistic ranting against the female body and instead identify a late antique body metaphor concerned for the social and political boundaries of a newly converted Roman Empire.[3] These writings rely particularly on the idealized virgin—disciplined through asceticism, sustained in chastity, and purified by God—to signify the orthodox, undefiled, and intact Christian church.

A similar body metaphor emphasizing purity instead of integrity evolved in Shi`ite Islam regarding Muhammad's prophetic status and the Imams' religious authority.[4] Some traditions explain that Allah formed the Prophet as pure light before he created time. This light is referred to as the *nur Muhammad*, which is the essence of the Prophet's being. With the light (*nur*) Allah engraved Muhammad's name on his throne.[5] The *nur* symbolizes Muhammad's favored status among the other prophets and his commission to transform a dark and corrupt world with Islam's radiance. After the creation of the heavens, earth, and humanity, Allah removed the light from his throne and translated it through the Prophet's ordained ancestry until it finally reached Muhammad's mother, Amina. During this conveyance, Allah carefully preserved the *nur* through a special covenant requiring all males to place the light only within the wombs of pure females. This provision was necessary because a woman's body might provide either an immaculate vessel for the light's containment and gestation or a ritual contagion if unclean, tainted, or impure.[6]

As Adam prepared to transmit the *nur Muhammad* to Eve, for example, he required her to perform ritual ablutions before sexual intercourse. When Eve finally conceived Seth, the light moved safely from Adam's loins to Eve's womb without contagion.[7] Adam later explained the responsibilities of the unique covenant to his son:

> Allah has ordered me to impose on you a covenant and a compact for the sake of the light on your face, to the effect that you shall deposit it only within the purest woman of all mankind. Let it be known to you that Allah has put upon me a rigid covenant concerning it.[8]

Allah commanded Muhammad's male ancestors to protect the divine light from the female body's potential threat.

Shi`ite sources employ the body metaphor to emphasize the transmission not only of the *nur Muhammad* but also of the preexistent Imams.[9] According to classical hadith esteemed by Twelvers, Allah created Muhammad, Fatima, and the twelve Imams as divine light and engraved all their names on his throne. Each light assumed corporal form only after miraculous conception, gestation, and birth free from ritual pollutants such as blood.

Fatima, as the only female sharing in the holy family's divine light, transcends mundane limitations ascribed to the female form: she neither menstruated nor experienced blood loss during childbirth. Fatima was born and continued to exist without impurities or pollution and, unlike Eve, presented the ever-immaculate vessel for the Imamate. Fatima's body, like Christianity's idealized virgin, presents a metaphor imbued with symbolic formulations of theological, political, and communal purity. While the virgin symbolized the church—immaculate, pure, and intact—Fatima signifies pristine Islam and the Shi`ite Imams' sublime status.

Although male authors translated Mary's and Fatima's virginal bodies into metaphors for communal identity and purity, these metaphors did not remain static. Hagiographers instead merged conflicting descriptions of purity and integrity with fecundity and creativity. The virgin's physical chastity ultimately led to spiritual fertility. Hagiographers revealed such dynamism by describing the virginal body and womb as a container, at once sealed from worldly contamination while prolific in spiritual works.

The womb itself is a multivalent symbol in sacred literature: it is the source of pollution and purity, chaos and order, darkness and light.[10] As the innermost female space, the womb pollutes through menstrual contamination,[11] yet can mediate sacrality as the inner sanctum of a cultic shrine (as in Christianity) or a domestic sphere (as in Islam). Because female reproductive space is occupied in sex and pregnancy, it is both honored and feared: it can contain new life, but, as an empty place, it might also be filled by malevolent forces.[12]

Ethnographers of traditional Islamic societies have also noted the symbolic relationship between the home and the womb. In traditional households women's quarters are at the back of the complex and masculine space is near the front courtyard. The female space, or secluded interior, can be called the *batn*, "inside, womb." Entry into this space proceeds through the *khashm*, or door, which also designates bodily orifices such as the mouth and nose.[13]

The womb symbolizes a sacred space, a sacred interior separated from the profane exterior. As an empty space, the womb invites penetration or occupation. In the ancient Greek context, for example, divinities bestowed the gift of prophecy on women by possessing their innermost spaces.[14] The female interior signified the potential for divine inspiration and presence within the community. Since unwelcome divinities, or *daemons*, associated with darkness and obscurity might dwell within the womb, female possession also conveyed potential threat.[15] Women (and their communities) might then benefit from divine favor or suffer from the potential chaos that lies within the female interior. Mary and Fatima provided such enigmatic figures for their own communities: virginal containers free from contamination, yet fecund with holiness.

Blessed Virgin Mary

Christian hagiographers fashioned their idealized virgin by transmuting Mary's mundane form into an extraordinary body. Mary's virginal flesh defied common laws of physicality and sexuality: Mary remained a virgin even after childbirth. Christian authors constructed this Marian icon as part of a complex ascetic theology that promoted the virgin's body as one symbolically transformed into the image of the resurrected Christ. Such a body trained through asceticism gains a glimpse of the spiritual form modeled by Christ and promised by the apostle Paul (1 Cor. 15.47–51).

The early Christian emphasis on self-abnegation and chastity functioned, at first, to distinguish the new community from its Jewish origins. The Jews celebrated sexuality and procreation as divine blessings from God; indeed, the Abrahamic covenant promised the patriarch offspring as numerous as the stars in the sky (Gen. 15.5). The covenant, as outlined by the Torah, demanded that the Jews worship Yahweh exclusively. In return, they were offered a promised land abounding in spiritual and material blessings. God pledged: "You [Israel] shall be the most blessed of peoples, with neither sterility nor barrenness among you or your livestock" (Deut. 7.14).[16]

The Christian canon diverges from the Judaic acclamation of procreation and family. Jesus (himself understood to be unmarried and celibate) promotes devotion to the "kingdom of heaven" wherein spiritual kinship supersedes physical consanguinity. In Mark 3.33–35, Jesus announces that "[w]hoever does the will of God is my brother and sister and mother," not his mundane relatives then summoning him at the door. Jesus even suggests that celibacy surpasses marriage in spiritual perfection: "but those who are considered worthy of a place in that age and in the resurrection from the dead neither marry nor are given in marriage" (Luke 20.34–36; also, Luke 20.29).

The Pauline epistles expand this virginal ideal by emphasizing the practicality of celibate life. Virgins, as Paul explains, simply have more time to devote to spiritual endeavors (1 Cor. 7). Paul wishes that "all were as I myself am [i.e., celibate]" (1 Cor. 7.7), although he carefully acknowledges that marriage does not constitute sin. Marriage instead signifies the spiritual relationship between Christ and his church: "Husbands, love your wives, just as Christ loved the church and gave Himself up for her" (Eph. 5.25). In a further correlation between the Christian household and the *ecclesia*, Paul commands wives to submit themselves to their husbands just as the church submits to Christ. Women within the marital bond thus represent a gendered image of the Christian community: submissive, domesticated, and redeemed by the salvific acts of the male "householder," Christ.

The second- and third-century church inherited from the Gospels and Pauline epistles this paradoxical view of virginity and sexuality wherein marriage is censured yet endorsed, criticized yet commended.[17] The early church promoted an equally complex ascetic theology: wildly popular narratives celebrated pious celibacy while theologians such as Clement of Alexandria (d. 215) called for moderation.

Soon after Paul's death (c. 150 CE), a number of apocryphal texts exclaiming the benefits of sexual renunciation circulated throughout the Christian world. The *Acts of Paul and Thecla*, perhaps the most prevalent, recounted the adventures of a young virgin named Thecla who, after hearing the melodious voice of the blessed Paul, renounced her fiancé and devoted herself to perpetual chastity.[18] For a time, Thecla provided a more popular virginal image than Mary herself. Thecla actuated her new vocation by cutting her hair, dressing as a man, and following after the apostle.

While this lifestyle certainly afforded Thecla more freedom to travel and even preach in the ancient world, the *vita* nonetheless subordinates the young virgin to the male apostle. Thecla appears as an amorous groupie who obsessively pursues her famous teacher; and after Paul finally commissions her to teach in Iconium, she secludes herself in a cave for seventy-two years sustained only by water and herbs. The *vita* popularized the notion of pious chastity while still relegating the female virgin to masculine supervision. Church fathers praised Thecla's astounding asceticism while encouraging other women (especially wealthy matrons) to become "new Theclas" and devote themselves, spiritually and financially, to the church.

Clement of Alexandria, on the other hand, proposed a broader understanding of sexuality and the body. He argued that Paul endorsed both marriage and celibacy equally and that fervent ascetics falsely exaggerated the rewards of virginity. Marriage represented the divinely ordained plan for procreation, although Adam and Eve, like two impatient adolescents, had originally rushed consummation. Because of their sexual enthusiasm, humanity inherited the desire and lust that sullies the sacred intent of the marital bond. Clement writes:

> A man who marries for the sake of begetting children must practice continence so that it is not desire he feels for his wife, whom he ought to love, and that he may beget children with a chaste and controlled will. For we have learnt not to "have thought for the flesh to fulfil its desires." We are to "walk honourably as in the way," that is in Christ and in the enlightened conduct of the Lord's way, "not in reveling and drunkenness, not in debauchery and lasciviousness, not in strife and envy."[19]

Married couples, Clement says, might practice sexual intercourse without guilt as long as they hold their desires in check.

Although even the more liberal fathers such as Clement sanction marriage, they share a general distrust of and profound ambivalence toward sexuality and the lustful body. Both Clement and Irenaeus of Lyons (c. 200) equate Adam and Eve's first sin not only with disobedience but also with the acquisition of carnal knowledge.[20] After Satan successfully tempted Eve and she shared the forbidden fruit with Adam, "the eyes of both were opened, and they knew that they were naked; and they sewed fig leaves together and made loincloths for themselves" (Gen. 3.7). Christian theologians easily assimilated sexual astuteness with the shame and disgrace of the Fall. Celibacy, on the other hand, negated the sinful scar manifest in the flesh and returned humanity to prelapsarian existence, untainted by passion and lust.

In the third- and fourth-century ascetic movement, desert anchorites exchanged their physical bodies for a new spiritual existence in an effort to gain such a prelapsarian form. Athanasius advanced this theme (*topos*) in his *Life of Anthony*, the sublime prototype for Western hagiography. Athanasius blends Old Testament images of desert asceticism with New Testament accounts of Christ's death, burial, and resurrection.[21] Antony at once becomes the new Elijah who found divine solace and preservation in the wilderness (1 Kings 19.4–8) and the image of Christ's resurrected body. After immuring himself in a tomb and combating his demons, Antony appears to his disciples transformed into a spiritual being.[22] He served as a visible icon of Paul's promise: "It is sown a physical body, it is raised a spiritual body" (1 Cor. 15.44). Antony and like-minded ascetics of the Egyptian and Syrian desert reclaim their paradisiacal form, released from fleshly bondage, and appear more angelic than human.

Although this desert theology enjoined celibacy and self-abnegation on both males and females, pious women expressed their ascetic heroism in vastly different ways.[23] The desert corpus advanced, in particular, the harlot-saint figure, holy women (usually former prostitutes) who had languished in their lust and finally redeemed their flesh by immuring themselves in caves and practicing radical penance. These "holy harlots," such as Mary of Egypt and Pelagia of Antioch, signified God's redeeming power as they transformed their bodies from corruptible Eves (harlot-temptress) to impenetrable Virgin Marys (cloistered behind cave walls and chaste).[24] The holy harlots' cave existence provided a symbolic replica of Mary's impenetrable womb. The Virgin Mary provided a didactic icon, exhorting women to reverse their fallen nature inherited from the temptress Eve.

As the ascetic impulse spread to the western regions of the empire (including Italy and Gaul) during the fourth and fifth centuries, Western theologians adapted the harlot-saint ideal to its new audience. Church fathers assimilated respectable Roman matrons to the desert icons and promoted Mary as a sublime model for female imitation. Mary presented a virginal ideal that advanced an ascetic theology: her pure, incorruptible body signified the redeemed flesh available (through asceticism) to the daughters of Eve. In constructing this Marian *exempla*, church fathers relied on already existing literary and theological traditions.

Popular extracanonical Christian works had displayed the fascination with Mary's virginity since the early second century. What details the Gospel accounts neglected, popular imagination soon supplied. In the *Odes of Solomon* (an early hymn book written in verse), the author embellished the Gospels' account of Jesus' miraculous conception and delivery. First, the Holy Spirit opened Mary's breast, combined her milk with God the Father's, and delivered the mixture to Mary:

> The womb of the Virgin took [the milk],
> And she received conception and gave birth.
> So, the Virgin became a mother with great mercies.
> And she labored and bore the Son but without pain,
> Because it did not occur without purpose.
> And she did not require a midwife,
> Because He caused her to give life.[25]

In this text the image of the virgin merges provocatively with the maternal nature of a lactating God and Mother. The virgin is neither barren nor desolate; she is "mixed" with God, produces milk, and delivers a son. Mary also escapes the indictment of Genesis 3.16: "I will greatly increase your pangs in childbearing: in pain you shall bring forth children." The *Odes of Solomon* provides Mary with prelapsarian flesh, freeing her from Eve's punishment for paradisiacal sin. Hagiographers thus confirmed that virginal asceticism leads to physical and spiritual transformation.[26]

The *Protevangelium of James*, another second-century apocryphal text, goes even further. Although controversial and even banned for a time in the Latin West, the *Protevangelium* effectively laid the foundation of late antique and medieval Marian theology. It emphasized Mary's Immaculate Conception, perpetual virginity, and childhood miracles. It also established a gendered metaphor of the virginal body by confining and containing Mary within temple walls and, later, Joseph's home (domestic space).

The *Protevangelium* depicted Mary as the ultimate sacred space. In imitation of Hannah's plea for a son (1 Sam. 1.9–11), the *Protevangelium* describes Anna and Joachim's desperation for a child (even a girl child). After Mary's birth the couple preserves the infant's room as a sanctuary and prevents any impurities from entering. When Mary was three years old, Anna and Joachim fulfill their pledge and consecrate her at the temple where she was "nurtured like a dove" and "received food from the hand of an angel."[27] After Mary reaches the age of menstruation and becomes a potential pollutant to the temple space, Joseph, a local widower, accepts her into his care. The childhood room, the temple space, and finally the private sphere of Joseph's guardianship maintains Mary's sacrality. She, like the space she occupies, remains impenetrable (except to the consecrated priest), protected, and contained.

In rendering Mary's body as sacred space, early hagiographers symbolically correlated her with the Hebrew temple constructed on the tabernacle prototype. Beginning in Exodus 25, God commanded Moses to construct this tabernacle (or dwelling place) for him in the midst of the Israelite camp. The tabernacle, consecrated to God, included an outer courtyard complete with an altar accessible to the Israelites, an outer sanctum accessible only to the priests, and an innermost Holy of Holies accessible only to the high priest. A fine curtain woven from blue, purple, and crimson yarns and fine twisted linens separated the outer sanctuary from the inner sanctum. In the Holy of Holies resided the ark of the covenant, and in the empty space between the cherubim mounted on the ark resided God himself.

Late antique hagiographers subtly transformed Mary's body into a tabernacle. Mary moves from her parents' public space to the temple's sacred space and finally to her restricted existence under Joseph's guardianship. Like the tabernacle's Holy of Holies, Mary soon holds God's presence within her innermost womb/chamber. The tabernacle's Holy of Holies can even be interpreted as a nuptial bedchamber; in that sacred space God united with Israel, his Bride.[28] In similar fashion Mary's womb becomes the locus of God's presence and union of humanity and divinity.

According to the *Protevangelium*, when Mary resided with Joseph the temple priests gathered "pure virgins of the tribe of David" to weave a new veil for the temple. The priests then cast lots to decide which virgin should weave what color: "And to Mary fell the lot of the 'pure purple' and 'scarlet.'"[29] When Gabriel later visited Mary and announced her pregnancy, Mary trembled and "took the purple and sat down on her seat and drew out [the thread]."[30] As she encounters the angelic messenger, Mary weaves the purple and red symbolic of divinity and martyrdom just as her womb would soon "weave" the flesh of the God-Man.

At the end of the *Protevangelium*, the midwife Salome questions Mary's sacrality and receives prompt retribution. Like the apostle Thomas in John 20.25, Salome doubts the physical integrity of the person before her: "As the Lord my God lives, unless I put [forward] my finger and test her condition, I will not believe that a virgin has brought forth."[31] After she inserted her hand, testing Mary's perpetual virginity, it withered (or caught aflame), restored only by the touch of the infant Jesus. Mary's flesh, as Jesus with the doubting disciple, proved incorruptible.

The church fathers included these Marian traditions in a larger rhetorical framework of feminine compliance and regulation. Ambrose (d. 397), bishop of Milan, for example, championed Mary as the "discipline of life," or the sublime model for Roman virgins to emulate.[32] He and other like-minded theologians confined females to private space just as Mary resided within imposed masculine boundaries throughout her own lifetime. Ambrose wrote:

> [Mary] was unaccustomed to go from home, except for divine service, and this with parents or kinsfolk. Busy in private at home, accompanied by others abroad, yet with no better guardian than herself, as she, inspiring respect by her gait and address, progressed not so much by the motion of her feet as by step upon step of virtue. . . . [As the Evangelists have shown,] she, when the angel entered, was found at home in privacy, without a companion, that no one might interrupt her attention or disturb her; and she did not desire any women as companions, who had the companionship of good thoughts.[33]

This ascetic Mary, cloistered within her *domus* (domestic space), no longer resembles the Hebrew girl of the New Testament Gospels who traveled to visit Elizabeth and participated in temple feasts. She instead reflects an immuring theology for females proscribed by episcopal authority. Female ascetics, as the Virgin Mary, resemble the Song of Solomon's "garden enclosed":[34] "You are a garden locked up, my sister, my bride; you are a spring enclosed, a sealed fountain" (4.12–13).

The female virginal body is transformed into sacred space, contained and secured. Ambrose even likens virgins to altars on which Christ "is daily offered for the redemption of the body."[35] Yet male agents ultimately mediate between that sacred space and the mundane world as altar servants. Ambrose continues: "Blessed virgins, who emit a fragrance through divine grace as gardens do through flowers, temples through religion, altars through the priest."[36] Theology concerned for Mary's virginity reveals not only a model for female imitation but also a rhetoric endorsing masculine agency and authority within the burgeoning church. The divine blessings of the female "altars" proceed only through the intercession of a masculine clergy.

Late antique theologians delineated Mary's sacred status through the use of container metaphors; Mary was a feminine vessel, a perpetually pure vessel, "possessed" by the divine God-Man. Such imagery confirmed her status as virgin (the purified inner sanctum) and mother (pregnant with the Divine Son). Theologians such as Ambrose and Jerome again invoked Old Testament descriptions of the Hebrew tabernacle, transforming Mary into an archetypal sacred container holding the Divine within her body.

Just as the Holy of Holies and the ark of the covenant marked the dwelling place of Yahweh in the midst of the Israelites, Mary's womb provided the empty space wherein the God-Man dwelled. The door or passageway remained sealed except for the divine High Priest. Ambrose, in *De Institutione Virginis*, asserts the Mary–tabernacle parallel explicitly while discussing the Book of Ezekiel. Ambrose identifies Mary as an exemplary model and transmutes her into the prophet Ezekiel's visionary New Temple:

> And later the prophet [Ezekiel] related that he had seen on a very high mountain the structure of a city whose many gates were revealed; one, however, was described as shut, concerning which he said: Then He (the Lord) brought me back to the outer gate of the sanctuary, which faces east; and it was shut. The Lord said to me: This gate shall remain shut; it shall not be opened, and no one shall enter by it; for the Lord, the God of Israel, has entered by it; therefore it shall remain shut (Ezek. 44.1–2) [Ambrose added]: Who is this gate except Mary, "shut" as a virgin? Therefore, Mary is the gate, through whom Christ entered into this world[,] . . . a gate which was shut, and is not opened. Christ passed through her, but did not "open" her.[37]

Ambrose explains that the *porta* is the womb's gate *(venter)*, inviolate for any ordinary man, yet miraculously penetrated by the God of Israel.

Mary's womb corresponds to the Temple's east door, accessible only by the Divine and sealed thereafter.

Jerome, too, relates Mary's body to the Hebrew temple. In his polemic *Against Pelagius*, Jerome defines Mary's womb as the temple's east door available only to the High Priest. The divine God-Man alone miraculously entered the womb, and it remained permanently closed after Jesus was born.[38]

Jerome's text reveals that Marian theology was still evolving in the West; for in an earlier treatise Jerome had explained that Christ, as the "first-born," had indeed opened Mary's womb.[39] This had compromised Mary's *in partu* virginity, or the notion that Mary's womb remained miraculously sealed and she remained (corporally) a virgin before, during, and after childbirth. Yet when Jerome wrote *Against Pelagius* in 415, he concluded along with Ambrose that Mary's womb remained perpetually closed like the tabernacle's east gate. Jerome and Ambrose successfully translated Mary's womb into a metaphor for permanent enclosure (like the tabernacle's inner sanctum). Not only did this argument boost the uniqueness of Christ's birth (i.e., a Christological point), but it also supplied a powerful prototype for the growing number of female ascetics to imitate: one of seclusion, purity, and impenetrability.

Marian texts extolling this immuring lifestyle, using the womb as a metaphor, ultimately served to curb the public and independent careers of imperial women recently converted to Christianity.[40] Late antique hagiographers advertised the *vitae* of wealthy patrician women who dedicated their money to the church, their lives to charity, and their bodies to a new spiritual Bridegroom while leaving the public rule of the church to male clergy. Hagiographers modified desert spirituality to a new form of elite asceticism wherein matrons and young virgins abandoned their fineries and delicacies in favor of a more austere lifestyle devoted to pious reflection, usually under the tutelage of male mentors.

Jerome's personal fondness and spiritual counsel for Roman matrons consecrated to the ascetic life is a significant example of this new elite asceticism. He paints a vivid picture of ascetic expectation in his *Epistle 22* to the young virgin Eustochium.[41] A good virgin, Jerome explained, exercised self-control regarding food and drink; she never evoked lust from a man's heart; and she never crossed the boundaries of her *domus*.[42] At the same time, however, Jerome encouraged holy women to imitate

Paula's excessive (and public) acts of charity. In his *Vita Paulae* (*Ep. 108*), Jerome said:

> Her liberality alone knew no bounds. Indeed, so anxious was she to turn no needy person away that she borrowed money at interest and often contracted new loans to pay off old ones. . . . "God is my witness," she said, "that what I do I do for His sake. My prayer is that I may die a beggar not leaving a penny to my daughter and indebted to strangers for my winding sheet."[43]

Paula, a noble woman descended from the Gracchi and Scipios according to hagiographic convention, subverts traditional Roman values by abandoning her family and relinquishing her patrimony to wed her new heavenly Bridegroom.[44] She becomes a new Mary, submissive, silent, and receptive to God's will, which is now mediated by a masculine hierarchy (i.e., Jerome).

The womb also provided theologians such as Ambrose and Jerome with a multivalent symbol. Blurring gender boundaries, the theologians used the womb not only as a metaphor for female purity and enclosure but also as an image of fecundity and birth. The soul, much like the womb, received the divine seed (or Jesus) and became pregnant. This divine (and intellectual) pregnancy transformed both men and women into spiritual beings; human gender proved irrelevant as God impregnated the souls of both sexes.[45] Origen proclaims that the soul represents the heavenly Bridegroom's beloved who "conceives from Christ, it produces children. . . . Truly happy, therefore, is the fecundity of the soul."[46] The soul, like the womb, bears "spiritual" fruit in works and deeds.[47] Mary, after all, had welcomed God's impregnation in an ultimate act of selfless obedience and, by this holy work (*sanctus labor*), gave birth to humanity's redeemer.[48] Every soul, then, should submit to the Divine Will, receive God's seed, and become fecund: in effect, believers should become "like Marys."[49]

Early medieval authors inherited this metaphor of the womb's spiritual fecundity and continued to promote Mary as an exemplar for both men and women to imitate. For female virgins in particular, Marian imagery articulated a clear message of feminine compliance and accommodation to the church hierarchy. Medieval authors, much like the church

fathers, encouraged religious women to confine themselves to the growing number of cloisters and bear spiritual children instead of corporal
progeny. Unlike their predecessors, however, early medieval authors
advised holy women to envision themselves as numinous mothers and
concentrate on their maternal responsibilities toward their family and
communities.

As Christianity expanded and stabilized in the post-Constantinian
era, wealthy female patrons offered the method and means of constructing new monastic foundations, educational facilities, and charitable
endowments. Virginal rhetoric again offered a social critique and theological response to female affluence and charisma. The exemplary virgin, displayed so eloquently by the Mother of God, extended a powerful
rejoinder to the pious female's complex (and perilously public) status in
addition to promoting an ascetic ideal.

Bishop Avitus of Vienne (d. 518) composed a poem addressed to
his sister, Fuscina, in praise of chastity and the celibate life. He assures
Fuscina that Christ has released her from the bonds of physical lust and
transformed her into his heavenly bride: "You are enrolled as a consort,
are wedded to a mighty king, and Christ wants to join Himself to your
beautiful form which He has selected."[50] Fuscina's physical sexuality is
eradicated by her spiritual (although strangely erotic) union with her divine Groom. As the Bride of Christ, she is now released from the perils of
mundane marriage, childbirth, and (hopefully) her own sexual nature.

Avitus then advises Fuscina that she must bear good works in her
soul/womb as evidence of her divine marriage. He persuades her to imitate Mary's conception of Christ through her own spiritual pregnancy:

> You may follow Mary who was permitted under Heaven's dispensa-
> tion to rejoice in the twin crown, that of both virgin and mother,
> when she conceived God in the flesh, and the Creator of heaven,
> revealing the mystery of His being, entered her inviolate womb. . . .
> But you, my sister, will not be without the glory of a deed that great
> if, as you conceive Christ in your faithful heart, you produce for
> heaven the holy blossoms of good works.[51]

Avitus carefully acknowledges that such conception is required of both
men and women: "mind and not gender carried off the palm of victory."[52]

But, for Avitus, spiritual pregnancy implies separate risks and responsibilities for the two sexes.

The pious bishop warns his sister against relapsing into her earthly vanities and lusts in a subtle castigation of what he views as woman's nature. He offers spiritual remedies to guard against her sensual proclivities; first and foremost he requires her to occupy both body and mind with good works. Avitus extols study (a *sanctus labor*) above all others but commands his sister to read "manfully" to avoid distraction and frivolous fantasies.[53] He also offers the life of Eugenia as one worthy of contemplation and emulation.

Eugenia was a Roman martyr who enjoyed intellectual debate and studying the Scriptures. As a young virgin, she dressed as a man in order to live in a monastery where her piety and devotion distinguished her among her colleagues. At the abbot's death, her brothers nominated her as his replacement; she declined, however, because custom prevented a woman from ruling over a man.[54] Eugenia's true identity was finally revealed publicly after she was falsely accused of rape.[55] Avitus thus reminds his sister that she may study as a man does and learn as a man does, but, in the end, she may not *become* a man. She should instead remain cloistered and protected, obedient to the church hierarchy, and fecund in spiritual deeds.

Bishop Fortunatus of Poitiers, a near-contemporary of Avitus, details the spiritual fertility of Radegund, founder of the Holy Cross convent at Poitiers. Radegund adopted Caesarius of Arles's monastic rule, which demanded complete claustration.[56] Fortunatus explained that Radegund devoted her immured existence to serving her spiritual family and the Frankish community with amazing displays of domestic piety. When Radegund died, her nuns could only watch from atop the convent walls as she was carried away, for, according to the rule, no consecrated nun should ever leave the convent's protection.[57]

Fortunatus's hagiography chronicles Radegund's radical acts of self-abnegation, displays of charity, and maternal care for her convent.[58] His poems also betray a close friendship with both Radegund and Agnes, abbess of Holy Cross. In one of his poems addressed to Agnes, he characterizes Radegund as the mother who had "given birth to both of us in a single delivery from her chaste womb, as though the dear breasts of the blessed mother had nurtured the two of us with a single stream of milk."⁵⁹ Fortunatus herein viewed his own spiritual life and friendship with Agnes as products of Radegund's spiritual fecundity. She, like Mary, gave birth to the church's saints.

The life of Galswinth, also by Fortunatus, presents another Merovingian queen distinguished by her domestic miracles and maternal deeds.⁶⁰ Galswinth's spiritual fecundity benefited her entire adopted Frankish community. Unlike Radegund, she lived outside the cloister and continually interceded between the poor and vanquished and her husband, King Chilperic (d. 584).

According to Fortunatus, Galswinth was a Visigothic princess far from home and family. Yet in perfect maternal fashion, she adopted her new community and served it willingly: "The maiden . . . earned the great love and respect of the people. Charming some by gifts, others by her words, she thus makes even strangers her own. . . . [T]he stranger, by her generosity to the poor was a mother to them."⁶¹ Galswinth's deeds (performed as one newly converted to Catholic Christianity) might be compared to the soul's fecundity, the spiritual womb giving birth to Christian charity.

One of Galswinth's postmortem miracles also attested to her revered position among her community. As her body was deposited in her burial chamber, a hanging lamp crashed to the stone ground yet remained intact and with its flame still burning.⁶² The lamp symbolizes Galswinth's beloved status as it parallels the parable of the ten virgins in Matthew 25.1–13. According to this parable, ten bridesmaids went to meet their Heavenly Bridegroom, but only five had sufficient oil for their lamps. When the Bridegroom arrived, he accepted the five virgins and escorted them to the wedding banquet. Like the alert and prepared virgins, Galswinth, with her lamp continually burning, too attained the Groom's rewards.

The lamp may also suggest Galswinth's maternal function by further assimilating her to the Marian archetype. Not only does the miracle echo the parable of the ten virgins but it also recounts God's command in Leviticus 24.2. According to this Old Testament edict, God required the priests to maintain lamps within the tabernacle symbolizing his perpetual presence. These lamps burned only the purest oil and sat in stands of pure gold. Galswinth, as a new tabernacle, held God's light within her own vessel-body even after it crashed to the ground. Fortunatus transforms Galswinth's body into a container for the Divine presence.⁶³

Fatima al-Batul (the Virgin)

While over the centuries Christianity popularized the virginal return to a prelapsarian state by circulating holy women's *vitae*, classical Islam never articulated a cosmogonic link between sin and sexuality. Asceticism flourished in Sufi circles and among pious mystics, but the Qur'an and hadith literature extolled the body and sexuality as divine gifts. As Christian virgins hoped to reclaim prelapsarian existence free from lust, medieval Muslims disavowed virginal piety in exchange for marital bliss.

The Muslim descriptions of paradise offer a sufficient glimpse into the exaltation of sexuality and sensual pleasures. In the next life Allah will reward the righteous with plentiful gardens, cool waters, luxurious mansions, and pure spouses.[64] The medieval exegetes Abd al-Rahman b. Ahmad al-Qadhi and Shaykh Jalal al-Din al-Suyuti further detail the heavenly vision by including the eight gates at its entrance, all constructed in precious stones, atop a ground composed of musk-clay, grass of saffron, and dust of amber.[65] In these sublime surroundings also reside heavenly houris (*huriyat*), or beautiful female creatures—seventy for each righteous male—who are flawless in their sensuality and femininity. Their bodies are composed of saffron, musk, and amber, and their cascading hair resembles raw silk. Allah assigns each houri to her Muslim husband and engraves his name on her chest. She then anxiously awaits her husband's arrival and weeps over his absence. Once there the Muslim man encounters perfect love, sensuality, and sexuality: the houris miraculously retain their virginal bodies at the same time that their sexual stamina increases.[66]

Muslim men also enjoy perfect sexual pleasure with their earthly spouses. They regain youth, vigor, and beauty while their pious Muslim women derive complete satisfaction from the eternal marriages. In accordance with Islamic law, even in paradise women may have only one husband whereas men collect many partners.[67] Although hadith maintain that both the male and the female achieve perfect sensual satisfaction through their respective experiences,[68] the obvious incongruity is difficult to ignore. This view of paradise exemplifies Islam's approach to female sexuality in general.

In paradisiacal descriptions, female sexuality is both marginalized and strictly contained while men languish in various sexual delights with wives, houris, and (in some poetry) young boys.[69] Islamic law ignores female sexuality as well; legal texts go to great lengths to outline legal expressions of male sexuality but are largely silent on women. Shi`ite Islam even permits a much-debated form of temporary marriage called *mut'a* to accommodate the male sex drive. Temporary marriage is a contract forged between a man and a woman, without legal documentation and often in private, that binds husband and wife for an established amount of time, from a number of hours to ninety-nine years. Supporters of temporary marriage argue that it gives men a religiously sanctioned method of sexual contact with the implicit supposition that they seek sexual pleasure more ardently than do women.[70]

From a Western perspective, this version of male sexuality expressed even in paradise might seem materialistic and oddly sensual. Late antique and early Christian theologians (who shaped medieval and even some modern expectations of the afterlife) viewed paradise very differently. Many of these authors, such as Irenaeus and Tertullian, agreed that the flesh itself will be resurrected; that is, human identity does not simply reside in the spirit or soul but also in the body's material continuity. Yet the resurrected flesh will be very different from the earthly body: according to 1 Corinthians 15.21–54, the resurrected body will be imperishable and incorruptible; in Matthew 22.23–32 the body will not marry but be like the angels; and in 2 Corinthians 5.4 the earthly body is but a burdensome tent/tabernacle compared with the immortal, heavenly dwelling. The resurrected heavenly bodies will not require food, sex, or sensual joys but will take pleasure in continually praising God.[71] According to Jerome and Augustine, sex organs will remain in heaven (unused) as part of a sublime gender hierarchy only because this hierarchy was so important in defining virtuous rank on earth.[72]

In Islamic religious consciousness, however, paradise is a logical continuation of the celebration of the body's senses: it celebrates even more fully the ways Muslims encounter Allah and enjoy his creation through the body. The flesh and sexual pleasures, far from being associated with primeval sin or obligatory redemption, number among Allah's creation and, therefore, his wondrous gifts. The Qur'an encourages sexual intimacy (within legal marital bonds) and even promotes marriage as a metaphor for Allah's unity.[73]

Although Islam releases humanity from the scar of original sin and the shame of sexuality, Muslims nonetheless struggle to maintain a state of purity required to commune with Allah. In this sense Islam resembles the halakhic traditions of Judaism, carefully outlining conditions of ritual purity and impurity. Pollution is not viewed as an ethical issue or sin problematic. Pollution or impurity works instead within legal traditions, separating the sacred from the mundane. Islam asserts a constant contention between sacrality and pollution on a daily, even hourly basis.

Islamic law regulates and routinizes the body's constant lapse from and return to purity. Throughout the day legal pollution occurs through biological functions of elimination, excretion, or emissions. After ritualized cleansing (either *wudu'*, lesser ablutions, or *ghusl*, complete lustration), the body returns to its pure state, again able to commune with God.[74] The impure body must remain outside sacred boundaries, dissociated from handling the Qur'an, prayer, or fasting. The female body also derives impurity from menstrua, pseudomenstral emissions, or lochia.

In contrast, the paradisiacal body realizes a state of constant purity and functions as a vehicle for divine communion with Allah. Instead of receiving redemption from its sexual sin and shame, the body achieves complete harmony with itself. The righteous, for example, consume food without digestion and excretion and experience sex without pollution (the emission of semen or other fluids), and women cease to menstruate.[75] From this paradisiacal state, Fatima or al-Batul (the Virgin) originates.[76]

Fatima's appellation, al-Batul, at first seems enigmatic considering that she bore four children who survived her: two sons, Hasan and Husayn, and two daughters, Zaynab and Umm Kulthum. Unlike the Virgin Mary, al-Batul need not indicate corporal integrity. Fatima as Virgin instead symbolizes paradisiacal purity through exemption from all ritual pollutants.

Certain Shi`ite hadith place Fatima in paradise, preexistent and formed of Allah's *nur*, prior to her earthly conception. There Allah stored her essence in a fruit (apple, date, or pomegranate) and commanded Muhammad to consume it during his famous night journey and ascent to paradise at the beginning of his ministry (*mi`raj*):

The Prophet said: When Gabriel ascended with me to the heavens, he took my hand, he admitted me to paradise, and he offered to me a date from it. And I ate it and it was changed to sperm in my loins.

When I descended to the earth and had intercourse with Khadija, she became pregnant with Fatima.[77]

In a scene reminiscent of the Christian Fall, Muhammad eats from the paradisiacal tree as commanded by God via Gabriel. The proffered (not forbidden) fruit contained Fatima's essence, and eating it led to her creation and birth. In contrast, Christian theologians viewed eating as humanity's pathway to sin. By consuming the fruit denied them in paradise, Adam and Eve brought death and destruction into the world. This imagery hints again at Islam's completion of the Judeo-Christian story. God invites Muhammad (unlike the biblical prophets before him) to eat the fruits of heaven, while Khadija, in another type of miraculous conception, receives Fatima's essence directly from paradise. Fatima, like Mary's immaculate conception and Jesus' virgin birth, is conceived free from sin, pollutants, or impurities.

Muhammad continuously recalls his daughter's paradisiacal nativity by calling her a human houri and reporting that he "smells from her fragrance of paradise."[78] Fatima characterizes eschatological perfection: like the houris who remain eternal virgins, Fatima's body displays the idealized feminine form. She emanates musk and amber, she never menstruates, and she bears her sons without blood loss or other contamination.[79] Instead of exemplifying corporal integrity, Fatima's status as virgin connotes paradisiacal perfection free from impurities. She is, by her essence, sacred.

Shi`ite hadith underscore this sacrality through linguistic exegesis of *batul* (بتول). According to one transmission, the Prophet designated *al-batul* simply as one "who has never seen red, that is, has never menstruated."[80] The transmitter further defines *virgin* by relating the root (verbal form), *batala* (ب-ت-ل, to cut off or sever), to its synonym, *qata'a* (قطع). Mary is a virgin, "cut off from man," devoid of passion for them or they for her. Fatima, however, is "cut off [separated] from women of her time."[81] The human houri thus surpasses the virtuous women on earth in both purity and divine favor.

Other hadith rank Fatima as superior to women not only of her own generation but also of all time. She is compared specifically with Maryam bint `Imran (Mary, daughter of Imran) and receives the appellation *Maryam al-kubra*, or Mary the Greater. This intertextual allusion asserts the supersession of Christianity by Islam. Mary along with other heavenly women attend Fatima's birth, symbolically conceding the infant's magnificent status:

> [And while Khadija was in labor] four tall, brown-skinned women came to her, as if they were women from Banu Hashim. And she feared them when she saw them. And one of them said: Do not grieve, Khadija, because we are messengers of your Lord to you, and we are sisters. I am Sara, and this is Asiya bint Mazīhim [the Pharaoh's righteous wife]. . . . [T]his is Maryam bint ʿImran, and this is Kulthum, the sister of Musa ibn ʿImran, [for] God has sent us to you. . . . And one sat to [Khadija's] right, and the other to her left, and the third in front of her, and the fourth to her back. She gave birth to Fatima, the Pure One, without ritual impurity.[82]

The sublime midwives, along with ten houris, then proceed to bathe and wrap the infant in water and linens from paradise.

The presence of the four holy women at Khadija's side attests to Fatima's significant station and Islam's completion of Judaism and Christianity. Sara, Asiya, Mary, and Kulthum all serve Khadija at Fatima's birth. Fatima, as Mary the Greater, promotes Islam's transcendence while also providing a feminine ideal of purity and virtue. This ideal does not stand alone, however, as Fatima also represents the sublime mother. Like their Christian counterparts, Islamic hagiographers emphasize fertility and spiritual fecundity alongside Fatima's ritual purity. Once again, hagiographers liken their holy woman to sacred containers, a metaphor most apt for the mother who held the Imamate within her womb.

Medieval Shiʿite cosmology presents the womb as an equally complex and multivalent symbol as does Christian tradition. The womb symbolizes both the pure inner sanctum where the sublime seed dwells and the locus of fecundity and familial loyalties. Christian exegetes related the sacred womb to spiritual vocation and enclosure, commanding its female religious to be both virgin and mother, chaste and pregnant. Shiʿite authors used the metaphor for different purposes. Instead of outlining the expectations of spiritual pregnancy and the individual soul, Shiʿite exegetes linked their communal identity to maternal kinship with Fatima.

According to Shi`ite cosmology, the pure womb protected Muhammad's divine *nur* (as well as that of the Imams) from pollution and contamination. Medieval hadith related that Allah fashioned the *ahl al-bayt* from his *nur* before the creation of the heavens and the earth. At the moment of creation, Allah placed Muhammad's *nur* and the Imams into Adam's loins and then required the angels to bow in symbolic submission to their spiritual authority. Allah transmitted the *nur* through Muhammad's Arabian ancestors with women serving as immaculate vessels for the light's "gestation." This enabled the Prophet to finally boast: "A whore has never given birth to me since I came out of Adam's loins."[83]

Allah continued to secure immaculate vessels for Fatima and the Imams; Muhammad, for example, impregnated Khadija immediately after his visit to paradise (*mi`raj*). Once in the womb, Fatima conversed with her mother in miraculous displays of maternal comfort. According to one hadith, Qurayshi women had rejected Khadija after she married Muhammad so that when she became pregnant she had no companions. Feeling her mother's intense loneliness, the preexistent Fatima consoled her by issuing proclamations against the Qurayshi women from the womb in her mother's defense. After Muhammad heard about these chats between daughter and mother, he revealed to Khadija a message from Gabriel: "He tells me that she is a female, and that she is the blessed, pure progeny and that Allah, Blessed and Exalted, will create my progeny from her . . . and Allah appoints them [as] His caliphs on His earth."[84] While these traditions emphasize Khadija's miraculous relationship with Fatima, they also illustrate Fatima's unique status as divine matriarch. Fatima nurtures and comforts her biological mother even before her birth, and she contributes the surrogate womb for Muhammad's sublime progeny, the Shi`ite Imams.

Fatima, unique among women, participates in the divine light and then later furnishes the vessel (her own body) for the Imamate. Muhammad b. Ya`qub al-Kulayni (d. 940–41) relates Fatima to the famous Qur'anic Light Verse (24.35):

Allah is the Light of the heavens and the earth, the parable of His Light is as if there were a Niche and within it a Lamp, the Lamp enclosed in Glass, the Glass as it were a brilliant star.

According to Kulayni's exegesis, Fatima serves both as the niche wherein the lamp (i.e., the Imams Hasan and Husayn) resides and the shimmering glass itself.[85] Fatima, unlike the women of her paternal ancestry, is both vessel and *nur*.

Shi`ite traditions associate Fatima with other ancient container archetypes as well.[86] Noah's ark prefigures the salvific force not only of Fatima but also of the entire holy family as a vessel of salvation. One hadith recounts the Prophet's words:

> The people of my house (*ahl bayti*) may be compared to Noah's ark; whoever rides in it is saved and whoever hangs on to it succeeds and whoever fails to reach it is thrust into hell.[87]

The ark imagery resonates with the figure of Fatima. She, also as a vessel, contains the hope of salvation—her progeny, the Imamate. This tradition provides a striking parallel to early Christian exegesis that acclaims Mary as the "new ark." Late antique authors first promoted Noah's ark as the Old Testament symbol for the church. Like the ark the *ecclesia* might be tossed and tried, yet never submerged or defeated. Early medieval authors such as Saint Hildephonsus of Toledo (d. 667) likened Mary to the wooden vessel: just as the ark held the hope of humanity, so Mary's body enclosed humanity's redeemer.[88] Theologians thus transformed both women into sacred vessels for their holy offspring.

According to Shi`ite tradition, Gabriel himself explained to Noah that his ark prefigured the holy family's salvific force. When Allah commanded Noah to build the vessel, the angel delivered five sparkling nails to aid in its construction (which resonates with the image of Christ's five wounds). As Noah received the first four, he rejoiced; yet he could only weep as he looked at the fifth.[89] Gabriel then reported that the nails symbolized the holy family: Muhammad, `Ali, Fatima, Hasan, and Husayn. The fifth nail, imbued with sorrow and pain, prophesied Husayn's martyrdom at Karbala.

After Noah completed the ark, God flooded the earth and set the vessel afloat. According to tradition, the ark soon experienced rough sailing: it began to toss as the waters and wind raged. Noah offered supplications to Allah and soon learned why the ark trembled so: it was then passing over the plain of Karbala.[90] Allah revealed the Shi`ite holy family's prophetic status and suffering; and as Noah recognized and even participated in those sufferings, he was symbolically transformed into a distant relative and brought aboard the ark of salvation. Just as Fatima's womb contained the light of the Imams, the ark embraced all the adoptive members of the *ahl al-bayt*.

Virgin Mothers?

Mary and Fatima provide both Christianity and Shi`ite Islam with the ultimate paradox: they are figures of incorruptible purity and virtue pregnant with spiritual deeds and piety. Both women personify ideals of feminine chastity; they transcend the limitations placed on mundane women and attain a paradisiacal form here on earth. Mary, the miraculous virgin, remains intact and uncorrupted while living a life of seclusion and charity in prelapsarian flesh. Fatima, *al-batul*, provides a pure vessel for the Imams within her undefiled body. Whereas early Christian authors elevated Mary as flesh transformed, Shi`ite transmitters hailed Fatima as flesh perfected.

While advancing these feminine ideals, Mary's and Fatima's hagiographers represented them as sacred space. As undefiled containers of sublime progeny, their bodies resembled the tabernacle, lamp, and ark of biblical tradition. The vessel metaphors also served to subtly promote masculine public authority and feminine compliance. Mary's *vita* modeled the secluded and privatized life intended for young Christian virgins to imitate; Fatima's paradisiacal form still deferred to the authority of her husband, `Ali. Taken together, the virgin mother is relegated ultimately to male agency evident both in a masculine clergy (who traverses sacred/profane and public/private space) and a patriarchal *ahl al-bayt* (Fatima's father, husband, and sons).

From another perspective, however, these models may reveal more about theology than human gender expectations. The church fathers command both men and women to become "like Mary" and transform their barren souls into fecund wombs through the conversion process. According to ascetic theology, Christ transmutes the sinful flesh of both men and women so they may be the spiritual consorts of the Heavenly

Bridegroom and dedicate themselves to good works. Fatima's womb, like an ark of salvation, contains the Imamate, the sublime descendants of Muhammad created by Allah. Fatima's purity confirms the Imams' status while offering security to all those who identify with the Shi`ite holy family. Mary's and Fatima's bodies thus effectively advertise the salvific powers of the church and Shi`ite Imams, their holy families, to their respective communities.

Chapter Four

Mothers and Families

In his work *The Body and Society*, Peter Brown poses this interpretive option for scholars of ancient texts: "Rather, they [the Apocryphal Acts] reflect the manner in which Christian males of that period partook in the deeply ingrained tendency of all men in the ancient world, to use women '*to think with*.'"[1] Brown's approach resembles Douglas's notion that considerations for the human body reflect larger concerns within the body politic. Drawing also on the conclusions of the structural anthropologist Claude Lévi-Strauss, Brown argues that male authors present women as a means to verbalize concerns for Christian identity in a seductive pagan society. His project, like current feminist scholarship, approaches women as literary constructions employed by male authors to didactic ends.[2] Cameron, for example, relates late antiquity's obsession with the virginal body to the political purity and security of the Christian empire.[3] Feminine imagery reveals not only social expectations of women but also political and theological designs promoted by a male elite.

Such a methodology affords a better understanding of how hagiographers and theologians of Christianity and Islam used the image of Mary and Fatima. Medieval writers certainly intended their models to provide guides for women to imitate; yet they also employed Mary and Fatima *to think about* matters of politics and theology. By using Mary and Fatima as symbols *to think with*, medieval authors articulated ideals of orthodoxy or rightness. Male writers developed the notions of right doctrine, right communities, and right gender.

Early Christian and Shi`ite theologians formulated their doctrinal orthodoxy by explaining Mary's and Fatima's role as holy mother to their holy families. Each group's rightness refers to the nascent religious identity evolving among their own ranks; it does not imply universal recognition of a true or pristine Christianity or Islam. In the specific case of Shi`ism, for example, Shi`ite Muslims were neither demographically dominant in the Muslim world nor (except for a brief time during the mid-tenth century) politically successful in the medieval period. Doctrinal orthodoxy applies to the specific theology and ideology shaped by religious thinkers about their own rightness, their own identity. By highlighting Mary's and Fatima's relationship with their sublime progeny, these authors fashioned feminine authorities on matters of theology and morality. Mary, as the mother of God, gave expression to the nature of Christ; and Fatima, as the Imams' mother, verified the status of the *ahl al-bayt*. Right doctrine became flesh in both Mary and Fatima.

As doctrinal orthodoxy developed and became a matter of identity, both the Christian and Shi`ite communities needed to clarify their boundaries and sharpen their polemics against the other or the heretic. Although cogent theological statements in the early medieval period certainly exist, many dogmatic statements and concerns are embedded in texts about women. As medieval authors distinguished their own nascent communities from unorthodox ones, they used identification with holy women as a marker.

Hagiographers reified Mary's and Fatima's heavenly attributes in terms of miraculous maternity and domestic deftness. As the female was increasingly identified as the core of the family unit, she also emerged as a politically galvanizing symbol for the group she represented. With the establishment of a matriarchal figure at its center, what might otherwise be just another political faction was transformed into a spiritual family—the social group that creates the deepest affective bond among its members. Although both groups sought to create a spiritual community, Christian and Shi`ite hagiographers exalted two very different styles of motherhood. The Christian theologians' Mother Mary extolled a more sublime maternal model wherein the bride wed a heavenly Bridegroom and often (but not always) adopted a life of chastity. This path was a path of perfection. Shi`ite authors offered Fatima as a more practical model for Muslim wives and mothers to emulate; Islam lauded temporal marriage and motherhood over the more symbolic, spiritual pattern followed by monastics.

The Merovingians employed the Christian maternal image to provide themselves with a political pedigree in the sixth and seventh centuries. The new Frankish dynasty converted to Christianity and vigorously employed Christian symbols as a means of authorization among the Gallo-Roman elite they supplanted. Frankish texts sanctioned female monasticism and Merovingian rule by adapting abbesses and queens to a Marian heavenly prototype, thereby identifying Merovingian holy women as maternal and nurturing intercessors. They remade their queens into royal mothers and their abbesses into new Marys. Those outside of Frankish royal bonds—the Goths, the laity, or the Arians—lacked membership in the elite and presumably blessed and favored group.

Classical and medieval Shi`ite texts likewise converted Fatima into the mystical nexus of the holy family, equating orthodoxy with familial membership. The early Shi`ite community envisioned itself as members (and defenders) of the *ahl al-bayt*, a type of extended family with Fatima at its center. While the community might be persecuted in this world, these righteous kin would certainly receive their reward in paradise. As sublime matriarch, Fatima identified her supporters and adopted kin and then cast all pretenders into the hellfire. Shi`ite hadith accentuated Fatima's maternal role with gendered images of miraculous parturition, suckling, and food replication.[4]

It is impossible to deny that theologians also intended Mary and Fatima as orthodox gender models for all pious women to imitate. As matriarchs (and idealized virgins, mothers, and brides), Mary and Fatima draw their authority from the private domestic sphere, a space ideally regulated by public male figures. Priests, Imams, and Shi`ite clerics arrogate to themselves public authority by symbolically negotiating between the domestic sphere and public space. Pious women, emulating Mary and Fatima, thus should yield (at least in theory) to the altar servants and religious scholars sanctioned by God.

Sublime Brides, Pious Mothers, and Holy Families

Even though early Christian theologians praised virginal asceticism, they also elevated marriage and motherhood as pious vocations. Even Jerome admitted that brides and mothers would inherit their heavenly reward, although it would be significantly less than virgins and chaste widows.[5] Theologians again found their didactic icon in Mary; the Blessed Virgin, elevated for her docile submission to God's will, also reigned as Christ's Bride and Mother.[6] As such she provided not so much a practical model for secular brides and wives but a spiritual ideal for Christ's monastic spouses. Though Mary's identification with the Bride of Christ only reached its zenith during the high and late Middle Ages, especially with the writings of Bernard of Clairvaux,[7] late antique and early medieval exegetes laid the theological foundation.

Christian Scriptures are replete with bridal images. Old Testament prophets often described the covenant between Yahweh and Israel as a marriage pact. Isaiah proclaims: "For as a young man marries a young woman so shall your builder marry you, and as the bridegroom rejoices over the bride, so shall your God rejoice over you" (62.5). Ezekiel and Jeremiah warn Israel not to forget her bridal responsibilities or commit adultery with other nations' gods (Jer. 2.32). Likewise, New Testament disciples identify Christ as the Bridegroom (Matt. 9.15; Mark 2.18–20; Luke 5.33–35) and Paul defines the church as Christ's bride (Eph. 5.25–33; 2 Cor. 11.2).

Early church fathers emphasized these nuptial images and furthered the Pauline metaphor by correlating the church/*ecclesia* with the Virgin Mary. They explained that the Song of Songs' bridal figure (already associated with the *ecclesia*) signified Mary herself. In a rather ironic twist, patristic authors thus identified the Virgin with the pure, unstained Bride from the canon's most sexual text.

The Song of Songs opens with the plea, "Let him kiss me with the kisses of his mouth," and continues with visions of perfumes, wine, beauty, and desire. Amid images similar to the Islamic paradisiacal description, the lover (Bride) and beloved (Bridegroom) express their mutual affections. The lover describes him: "His head is the finest gold; his locks are wavy, black as a raven. His eyes are like doves beside springs of water, bathed in milk, fitly set" (Song of Songs 5.11–12). He is like "a bag of myrrh that lies between my breasts . . . a cluster of henna blossoms in the vineyards of En-gedi" (1.13–14). The beloved extols his bride's beauty: "Your lips are like crimson thread, and your mother is lovely. . . . Your two breasts are like two fawns, twins of a gazelle, that feed among the lilies. . . . You are altogether beautiful, my love; there is no flaw in you" (4.3–7).

The Song of Songs boldly approaches sensuality and sexuality and develops intense emotion between two equal participants. The bride and bridegroom's mutual desire, however, remains unsatisfied. As the bride searches the streets for her beloved and as the bridegroom disappears from the lover's door, they only contemplate each other's charms. Unlike the Islamic paradisiacal promotion of sexual bliss, love's power remains in its desire: "love is strong as death, passion fierce as the grave. Its flashes are flashes of fire, a raging flame. Many waters cannot quench love, neither can floods drown it" (8.6). Christian exegetes argued that the Song of Songs promotes an eschatological vision of the church's own anticipation for the return of its beloved Bridegroom. Even in this context of sensuality and desire, the church (and Mary) retains its virginal purity only in expectation of its heavenly consummation.

Ambrose was perhaps the first church father to correlate Mary with the Song of Songs' perfect, spotless bride. He compared the first display of desire, "Let him kiss me with the kisses of his mouth," (1.2) with the Annunciation event. The "kiss" of the Holy Spirit encompassed Mary and she conceived the God-Man.[8] Song of Songs 1.2–3 continues, "your anointing oils are fragrant, your name is perfume poured out." This, Ambrose said, further signifies the anointed Mary and the virgin birth: "she conceived as a virgin and as a virgin brought forth good odour, that is to say the Son of God."[9]

A fifth-century student of Augustine expanded the exegetical correlation between Mary and Christ's bride by identifying her with the woman mentioned in Revelation 12.1: "a woman clothed with the sun, with the moon under her feet, and on her head a crown of twelve stars."[10] This apocalyptic figure had only been recognized as the church that would descend as the new Jerusalem, or "the holy city . . . prepared as a bride adorned for her husband" (Rev. 21.1). The fifth-century conflation of Mary and the eschatological woman of Revelation—previously labeled the church—underscored her identification with the heavenly *ecclesia*.

Ambrose and Augustine transformed Mary into a symbol of the church most thoroughly. In his exegesis on Luke, Ambrose examined Christ's final words to Mary and John: "'Woman, here is your son.' Then he said to his disciple, 'Here is your mother'" (John 19.26–27). He suggested that Christ's pronouncement correlated Mary with the church: Mary now acted as the universal matron of all disciples, represented by John, and as Christ's Bride.[11]

Both theologians also emphasized Mary's maternal fecundity without jeopardizing her perpetual virginity.[12] As a metaphor for the church, Mary provided for the intersection of fecundity and virginity. Just as Mary delivered Christ, pure and sinless, so too would the church produce pure Christians. Augustine provides the most detailed image of the Mary-church parallel:

Let your heart accomplish in the law of Christ what Mary's womb wrought in the flesh of Christ. How are you not included in the child-bearing of the Virgin since you are members of Christ? Mary brought forth your Head; the church, you His members. For the church, too, is both mother and virgin: mother by the bowels of charity, virgin by the integrity of faith and piety. She brings forth diverse peoples, but they are members of Him whose body and spouse she is, and even in this respect she bears the likeness of the Virgin because in the midst of many she is the mother of unity.[13]

The church and Mary share the same pious duties. Both remain pure in body and soul yet fertile in charity and conversion.[14]

The church fathers' expansion of Marian imagery in an emerging Christology and ecclesiology also offered a feminine image of submission and obedience. By surveying Mary's actions as mother, the Fathers articulated a feminine ideal of radical compliance. When the angel Gabriel appeared to Mary and announced her impending pregnancy, she replied: "Here am I, the servant of the Lord; let it be with me according to your word" (Luke 1.38). Mary's acceptance became the exemplary model for all the "Lord's handmaidens," both virginal and married.[15]

Arabo-Muslim culture has also promoted marriage and motherhood as sacred vocations; and, as in Christianity, the status of bride and mother can be viewed as both empowering and confining. According to Muslim theology, for example, the male and female complement each other as two aspects of a single being. Qur'an 4.1 states, "O humanity! Fear your Guardian Lord, Who created you from a single person, created, out of it, his mate, and from them twain scattered (like seeds) countless men and women." Before created time males and females composed a single being and will be reunited in the marriage contract: husbands and wives essentially complete each other. Marriage represents an expression of *tawhid* (divine unity)—returning to the oneness of creation from diversity and division.[16]

While marriage between men and women might symbolize cosmogonic unity and completion, social mores nonetheless make strict distinctions between men and women and masculine and feminine space. Tradition relegates women to home and hearth, identifying the feminine with the private and secluded. In like manner tradition proclaims this female space forbidden (*haram*) to men outside the proscribed kinship boundaries. Strict clothing customs also enforce the social demarcations between the sexes. Men must cover the area between navel and lower thigh; women are removed from the masculine gaze by means of veiling or complete seclusion.[17]

The gendering of space and dress firmly establishes expectations of the sexes: males, in the end, should look and act like men, and women should look and act like women.[18] This operates in a larger, divine hierarchy revealed by Allah wherein the woman resides under masculine authority and maintenance. Male householders able to negotiate between private and public space are commended as "the protectors and maintainers of women, because Allah has given the one more (strength than the other), and because they support them from their means" (Qur'an 4.34).

The house (*bayt*) serves as feminized space and the locus of domestic sacrality. Herein Allah bestows grace and blessing via progeny, especially male progeny. Marriage socializes the theology of completion and in certain respects objectifies women as childbearers. Women purvey divine favor by producing offspring while residing under the male householders' custodianship. Mothers receive recompense in the afterlife; the Prophet, for example, proclaimed that "paradise is under the heels of the mother."[19] Women who die in childbirth receive the same heavenly rewards as those warriors who die in jihad. Women resume their earthly domestic status in paradise as they remain faithful to their husbands and nurturers to their children.

Fatima, as archetypal mother, displays many of these attributes: she remains closely aligned with the domestic sphere, she bears coveted male children to the Imam `Ali, and she ultimately submits to `Ali's custodianship. The Prophet emphasizes Fatima's submissive qualities in one description of her eschatological duties. According to Shi`ite tradition, Muhammad will lead and intercede on behalf of faithful Muslim males before Allah's throne on judgment day. He commissions Fatima to lead the faithful women who not only perform the ritual requirements of Islam (prayer, fasting, alms, and hajj) but also "obey their husbands."[20] Fatima's submission to `Ali provides a sublime example for women to imitate. One transmitter noted that Fatima's appellation *al-haniya*, the compassionate, indicates her sympathy for her children and obedience to her husband.[21] Unlike Mary, Fatima provides a practical model for women to imitate, available for all wives and mothers instead of a monastic audience married only to a spiritual bridegroom.

The circumstances surrounding Fatima's marriage to `Ali are sometimes difficult to distinguish. Both Sunni and Shi`ite hadith describe the marriage contract and wedding ceremony between Fatima and `Ali, although they vary as to when the union actually took place. Most accounts claim the marriage occurred in 623 after the Battle of Badr (the early Muslims' first significant victory against the still unconverted Meccans).[22] There is even less agreement as to Fatima's age at the time of betrothal: various authors place her between nine and twenty-one years old.[23] All sources, however, confirm that the wedding was most distinguished by the poverty of the Prophet's family.

According to hadith, `Ali provided a meager dowry of either his coat of mail (*dir`*, worth 4 dirhams, 300 dirhams, or 400 dirhams), or a sheepskin and a garment.[24] On `Ali and Fatima's wedding night, Muhammad visited and blessed their marriage by sprinkling water across their upper bodies.[25] That night, and many others as well, the young couple slept atop an untanned sheepskin with a covering too small to reach from head to toe.[26]

Shi`ite hadith embellish descriptions of terrestrial poverty with cosmological significance. Before `Ali proposed, for example, other suitors approached Muhammad offering extravagant dowries for Fatima.[27]

Muhammad shunned their display and tossed pebbles at one of the suitors that miraculously became precious pearls.[28] The act reveals the Prophet's true wealth and favor with Allah, not measurable against material fortune. Gabriel then descends and announces that Allah has already ordained Fatima's marriage to `Ali.

The earthly poverty of Muhammad's family is then refunded by celestial participation. According to one tradition, the paradisiacal wedding occurred in heaven forty days before the Medinan ceremony with Gabriel acting as the public speaker (*khatib*), Allah as guardian (*wali*), and angels as witnesses. The dowry (*mahr*) in heaven reflected the holy family's true wealth: Fatima possessed one-half of the earth along with paradise and hell.[29] After the ceremony Allah caused the *tuba* tree in paradise to shed pearls, precious stones, and luxurious robes, which the houris gathered and continue to hold for Fatima until the day of resurrection.[30] Such a ceremony indicates not only the family's divine favor but also Fatima's eschatological significance: she presides over paradise and hell and consigns her family's supporters to one and their enemies to the other.[31]

The terrestrial ceremony was no less significant. Shi`ite traditions relate the appearance of heavenly maidens and houris transporting perfumes, exotic fruits (not tasted by mortal man since the time of Adam), and various spices. Gabriel and/or Michael attended, calling down from heaven the *takbir*, or "God is Great, *allahu akbar*."[32] According to Shi`ite exegetes, this terrestrial ceremony simultaneously reflects the family's wealth in paradise and contributes the community's *sunna* (custom). In contemporary marriage celebrations, for example, the exclamation "Allah is Great" is recited, and the dowry might be modeled after `Ali's gift.[33] Fatima's wedding provides the archetypal ceremony for Shi`ite brides to imitate as well as heavenly rewards for which to strive.

Shi`ite traditions acknowledge that Fatima's engagement and wedding were not completely without friction. Medieval transmitters such as al-Tusi, al-Kulayni, and al-Qummi report Fatima's reluctance and even hostility toward `Ali's proposal.[34] Fatima cries when Muhammad introduces her future husband and complains that he is unattractive and too poor. Muhammad then lists `Ali's virtues and explains that Allah commands the union. Fatima, like the obedient Mary, piously accepts `Ali and expresses her happiness. Such rhetoric not only advances `Ali as Allah's chosen and righteous agent but also models Fatima's feminine compliance as she accepts both her father's will and `Ali's spousal authority. Legal scholars, both medieval and modern, use her wedding as proof that a woman's permission is necessary in marriage.[35]

Fatima's largely traditional marriage does not completely distract from her unique status. She maintains her divine knowledge and prophetic insight, even to `Ali's surprise. According to one tradition, Fatima received a book from paradise after her father died that outlined all world events from the beginning to the end of created time.[36] In another tradition, dated before Muhammad's death, `Ali met Fatima and she said: "approach, [so that] I [may] tell you of what was, and what is, and of what is not until the day of resurrection when the [last] hour is manifest."[37] `Ali was so surprised by his wife's prophetic abilities that he immediately went to the Prophet and asked how she acquired them. Muhammad, without hesitation, reminded the Imam that Allah created Fatima from the same *nur* as themselves. This shared divine essence enabled Fatima to share many of the charismatic talents of the Imamate.

Shi`ite traditions elevate Fatima as the Mistress of Sorrows.[38] Fatima weeps, wails, and mourns the deaths of both her father and her son. In 632 Muhammad first tells Fatima of his impending death and then consoles her by promising that she shall soon follow (i.e., she will not be without him for long).[39] According to Shi`ite tradition, he then warned his daughter of the pathetic sufferings she would experience after his death. Abu Bakr and `Umar refused to recognize `Ali as Muhammad's successor and, in an ultimate act of disgrace, denied Fatima the oasis of Fadak, land she claimed according to birthright.[40] After public humiliation, beatings, and a miscarriage, Fatima died as the Prophet foretold only six months after his death.

Fatima suffered most poignantly over her son Husayn's martyrdom at Karbala. According to tradition, Fatima witnessed the Karbala tragedy from paradise. Ja`far al-Sadiq, the sixth Imam, described her reactions:

> [F]or truly Fatima continues to weep for [Husayn], sobbing so loudly that hell would utter such a loud cry, which, had its keepers [the angels] not been ready for it . . . its smoke and fire would have escaped and burned all that is on the face of the earth. Thus they contain hell as long as Fatima continues to weep . . . for hell would not calm down until her loud weeping had quieted.[41]

Fatima wails so loudly that neither paradise nor hell are able to ignore Husayn's catastrophic death.

As the weeping mother, Fatima reflects the gendered expectation of women in Arabo-Muslim death rituals.[42] Women traditionally wail and lament in public displays after the deaths of close family members. Many Muslims condemn this practice because it focuses on earthly instead of heavenly familial bonds, seems to challenge the will of Allah, and reveals a lack of faith. These critics point to several hadith that disparage loud and extravagant exhibitions and instead promote female saints who refused to wail after their children's deaths.[43] As wailing is recognized as a female occupation, this contentious discourse casts women in the role of pious inferiority because they fail to accept tragic events as God's plan.

At the same time women's participation in funerary rites complements the usually male-identified methods of mourning, which include prayer and verbal compliance to Allah's will. Women's wailing affords a visual (and auditory) display of kinship ties, familial loyalty, and human emotion. In this sense, Fatima as the Mistress of Sorrows reveals a powerful and approachable archetypal mother who grants access to the *ahl al-bayt*: she recognizes those who share in Husayn's sufferings and welcomes them into the "family of sorrows."[44] This gendered discourse simultaneously contains feminine authority by relating it to the domestic and emotional spheres. Fatima's position as virgin and mother thus complement each other: as virgin, Fatima signifies the perfectibility of paradise; as mother, she binds the terrestrial family of the Prophet to its paradisiacal counterpart. Joining the house of sorrows (*bayt al-ahzan*) on earth ensures a position in the house of sorrows in paradise through association with its most suffering Mother.

Right Doctrine

Medieval Christian and Shi'ite authors carefully crafted Mary and Fatima as holy matriarchs, continually mindful of their respective households, the church and *bayt*. Yet exact membership in those households needed explanation. What beliefs identified the true members from pretenders? Who really belonged in the sublime families? By exploring the relationship between matriarch and kin, theologians articulated their spiritual precepts more fully. In Christianity, for example, Ambrose and Augustine explained their Christology by depicting Mary's miraculous conception and parturition; they also developed an ecclesiology by correlating Mary's body with the church body (virgin and mother, pure and fecund).[45] Merovingian theologians were no different; they also devoted considerable effort to both defining Christian orthodoxy and locating potential heretical threats by invoking Marian rhetoric.

Gregory of Tours, for example, defends the doctrinally pure Catholic clergy against fraudulent Arians by describing their various miracles. In *Glory of the Martyrs*, he described the Arian-Huns' siege of Bazas and the local bishop's triumph through prayer. According to Gregory, the bishop prayed for relief from the enemy onslaught and God sent "men dressed in white" and a "great ball of fire" to frighten the enemy king Gauseric. After the Huns deserted the battlefield, the bishop celebrated mass and noticed three drops, similar to crystal, hanging from the altar. He gathered them together and the three fused to form one exquisite gem.

> By an obvious deduction it was evident that this had taken place in opposition to the evil heresy of Arianism, which was hateful to God and which was spreading at that time. It was furthermore acknowledged that the holy Trinity was bound in a single equality of power and could not be pulled apart by chattering [arguments].[46]

By miraculous intervention, God revealed the real motivation behind the bishop's success; it was a victory of orthodoxy over Arian heresy.[47] Hagiographers also emphasized orthodox theology against the Arians by repeated appellations of Mary and her role as the God-Man's mother. These statements, ubiquitous and formulaic, introduced Christ in incontrovertibly orthodox terms. Gregory once presented Christ as one who, in the end, "deigned to be enclosed in the womb of Mary, ever virgin and ever pure, and the omnipresent and immortal Creator suffered Himself to be clothed in mortal flesh."[48]

Sometimes Mary played a more active role in the defense against heresy. Gregory recounts one Marian miracle that occurred "in the East" wherein a young Jewish boy attending mass with his friends received the holy Eucharist.[49] When he returned home, the young boy revealed his actions to his father, "an enemy of Christ and Lord and his laws."[50] The

Jewish father immediately tossed the boy into a blazing furnace despite the frenzied pleas of the mother. Neighboring Christians finally realized what was happening and interceded; they found the boy lounging unhurt on the flames "as if on very soft feathers."[51] While God had protected the young boy just as he had protected the three Hebrews of the Old Testament, he condemned the father to the anguishing flames.[52] The boy professed afterward that "the woman sitting on the throne in that church where I received the bread" protected him inside the furnace.[53] Gregory concluded that the blessed Mary guarded the young communicant who then, "having acknowledged the Catholic faith, . . . believed in the name of the Father and the Son and the Holy Spirit."[54] Mary's intervention expressed the Trinitarian orthodoxy, the potency of church sacraments, and salvific hope for "heretical" Jews.

The miracle story also might have been Gregory's attempt to warn Jews against interfering with conversion. In the sixth century a renewed wave of anti-Semitism swept through Gaul: the Council of Agde (506) reiterated earlier restrictions against Jews and Christians intermarrying and eating together;[55] and Bishop Avitus of Clermont introduced forced expulsions and conversions in 576. Gregory, who had written several texts supporting the efforts to convert Jews, might have intended his miracle story as a warning against Jews in Clermont who sought revenge against the conversion efforts.[56] The Marian miracle promised swift and divine retribution for those who tried.

Merovingians also emphasized Mary's role as mother and nurturer as they transformed themselves into Christianity's new champions. Frankish women, in particular, became powerful Christian envoys resembling Christ's Bride and Mother. Whereas late antique authors had demanded that women deny their sexuality, embrace virginity, and forsake their families (and pledge their patrimonies to the church), early medieval hagiographers positioned most holy women at the center of the family unit, both mundane and spiritual. This reflects the Frankish political milieu in which royal power resided in familial connections.[57]

To recognize that hagiographers relegated their female subjects to the domestic sphere does not negate the influence and command that Frankish women wielded.[58] Uniquely, holy women shared this domestic space with their royal kings and kin. A woman's power at court, for example, often depended on her loyal household servants, the strength of her regency over a minor child, and her family connections, not to mention her wealth. According to Frankish law codes, women could own land, and royal women often received land as part of their *morgengaben*, or bride-price. Personal land and control of royal treasuries translated into substantial power.[59] Hagiographies thus reveal a strong domestic core of royal might, with the holy woman, the sublime matriarch, carefully poised at its center. Although each royal household differed and each holy woman's family and domestic experience was somewhat different, most biographers developed this matriarchal image by emphasizing their conversion efforts.

Merovingian authors hailed holy queens as great missionaries and peacemakers by recognizing and glorifying their efforts in the conversion of Frankish kings and subsequently their families. During the fifth and sixth centuries, residents of Gaul, faced with the Roman Empire's transformation, had merged with the invading Franks to form a unique cultural experiment. By necessity, Gallo-Romans and Frankish "barbarians" united in one community ultimately defined by Christianity.[60] Queens usually transmitted this new faith, converting first their pagan kings and then their new communities.[61]

Gregory of Tours describes the conversion of Merovingian King Clovis (d. 511) by transforming him into the "new Constantine" destined to convert his empire to Christianity.[62] Gregory merges Clovis's spectacular victory over the Alamanni in 496 with Constantine's legendary triumph at Milvian Bridge in 312; both received divine visions from God that led to conversion. After that conversion Clovis aligned himself with Saint Martin of Tours, the most popular of the Gallo-Roman patrons. He frequently visited Saint Martin's relics, sent gifts to the saint's shrine, and patronized the construction of various new pilgrimage sites.[63]

Gregory also explains Queen Clothild's persistent missionary fervor that prepared Clovis for his visionary experience. Clothild, of Gallo-Roman and Burgundian ancestry, appears as the archetypical nagging wife throughout Gregory's history and her hagiographies.[64] When she married Clovis she constantly urged him to convert to orthodox Christianity for obvious spiritual and even political reasons.[65] Her ninth-century hagiographer commended her as the church's protectress and missionary responsible for diverting Clovis from idolatry and Arianism.

Queen Clothild funded several basilicas and churches throughout Gaul and also sponsored the Parisian cult of Saint Genovefa, a fifth-century Gallo-Roman virgin who miraculously protected Paris against the Huns.[66] By associating the two holy women, hagiographers correlated Clothild's own struggles against Germanic Arianism with the young saint Genovefa's contentions with Hunnish barbarians.

Not only did Clothild serve as a fearless Genovefa against the Arian onslaught, she also offered her maternal care to her extended family in the newly conquered Frankland. In constructing this feminine ideal, hagiographers adopted a Marian vocabulary of virgin, mother, and bride and fashioned their queen as a numinous matriarch. Queen Clothild becomes a new Mary as the mother of the church. Her hagiographer describes the king's baptismal scene: "For as was fitting in the pagan king's approach to baptism, Saint Remigius took the lead as they entered playing the role of Jesus Christ and the holy Queen Clothild followed as the embodiment of God's church."[67] Just as Mary signified the redemptive body of the church, so too Queen Clothild offered redemption to the Frankish empire through the king and conversion efforts. Her hagiographer says, "Her sweetness softened the hearts of a pagan and ferocious people . . . and she converted them through blessed Remigius with her holy exhortations and unremitting prayers."[68] Queen Clothild reflects Mary's own salvific acts as mother of the church: each is hailed as queen and submissive handmaid.[69]

Doctrinal regulation for both spiritual and political ends took a different path in Shi`ite Islam. Instead of proliferating lives of specific holy women, Shi`ite hagiographers emphasized the sublime status of Fatima and the holy family. Recognition of and acceptance into the *ahl al-bayt* served as an identity marker in early medieval Shi`ism much like baptism in Christianity. Through associating with the house of sorrows and participating in its suffering, initiates joined a sacred family that offered salvation and intercession in paradise. After the tragedy at Karbala, the Shi`ite community was not just a political movement fighting to avenge Husayn's murder but an extended family mourning the Prophet's grandson and grieving with their kin.

Medieval hadith designated `Ali and Fatima's children as Muhammad's own and extolled their family as the cosmological link between the

Prophet and his community. To love Muhammad's family was to love Muhammad. In one hadith, the Prophet explained to `Ali:

> Oh `Ali, Fatima is part of me and she is the light of my eye and fruit of my heart. What saddens her, saddens me, and what makes her happy, makes me happy. . . . Be good to her after me, and as for al-Hasan and al-Husayn, they are my sons and my two offshoots, and they are the masters of the youths of the people of paradise. They are as precious to you as your hearing and your sight.[70]

The Prophet explains the intimate bond between himself and his daughter: he feels what she feels; she abides, literally, as part of his body. More than just a daughter, she provides the surrogate womb for his heirs. The *shi`at `Ali* is more than just the party of `Ali; it is the party of the family.

Early Shi`ite cosmology even promoted a celestial link between the souls of the larger Shi`ite community and the ancestry of their Imams. According to one tradition, Allah constructed bodies for the Imams' divine light out of clay. He then separated some of that clay, which was then imbued with the Imams' essence, and created the souls of the *shi`at `Ali*. After Allah assembled the souls, he removed clay from beneath his throne and formed the community's bodies. The entire Shi`a family, of all time and all places, share the Imams' essence through this celestial generation. When one part of the family suffers or experiences joy, the others share in that experience.[71] They are joined by spirit rather than blood.

Allah, as well as Muhammad, recognizes this familial bond in the Shi`ite community. According to one report, Allah "is angry for [Fatima's] anger, and is pleased with [her] contentment."[72] Fatima is an access point to the Divine; she, in effect, links the earthly community with the sublime. Whoever offends Fatima, or threatens her favored status in the *ahl al-bayt*, also faces Allah's punishment. Muhammad extended the condemnation of his enemies to include those of his beloved daughter: "whoever injure[s] her in my lifetime [or] injure[s] her after my death [will receive the same penalty]."[73]

Fatima the matriarch, the intimate of the Prophet and Allah, offers entrance into the holy family itself. She functions as the loving mother, welcoming her "adopted" children into the extended kinship group. Medieval exegesis associates her name's root meaning with this maternal imagery: ﻓ-ﻄ-ﻢ (*f-t-m*) designates the process of weaning. The scholars explain, "[She] is named Fatima on earth because she weans her *shi`a* (party) from the hell-fire."[74] Fatima's adopted children receive eternal reward through their devoted mother.

Imami hagiographers emphasize Fatima's role as matriarch and locate her within the home (*bayt*) by assigning her various domestic miracles, particularly those of food preparation. These miracles have an important precedent in Qur'an 19.22–26: Allah miraculously provides Mary, in the pains of childbirth, dates and water. In like manner Allah, through Fatima, provides his community with divine sustenance. According to Shaykh al-Mufid, (b. 948/950), God honored the charitable deeds of Fatima and the entire *ahl al-bayt* by sending down Qur'an 76.8–10: "And they feed, for the love of Allah, the indigent, the orphan, and the captive; (saying) 'We feed you for the sake of Allah alone: No reward do we desire from you nor thanks.'"[75] In one example Fatima forgets to prepare her family's meal because she is busy with obligatory prayer (*salat*). When the Prophet and `Ali enter, they see a boiling pot of meat settled beside her prayer chamber.[76] Fatima turns and is amazed by Allah's providence.[77]

In another miracle account, the Prophet, weak from hunger, staggers into Fatima's home. He asks his daughter for a meal, but she has little food in the house. She prepares what she can and offers her father and family meat and bread. Allah then miraculously multiplies the provisions so that the bowls never empty and the food tastes "as nothing ever tasted before." Fatima, aware of Allah's bounty, takes the food and distributes it to her neighbors.[78] As matriarch, she supplies her family's nourishment and dispenses divine blessings while she also tends to the surrounding community, symbolically assimilating them to her maternal care.

Shi`ite hagiography pitted Fatima against a specific enemy to the faith, Eve or Hawwa', who ultimately failed to recognize the family's sublime authority. According to early Christian theologians, sin entered the world through Eve's disobedience to God's paradisiacal law, and Mary's obedience later reversed the shameful taint. For Shi`ites, Eve/Hawwa' committed the severest heresy of all: she failed to confess the superior status of the holy family and envied Fatima's position in it.

The Qur'an is mostly silent regarding Eve/Hawwa', naming her only "Adam's wife."[79] Allah placed Adam and his wife in the Garden, both yielded to temptation, and Allah finally banished them after their disobedience. Adam alone received specific blame for their sin (Qur'an 20.120–22), and he alone repented (2.37). Islam absorbed traditions of Hawwa' through Isra'iliyat, which consisted of Jewish haggadah and early Christian apocrypha. These traditions, especially in the tales of the prophets (*qisas al-anbiya*), contributed a plethora of extrascriptural, hagiographic narratives to the Qur'anic story. The medieval author al-Kisa'i described Hawwa's appearance before her disobedience or betrayal of Allah:

> Eve [Hawwa'] was as tall and as beautiful as Adam and had seven hundred tresses studded with gems of chrysolite and incensed with musk. She was in the prime of her life. She had large, dark eyes; she was tender and white; her palms were tinted, and her long, shapely, brilliantly colored tresses, which formed a crown, emitted a rustling sound. She was of the same form as Adam, except that her skin was softer and purer in color than his was, and her voice was more beautiful. Her eyes were darker, her nose more curved, and her teeth whiter than his were.[80]

Medieval Qur'anic exegesis and hadith, drawing on these hagiographic traditions, expanded the Qur'anic account of Hawwa' and revealed her role in Satan's ploy against Adam. Qur'anic commentators filled in the narrative gaps by conforming Hawwa' to her Christian prototype. For example, Allah molded Hawwa' from Adam's crooked rib as a helpmate and comfort.[81] She received the name Hawwa'—as the mother of all the living (*hayy*) and as one who was formed from a living being, Adam.[82] Although liberated from causing the Christians' original sin (absent in Islamic theology), theologians still maintained that Hawwa', a beautiful temptress, led Adam into rebellion against Allah. Because of this error, Allah cursed her with menstruation, pain in childbirth, and weak mental abilities.[83] Women, like their mother Hawwa', became a potential curse to their husbands instead of a comfort: they represented an intellectual and spiritual liability.[84]

Shi`ite tradition expanded Hawwa's (and sometimes even Adam's) sin of disobedience and betrayal of Allah to include the betrayal of the *ahl al-bayt* as well. To define Hawwa' as a failed woman and enemy of the family, hagiographers juxtaposed her to the feminine archetype of Fatima. Shi'ite traditions reported that Allah favored the Imams above all creation and placed them on his throne. He regarded the divine light, embodied in the holy family and Imams, as his most beloved and chosen regents on earth. By extension, he rewarded their supporters and punished their enemies. Any enemy or pretender who falsely claimed the Imam's station, or even consorted with tyrants, committed *shirk*—the unpardonable sin of "associating," or maligning Allah's Oneness (*tawhid*).[85] This transgression ultimately led to Adam and Hawwa's expulsion from paradise.

After their creation, Allah continually warned the couple not to look upon the *ahl al-bayt* with the "eye of envy." Yet, overcome by temptation, Adam and Hawwa' desired the holy rank Allah never allotted them. They became pretenders (sing., *mudda'in*) to the light of Allah; both, equally liable, gazed upon the holy family's exalted status. For Hawwa' this narrative twist permitted temporary exoneration from the role of temptress. Since eating from the forbidden tree no longer constituted the pivotal moment of sin, Hawwa's temptation of Adam appeared only secondary. In most accounts, Adam and Hawwa' ate from the forbidden fruit as a result of their envy; Adam usually ate first.[86]

Hawwa's emancipation from the role of temptress did not continue unopposed. Shi'ite tradition maintained her inherent impurity and inferiority through constant contrasts to the idealized female: Hawwa' ultimately opposed the Mistress of the Women of the World, Fatima. Muhammad's daughter, like Mary with Eve in Christian tradition, served to amend Hawwa's mistakes and provide the idealized feminine figure. Hawwa' even appeared painfully aware of Fatima's superiority:

And [Satan] overcame Hawwa' to look at Fatima with the eye of envy until she ate from the tree as Adam had eaten. And Allah, mighty and exalted, expelled them from His Paradise, and sent them away from [their position] near Him to the earth.[87]

Hawwa' coveted not only the rank of the *ahl al-bayt* but also the specific position of Muhammad's daughter. This established a textual dichotomy of feminine imagery exposing Hawwa's weaknesses compared with Fatima's strengths, Hawwa's heresy with Fatima's orthodoxy.

Fatima's role as pristine matriarch verified her perfection and authority within the holy family; Hawwa's life, in contrast, seemed a failure. Fatima experienced no menstruation, had shorter gestation periods, and gave birth without blood or impurities whereas Adam demanded that Hawwa' ritually cleanse before intercourse to ensure her purity. According to one report, Fatima as sublime matriarch even appeared to Adam and Hawwa' while still in paradise, mystically adorned with her children and family: Muhammad her crown, `Ali her necklace, and Hasan and Husayn her earrings.[88] Eve received only the earthly adornment of jewels and precious metals, which fell away after she disobeyed Allah.[89] Fatima later wept at the death of her beloved father and son Husayn; Hawwa' only mourned the loss of paradise and her own foolishness.

Fatima's birth narrative, wherein Muhammad travels to paradise and ingests the fruit filled with her essence, resonates with this imagery. Medieval theologians, by depicting Muhammad eating the fruit of his daughter, associated Fatima with the tree of knowledge once denied to Hawwa' and Adam. This knowledge, in Shi`ite exegesis, referred to the Imam's authority and the exalted status of the *ahl al-bayt*. Fatima resided in paradise—part of the tree, part of Allah's knowledge, part of the holy family. Hawwa' remained alienated from all such grace: she was forbidden the tree and only a pretender to the rank of heaven's Mistress. Only extended family members who recognized Fatima's exalted position accessed the *nur Muhammadi* and gained hope of salvation: Hawwa' simply never belonged to that elect group.

An important parallel developed in Merovingian hagiography that also pitted a holy woman against her antithesis. Frankish queens were patterned after Jezebel, the famous villain of 1 Kings, the heretical and treasonous wife of Ahab, king of Israel. Jezebel killed God's prophets and priests, incited her husband to idolatry, and finally threatened the security of God's kingdom.[90] She proved to be the opposite of the matriarchal queen who converted her community and then interceded for them both on earth and in heaven.

Queens such as Brunhild (b. ca. 545–50), wife of Sigibert (r. 561–75), in like manner interfered with the conversion efforts of Columbanus, an Irish missionary preaching reform throughout Gaul and, according to some accounts, arranged the murders of several bishops.[91] Hagiographers transformed what might have passed for political savvy and shrewd

palace machinations for a male into heretical deeds and spiritual de-
pravity for the female.

Balthild (d. 680), Neustrian queen and wife of Clovis II (r. 639–57),
also received the opprobrious epithet from an English hagiographer.[92] In
the *Life of Wilfrid*, he reported the second Jezebel's persecution of God's
church and holy men (nine bishops plus various priests and deacons).[93]
Yet in Gaul Balthild received high praise for her piety, charity, and support of monasteries; she was, in fact, a saint.

Balthild's hagiographer in Gaul, probably a nun at Chelles (a monastic house founded by the queen), invoked the familiar vocabulary of
virgin, mother, and bride to describe her saintly subject. Balthild at first
desires only a spiritual bridegroom, but she soon submits to "Divine
Providence" and marries Clovis.[94] She then evolves into the sublime matriarch, acting as "a mother to the princes, as a daughter to the priests,
and as a most pious nurse to children and adolescents."[95] She dutifully
adopted the community around her as she "ministered to priests and
poor alike, feeding the needy and clothing the naked [and] . . . funneling
large amounts of gold and silver through [the king] to convents of men
and virgins."[96]

Taken together, the lives of Brunhild and Balthild reveal the peril-
ous position of most Frankish queens. Hagiographers recounted their
missionary efforts, their charitable deeds to both consanguineous and
spiritual kin, and even their miraculous deeds, revealing sublime matriarchs reminiscent of Mary and all her glories. In the end, however, a
woman's legacy ultimately remained in the masculine hand or patriarchal
expectations that shaped it. The matriarchs could not escape the political
realities of court that demanded firm regencies, noble allies, and enough
movable wealth to secure their power. Often such political vicissitudes
raged against the queen at court and produced a new Jezebel instead of a
Holy Mother.[97]

In both Christian and Shi`ite theology, then, women might signify
doctrinal distinction and political legitimacy only with the aid of a sympathetic hagiographer. While Mary and Fatima might reveal religious truths
for their communities, as archetypes crafted largely by male authors they
never move beyond their appropriate gender designations. The archetypes of Eve/Hawwa' and Jezebel served as a reminder of what could happen should holy women fall out of favor with masculine authorities.

Right Communities

Theologians and hagiographers employed the feminine ideal as a rhetorical tool to sharpen communal boundaries as well as doctrinal distinctions. In early medieval Christian exegesis, community identified not just the elite membership in the orthodox church but also a new vocation among one of the many monastic houses quickly being established across Gaul. Frankish men and women dedicated themselves to their new spiritual communities, theoretically forfeiting their worldly status and possessions. Marian rhetoric helped to define those monastic families and boost Merovingian claims to authority.

Christian authors had always used Mary as a primary example for the chaste life; popular narratives even from the second century advanced Mary, mother of Jesus, as a perpetual virgin.[98] The Merovingian identification with Mary and the monastic life was certainly nothing new. Yet the models of Mary from both late antiquity and the early Middle Ages shifted emphasis in terms of the female body and maternal expectations.

The feminine ideals of late antiquity had promoted masculine prototypes as well as the virginal Mary. Three particularly popular lives had outlined feminine virtues worthy of emulation that effectively transformed women into men.[99] First, the martyr text of Saints Perpetua and Felicitas demonstrated maternal sacrifice for the Christian faith. Both women forsook their husbands, children, and families for their Christian beliefs; Perpetua even transformed into a man in a dream sequence. Both saints chose martyrdom over recantation. Second, Saint Thecla abandoned an arranged marriage (despite her family's reaction) and opted for a heavenly bridegroom as she traveled the countryside dressed as a man. Third, Saint Eugenia not only cast aside her mundane family but also donned male clothing and entered a monastery.[100] These hagiographies had advertised Christian conversion narratives as well as gendered models of feminine piety. In all these models, the women traded their femaleness for the male ideal: they "became like men" in the service of God.[101] Mary's body, too, advertised an ascetic theology of enclosure and impenetrability that effectively negated many feminine gender expectations. Early church fathers had equated Mary's chaste womb with claustration, encouraging other virgins to remain separated from community and family (and all the temptations that implied).

Merovingian hagiography, on the other hand, replete with maternal imagery, elevated Mary's body as a paradigm for the monastic community. Hagiographers encouraged abbesses to first become brides of
Christ and then, along with abbots, to act as mothers and extend their
maternal care to both their natural and spiritual families. Hagiographers
equated the care given by monastic leaders with Mary's own nourishment from the womb. One monastery, for example, feared they would
starve after their wheat supply was depleted, but the abbot assured them,
"[I]t cannot happen that there is insufficient wheat in a monastery dedicated to [Mary] who offered from her womb the fruit of life to a starving
world."[102] The monks, under the abbot's direction, then prayed together
into the night and awoke to find their granaries filled with wheat. The
abbot's obedience in prayer brought food to his family just as Mary fed
humanity through her Son. Mary provides a maternal paradigm that defines the monastic life.

Similar to Mary, Merovingian women continued to nourish their
new Christian communities after conversion. Hagiographers demonstrate that these new matriarchs assume spiritual responsibility for their
extended families that guaranteed the Franks more than just spiritual
rewards. For the Gallo-Romans and Franks just joining the ranks of
Christian leadership, holiness offered an avenue of social mobility and
preservation of familial fortune.[103] Secular and religious authority fused,
and the Frankish ruling class invested vast wealth in the church.

Holy women performed an important role in this conversion drama
as they translated landed estates into monastic communities, immune
to patrimonial division, episcopal and royal control, and some tolls and
taxes.[104] A saintly career thus offered a variety of opportunities for women
as they funded and ultimately supervised family lands. These royal saints
often worked closely with episcopal authorities who, often enough, were
their brothers and uncles. Female sanctity eventually reflected the idealized queen, the spiritual mother, who possessed and distributed wealth
not only among her family and church but also the community at large.

Such a model of sanctity based implicitly on possession of means
and wealth challenges the desert ascetic theology of late antiquity.[105] The
much earlier life of Saint Antony, for example, reported Satan's various attacks on the Egyptian hermits with visions of gold.[106] Personal renunciation of wealth drew on biblical precedents wherein Christ warned

that riches barred the path to heaven and later purged the Temple of moneylenders.[107] Holy men and women who sacrificed everything to the church demonstrated the perfect path of self-denial, the path arguably unattainable (and undesired) by all Christians yet much needed by the church economy.[108] The holy woman Melania the Younger, for example, gave a local church "revenues as well as offerings of gold and silver treasures, and valuable curtains, so that this church, which formerly had been so poor, now stirred up envy on the part of other bishops of the province."[109]

Frankish holy women, unlike their late antique counterparts, did not necessarily renounce their family ties and forsake their earthly treasures. Hagiographers did require saintly separation from secular lusts by depicting holy women's disregard for fine clothes and jewels. Each time Saint Radegund entered a new church she piled her royal attire, complete with purple garb, gold jewelry, and precious gems, on the altar for "the relief of the poor" (without disapproving glares from the clerical elite).[110] Frankish women thus provided a means of consolidating landed property through their monastic complexes and estates; and, perhaps more significantly, they channeled royal wealth to the surrounding community. Merovingian holy women present paragons of maternal comfort and provision to their mundane poverty-stricken communities and their spiritual kindred.

Hagiographers also explain that Frankish saints dared to cast aside their royal privileges and become submissive "holy handmaids" (such as Mary) by performing common domestic deeds. Radegund's homey miracles permeate her *vita* as she ventures outside her royal confines to tend to the sick and poor. She advances beyond the wealthy patron who simply funds charities and transmutes into a royal servant. She bathes the bodies of the poor, "scrubbing away whatever she found there," combs their hair, and washes their feet. During their meal, which she also prepares, Radegund cleans "the mouth and hands of the invalids herself."[111] With this inversion *topos*, Radegund like Christ becomes the pious servant of the poor and a "new Martha" who busies herself with her household.[112]

In a more spiritual display of maternal attention, Radegund provides saintly intercession for one female pilgrim named Mammezo suffering from a vision problem. Mammezo's prayer to Radegund resembles the Ave Maria in both form and content:[113]

Lady Radegund! I believe that you who follow God's will above man's are full of God's virtue! Good lady, full of piety, have mercy on me. Help an unhappy woman, pray that my eye will be restored for my spirit is grievously stricken by this tormenting pain.[114]

Like the Ave Maria, Mammezo's prayer begins with an appellation and praise (Hail Mary, full of grace, blessed are you among women) and ends with a petition for intercession (pray for us now and at the hour of our death). Radegund, as Mary with her Son, becomes the intermediary for her adopted kin. Gregory of Tours compared Radegund's countenance at her death with the "Lord's holy mother herself."[115]

Monastic complexes especially provided important venues for Merovingian holy women to display their maternal and spiritual authority. Not only did these women (as abbesses) distribute wealth to the poor and establish important pilgrimage sites, but they also served as the mother (*mater*) for their new daughters. As leaders and spiritual guides, they supplied food, clothing, and miraculous healing for their extended families. Rusticula, abbess of Arles (d. ca. 632), tended her household with such pious zeal that "all called her lady and pious mother."[116] At her death, her body was placed in Saint Mary's Basilica, at the right side of the altar, dedicated in her virginity.

Instead of providing a monastic paradigm, Fatima's authorization of Shi`ite doctrine enabled the increasing identification of those within the family and those without, that is, those members of the Shi`a and then everyone else. As the dialectic between Shi`ite and Sunni theology evolved in the tenth century, theologians relied on Fatima to herald Shi`ite orthodoxy. Sectarian literature frequently promoted Fatima as the Muslim community's most excellent woman in opposition to the Sunni affection for `A'isha, Muhammad's beloved wife. The conflicts between Fatima and `A'isha reflected more than just familial jealousies and contentions; they exposed questions of political authority posed by each sect's interpretation of who should act as Muhammad's legitimate successor.

Sunni theologians challenged the Shi`ite exaltation of the holy family by honoring the Prophet's beloved companions, Abu Bakr, `Umar, `Uthman, and `Ali (the four Rightly Guided Ones, or *Rashidun*). According to Sunni traditions, the Prophet appointed Abu Bakr as his legitimate successor with no preference for `Ali; Abu Bakr and the following three caliphs, as companions, were the most excellent choice.

As Sunni authors exalted Abu Bakr, they also advanced `A'isha bint Abi Bakr, Abu Bakr's daughter and Muhammad's young wife, as the feminine ideal. Reports linked Abu Bakr's and `A'isha's legitimacy through parallel honorific titles. Abu Bakr, for example, is known as the truthful man (*al-siddiq*); `A'isha becomes the truthful woman (*al-siddiqa*).[117] Another tradition relates that Muhammad designated `A'isha as his most beloved among the people and her father as the most beloved among men.[118]

Shi`ite traditions, to the contrary, present `Ali as Muhammad's rightful successor and Abu Bakr as a usurper. Shi`ite rhetoric also transforms `A'isha from the Prophet's beloved wife into Fatima's antithesis by detailing her jealousies, adulterous tendencies, and political deceits. Instead of representing the virtues of virgin, mother, and bride, `A'isha exemplifies corruption.

Shi`ite authors emphasize one episode that casts doubt on `A'isha's loyalty to the Prophet (known in the texts as the tradition of the lie, or *hadith al-ifk*). According to this account, the Prophet and his young bride were traveling together after a raid on the Banu Mustaliq and stopped to rest during the night. During the repose, `A'isha realized she had lost the necklace she was wearing; so she exited her litter and began to look for it. When the caravan began to move again, no one realized `A'isha's absence (apparently she was light).[119] One of the Prophet's soldiers traveling behind the caravan found her and accompanied her back to the army. The Medinans heard about the adventure, placing the Prophet's wife alone in the presence of a male, and began to make accusations against her. According to Sunni interpretation, the Prophet then received the first of nine Qur'anic verses (24:11) that defended `A'isha:

> Those who brought forward the lie are a body among yourselves; think it not to be an evil to you; on the contrary it is good for you. To every man among them [will come the punishment] of the sin that he earned, and to him who took on himself the lead among them, will be a grievous chastisement.[120]

Allah himself (via Muhammad) exonerated `A'isha from the lies and rumors circulating about her adulterous affair. For Shi`ite interpreters, the event provided a powerful opportunity to question the loyalty of `A'isha and, implicitly, some of the Prophet's closest companions.

In retaliation against Shi`ite suspicions, Sunni authors maligned a genre of hadith allegedly promulgated by the Shi`ites against the Prophet's companions (*sahaba*). From the Sunni perspective, the earliest Shi`ite community wrongfully denounced and even cursed the Prophets' closest and most beloved associates, thus implying their blasphemy and disloyalty. This accusation is not entirely a rhetorical ploy. The early Shi`a did question the loyalty and honesty of the first Islamic generation—men such as Abu Bakr, `Umar, and `Uthman.[121] If after all Muhammad designated `Ali as his rightful successor, then these so-called companions had betrayed that designation and seized `Ali's position. One tradition recounts the event of the mountain pass, al-`Aqaba, wherein the Prophet's companions and his beloved wife plotted to destroy him.[122]

According to the account of al-`Aqaba, Muhammad realized the end of his life was approaching and related to `A'isha that he planned to publicly appoint `Ali his successor. `A'isha then disclosed the news to `Umar's daughter Hafsa and other conspirators who planned to prevent Muhammad's acknowledgment of `Ali and the *ahl al-bayt*. They then planned to ambush the Prophet at the Harsha pass along the Mecca-Medinan road. The angel Gabriel interceded and commanded the Prophet to announce his decision earlier than planned at Ghadir Khumm. After the disclosure the companions decided to continue their plot, hoping to disrupt `Ali's designation.

At the mountain pass Allah again intervened and saved the Prophet from his companions and treacherous wife. The plotters released a number of crawling insects in the hope that Muhammad's she-camel would become crazed and throw him off. As the beast became frightened, Muhammad soothed her, and Allah caused her to speak and promise that she would never be diverted from her path as long as she bore the Messenger of God.[123] Lightning then flashed through the heavens and revealed the traitors, including Abu Bakr, `Umar, `Uthman, and Talha. The Prophet decided not to execute them to retain unity within the community (*umma*). `A'isha, the most revered woman in Sunni circles (second, perhaps, only to Khadija, Muhammad's first wife) and the transmitter of so many hadith, joins the ranks of conspirators against the Prophet's life.

Sunni and Shi`ite hadith transmitters also projected their struggle for legitimacy into the domestic sphere as they set `A'isha and Fatima in personal opposition. In Sunni hadith collections, such as al-Bukhari, Fatima appears as a weak and spoiled daughter of the *umma*'s prominent leader.[124] In one account Fatima went to her father complaining about the blisters on her hands from grinding a stone hand-mill. She had heard that the Prophet recently received additional slave girls and hoped that he would provide her with help. Because her father was not home when she visited, Fatima related the message to `A'isha, who later conveyed the request to the Prophet. That night the Prophet visited `Ali and Fatima and admonished them for their laziness. He commanded them to recite Allah's name and praises instead of seeking servants.

Shi`ite hadith collectors provided a provocatively different description of Fatima's character and relationship to her father. In a similar transmission, Fatima faithfully ground barley for her family while the wheel caused the skin on her hand to tear and bleed. She persevered. When `Ali and the Prophet later arrived, they found Fatima asleep at the wheel, nursing her son at her breast, while the mill miraculously moved by itself (or by the hand of an angel). The Prophet wondered at Allah's care for his daughter and then reassured her (and the family) that the sufferings they endured in this life would disappear in the next.[125] This hadith identifies Fatima as the mother, nurturer, and provider while also promising her family (i.e., the Shi`a) eternal rest and reward.

Medieval Shi`ite authors effectively transformed Fatima into an identity marker for their community. As the Shi`a defined itself, its origins, and its political agenda, it had to set itself apart from other sectarian groups. One of the most important ways to achieve this identity was to emphasize the *ahl al-bayt* and Fatima's role therein.

Shi`ite hadith replaced any mundane understanding of the Prophet's family with the sublime understanding of the preexistent Imams. Sunni traditions also pitted `A'isha's piety against Fatima's weakness, `A'isha's loyalty against Fatima's groanings. Shi`ite scholars presented their own picture of Fatima's sublime character based on her miraculous origin and absolute purity. These scholars invoked `A'isha and Fatima *to think* about their orthodox theologies and to further define the boundaries of their communities.

Right Gender

Medieval male authors used Mary and Fatima *to think* about theological and political matters. Their textual bodies became commentaries and directives regarding doctrinal formulations, sectarian identities, and communal boundaries. At the same time there remains the agenda to regulate and reestablish traditional notions of gender, authority, and power. Male authors identify Mary's and Fatima's central (even miraculous) positions in the domestic sphere as virgins, mothers, and brides, but they also betray an attempt by patriarchal forces to arrogate to themselves the sovereignty of that sphere.

In early medieval Gaul, Mary and the maternal paradigm defined many of the evolving orthodoxies among the clergy and royalty alike. Mary's miracles confirmed Catholic orthodoxy against Jewish and Arian opposition; this also offered implicit sanctification to the Franks since many of their enemies, including the Goths, remained Arian. New monastic houses trained their abbesses and noblewomen to act as holy mothers on the model of Mary. Mary provided the sublime archetype for the cloistered life: according to the *Protevangelium of James*, she had resided first within the Temple walls and then Joseph's *domus*. Caesarius's *Rule for Nuns*, which required strict claustration, promised his virgins they would "receive crowns of glory together with holy Mary" in paradise.[126]

On the one hand, Marian rhetoric opened the way for change: consider the freedoms available to consecrated women entering the monastic life. Many women fled forced marriages by entering the convent and becoming mystically united with the Virgin Mary as new brides of Christ.[127] Wealthy noblewomen often served as abbesses and maintained control over the convent's finances as well as, in many cases, their family's property donated as the house's foundation. That property remained protected as abbesses named sisters, daughters, and nieces as the community's succeeding mothers.[128] The monastic life presented many wealthy noblewomen with the means to control their wealth, status, and authority; and perhaps even women of lower social status found a way to survive on their own.[129] Once again, the early Middle Ages uniquely allows public/private power to coincide; women's access to heavenly privilege often depended on her earthly position within the family.[130] More often than not, abbesses and female saints harmonized with the institutions of motherhood and royal marriage.

On the other hand, some monastic *regulae* seem to curb the potential for female autonomy and spiritual independence by instructing holy women to eschew their mundane families and wealth to embrace their new spiritual kin as equals.[131] Caesarius maintains that nuns should not receive anything personal from family members, whether it be a letter or gifts, unless it is thoroughly reviewed by the abbess.[132] He also required that familial visits be supervised by a senior sister if not the abbess herself.[133] By promoting a spiritual equality among a spiritual kin, monastic rules sought to weaken that very privatized power that Merovingian women wielded through their earthly families. Perhaps because consanguinial relationships were so important and the women's position within them so imperative to their spiritual power, these spiritual ideals remained just that, ideals. Aristocratic women continued to claim their place as leaders of estate-monasteries, disregarding the piety of lowborn sisters, even if that meant public scandal.

Monastic rules of the Merovingian period, including the rules of Ceasarius of Arles and Donatus of Besançon, managed to curtail the influence of female monastics more effectively by requiring strict claustration in women's houses.[134] This certainly reflected a real, physical danger to women's houses as targets of violence and rape; chronicles and histories alike repeat the threats of tribal rivalries and (later) Viking raids. These rules recognized the need to provide convents with additional protection, especially within city walls.[135] Yet the prominent bishops and clerical leaders who formulated the rules moved beyond practical concerns for women's lives and promoted a notion of right (or acceptable) gender roles.

Merovingian monastic rules and church councils, by delineating so exactly the expectations for nuns, effectively denied alternative forms of the consecrated life such as widowhood and clerical offices. Although early church practices had esteemed the ranks of widows and deaconesses, Merovingian theologians argued that life outside the monastery was indeed too dangerous and less perfect. Church councils made it clear that only the clergy could grant the privilege of living a consecrated life outside the convent walls. Some councils even made provisions for failure: the Council of St.-Jean-de-Losne in 673–75 ordered that women who did gain priestly permission to live a religious life at home be incarcerated in a monastery should they disregard their chastity.[136] The Council of Orléans, 533, proclaimed that women were too weak to perform any type of semipriestly work amid the struggles of the secular world and decreed that "after this no women are to be granted the diaconal benediction because of the fragility of their condition."[137] Expectations of and possibilities for religious women effectively dwindled under episcopal legislation.

The male clergy also arrogated to itself the traditional notions of domestic authority and household management. Even under the rule of strict claustration, priests (who were not necessarily monks) were required to consecrate the Eucharist.[138] No matter what the ideals of separation, purity, and enclosure, the community had to allow at least one male to enter its walls. The priest symbolically appropriated to himself the domestic space of the mother/abbess and her family; he both consecrated and fed the community as an altar servant. Mary's nurturing role had been usurped by her male sons. Even in economic terms, bishops and priests increasingly ignored Caesarius's inclination to allow the abbess financial autonomy and instead appointed kings' officers and bishops as overseers and procurators for the female communities.[139]

A similar rhetorical twist occurred in Shi`ite Islam as medieval theologians and scholars successfully seized Fatima's authority as the *ahl al-bayt*'s sublime matriarch. At first Fatima's influence within the family seemingly challenged traditional notions of gender designations. Muhammad miraculously "conceived" Fatima from paradise after ingesting a beautiful fruit; Allah favored her above Hawwa', which resulted in the first sin of envy; Fatima remained perpetually pure, avoiding menstruation, rendering her symbolically male; she identifies who belongs within her beloved (and spiritual) family; and on judgment day she will intercede for her progeny and rescue them from the hellfire. Fatima, like Mary, defines the boundaries of her spiritual and mundane communities because of her domestic authority.[140]

Also like Mary, Fatima's male heirs assimilated to themselves the matriarch's authority from the domestic sphere and emphasized Fatima as the obedient and submissive virgin, mother, and bride. The leaders of the Shi`ites had always been the Imams; Fatima and her sons provided the spiritual and sometimes political guidance for their community. Shi`ite theologians labeled them infallible (*`isma*) and responsible for spiritual guidance (*walaya*). After the twelfth Imam went into hiding, or occultation, the community faced a crisis of leadership. From that crisis the Shi`ite scholars, or the *`ulama´*, asserted their authority.[141] The scholars and theologians, rather than a centralized Christian clergy, decided on legal questions and theological matters through logical reasoning (*ijtihad*).

The *`ulama´*, the symbolic heirs to the *ahl al-bayt*, also promoted the theology of agreement (*ijma`*). When the community of scholars reaches consensus it must be correct because the Imam would never allow his community to deviate into error. The scholars are educated males, trained at religious colleges (*madrasa*), promising to lead the Shi`a for the Hidden Imam.[142]

As with Mary, the authority of the domestic, the family, passes from their powerful matriarchs to the male heirs, those bishops, priests, and Shi`ite clerics who negotiate between the public and private spheres. Mary and Fatima provide the right gender model for women to emulate: active within the domestic sphere as virgin, mother, and bride, yet yielding to masculine, public authority as holy handmaids.

Despite male hagiographers' placement of Mary and Fatima largely in the domestic sphere, their adoration became very public throughout material culture. While the authors' texts successfully advertised Mary's and Fatima's holy prowess, material objects spoke a language of piety all their own. Christians and Shi`ite Muslims constructed edifices, ritual items, and simple articles of beauty that not only reinforced but also shaped identity.

Chapter Five

Sacred Art and Architecture

Holy Women in Built Form

Early medieval Christians and Muslims created artistic images to illustrate their cosmologies and theologies in the social sphere. Much like hagiographers and theologians, artists and architects employed Mary and Fatima as symbols in their chosen space to depict constantly shifting theologies, political agendas, and gender expectations.[1] Material culture—including Christian churches, Muslim mosques, and Shi`ite amulets—conveyed these cues that continuously shaped and reinforced communal identity. As early Christian artisans pictured Mary holding Jesus instead of oriental gods and goddesses and Safavid royalty commissioned the *ahl al-bayt*'s names engraved in mosques, they effectively evoked a religious orthodoxy for their communities to recognize.[2]

The creation of such visual displays and material culture did not proceed without considerable debate and even bloodshed. Since each group was rooted in monotheism and revered the commandment that proclaimed God's oneness and prohibited strange gods, each had to negotiate the conflict between its desire for certain representations and this ancient law against them.[3] In the end, they came to different conclusions: Christians allowed material and artistic displays because they saw their pedagogical value.[4] Muslims rejected images as idolatrous, holding essentially the same ideals that one can find in ancient Judaism, although

99

eventually Islam found a way to translate its beliefs into built form.[5] Where Christians used statues and icons; Muslims defined sacred space and piety in calligraphy, geometric and floral designs, and grand architectural schemes.

When Christians and Muslims in the early medieval period searched for appropriate ways to "picture" their relationships with God, they were drawn to Mary and Fatima whose stories and reputed powers linked them and their families with intercessory and religious authority. Although their theologies and traditions had different approaches to the use of religious images, architects and artists transformed these holy women into holy heroines of visual culture. The hagiographic tales and rhetorical twists narrated by medieval texts came alive in pictorial displays, sculpture, religious artifacts, amulets, and architecture.

Christian and Islamic artists and architects emphasized their particular theologies as they transformed Mary and Fatima into visual form. Some of the earliest Western depictions of Mary appear in the third-century Roman catacombs and the Italian basilica Santa Maria Maggiore. This church contains fifth-century mosaics of both Old and New Testament scenes that either foreshadow or reveal Christ's birth along with Mary's miraculous participation. Unfortunately, no Merovingian counterparts survive aboveground. Several hagiographies, however, do describe architecture and artifacts dedicated to Mary, and many of the chapels boasted of Marian relics.

Shi'ite artists and architects presented Fatima in much more symbolic terms and usually along with the *ahl al-bayt*'s other members. In some hadith Fatima assumes the function of a *mihrab* (the prayer niche in mosques that points toward Mecca). According to one transmission, Fatima stood in her prayer chamber and emitted a light that permeated the city. Muhammad instructed his community to orient themselves toward Fatima's light while praying.[6] This miracle illustrates one of Fatima's most famous epithets, Fatima al-Zahra (the Radiant). Some Shi'ite hagiographers later associated that mysterious light with the lamps that hang from prayer niches in mosques.[7] Fatima, symbolized by the lamp, also marks the way to the Ka'ba. She stands in the space between the profane and the sacred, the supplicant and Allah, earth and paradise.

Shi'ite calligraphers recalled the holy family's sublime authority by inscribing Qur'anic verses, prayers, Shi'ite hadith, and the Imams' names throughout mosques. Two Iranian mosques constructed in the medieval period provide evidence of Shi`ite Muslims' adoration for the holy family. The mosque/mausoleum Gunbad-i `Alawiyan at Hamadan incorporates popular Shi`ite verses into its architectural design; and Fatima al-Ma`suma's shrine (the eighth Imam's sister) also contains calligraphic inscriptions praising the *ahl al-bayt*.[8]

Shi`ites also celebrated the family's power in a (perhaps) less subtle manner; amulets of the human hand signified their status and served as talismans against malevolent forces, or, more specifically, the evil eye. In Middle Eastern culture, the evil eye is associated with envy, much like the envy Eve cast to Fatima's preexistent form in paradise. According to Shi`ite interpretation, each digit on the talisman represents a family member: Muhammad, Fatima, `Ali, Hasan, and Husayn. These amulets, popularizing the holy family's authority, appear on everything from legal documents to jewelry.

Whether in churches or mosques, relics or amulets, Mary and Fatima enshrined basic issues of theology, politics, and gender designation. Their depictions in social (and sacred) space elevated these holy women as symbols of sublime truth, representatives of God, and promises of paradise.

Images or Idols?

It might at first seem odd to find amulets, statuary, and some representational images of holy men and women in traditions that were rooted in a radical monotheism that recognized and worshiped only one God and forbade graven images. Yet for both Christians and Muslims, *intent* ultimately defined the image as licit or illicit. In early Christianity licit use enhanced the petitioner's memory of God and the saints, whereas illicit images distracted from God and pointed to another (usually demonic) source of power.[9] Christian apologists even argued that God sanctified matter as witness to his divinity: pieces of the true cross provided the most popular case in point. Jesus' direct contact transformed these bits of wood into holy relics. While the Jews might view them as wooden idols, Christian theologians argued that the wooden slivers were licit because of their allusion to the crucifixion. Any aspect of material culture could ultimately serve as a medium for the creature to worship the creator.

Unlike Christianity, Islam regarded any human or animal figures in sacred space (both public and private) as illicit[10] and promoted geometric, floral, and epigraphic ornamentation as its own distinctive pattern of symbols.[11] This rejection of figural displays reveals much about Islamic theology and society beginning with its most holy text, the Qur'an.[12] The Qur'an, unlike the Christian Bible, lacks a principal narrative strain. Because it contains discriminate injunctions, poetry, laws, and fragmented tales of prophets and pious heroes, the Qur'an does not lend itself readily to pictorial display. The Bible, on the other hand, tells a series of stories that beg to be transformed into visual form. The Qur'an is experienced most profoundly in an aural medium—hearing the word of Allah, memorized and recited aloud.

Islam (as both a religious and social movement) burst onto the historical stage as a world power in the seventh and eighth centuries. Maturing alongside the Byzantine Empire, Muslim theologians and lawgivers considered similar questions to those that vexed the Byzantines.[13] At that historical moment, the iconoclast movement split the political and theological Byzantine world into opposing groups. Muslim theologians, after observing their neighbors' strife, discouraged the fabrication of images. One collection of hadith recounts:

> The angels will not enter a house in which there is a picture or a dog. Those who will be most severely punished on the Day of Judgement are the murderer of a Prophet, one who has been put to death by a Prophet, one who leads men astray without knowledge, and a maker of images or pictures. . . . The Sorcerer is he who has invented lies against God; the maker of images or pictures is the enemy of God; and he who acts in order to be seen of men, is he that has made light of God.[14]

Theologians thus doomed the image maker, whether Arab or Greek, to Allah's eternal wrath. In so doing, the Islamic empire further segregated itself from the Byzantine world.

By rejecting images and icons, Islamic theologians were not simply joining the ranks of the iconoclasts. Islam opposed not so much the image as the image maker. In several diatribes on images, Muslims argued that the creators of images or icons actually competed with Allah as the sole fashioner of creation.[15] To generate an image impinged on Allah's One-ness (*tawhid*) in the grave sin of idolatry (*shirk*). The Islamic community thus articulated both theological and political tenets through its artis-tic displays. Its distinctive, aniconic theology distinguished it from its Christian, Jewish, and Zoroastrian competitors. Through material cul-ture, the Islamic community discovered another venue to both formulate and assert its identity.

Mary in Built Form

Some of the earliest images of Mary in Western art functioned in just such a way by alluding to biblical narratives and theological orthodoxy. Some historians claim that early Christianity borrowed symbols from an-cient mother-goddesses in an attempt to acclimate pagan audiences to this new religion.[16] The Virgin, so the argument goes, replaced the feminine principle that pagan religions associated with the earth and fertility cults; her image, a new Divine Mother, made Christianity familiar and more attractive to prospective converts. The earliest images of the Madonna and Child, for example, bear a striking resemblance to Isis and Horus ef-figies: Isis, the Egyptian goddess who resurrected her murdered husband, Osiris, with her beloved son, a god of the underworld, Horus.[17]

While ancient goddesses might serve as prototypes for Marian im-ages, Mary certainly represented something very different for her Chris-tian audience. The earliest Western representation of the Madonna and Child is found in the Priscilla catacomb in Rome, a fresco presumably constructed in the third century. In this depiction Mary as Mother holds the Christ child, apparently nursing him at her breast (fig. 1). This por-trayal suggests an intercessory function; Mary, the mother of God, pro-vides a type of bridge that reaches from divinity to humanity.[18] Not only did her Son fill that abyss, but the supplicant can also reach the Divine through the mother's intercession. The cult of Mary's breast milk con-firms her intercessory role—this relic probably circulated as early as the seventh century.[19] Through adoration of the Mother's milk, pious Chris-tians gained access to the throne of God.

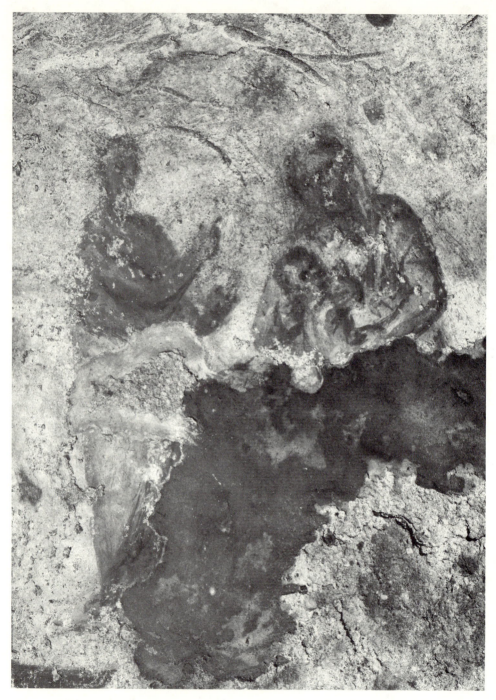

Figure 1. Fragment of fresco with Madonna, Catacomb of Priscilla, Rome. Photo courtesy of Art Resource.

Marian imagery continued to proliferate throughout the early medieval period and benefited from the artistic influences of northern Africa and the Greek East. These influences, including some distinctively
Greek aspects of Marian iconography, make early medieval architecture
particularly diverse. Early medieval architects, for example, included several variations on the standard T-model basilica—a central nave divided
by four aisles and a long, narrow transept ending with the apse—first
appearing in St. Peter's Basilica.[20] Santa Maria Maggiore provides a perfect example of early medieval variance as it surrendered its transept and
introduced new forms of adornment.[21]

Santa Maria Maggiore, a grand Italian edifice dedicated to the Virgin Mary by Pope Sixtus III (432–40),[22] celebrated the recent Council
of Ephesus's pronouncement that Mary was indeed the Theotokos. According to tradition, Mary also played a part in the church's construction;
she appeared to a patrician Roman couple and instructed them to erect a
church dedicated to her. The morning after that miraculous encounter,
August 5, the couple found snow on the Esquiline hill. The Virgin had
also visited Pope Liberius (352–66), who marked the outlines of the original church in the snow and then ordered its completion. Pope Sixtus III
later carried out the sublime request. The church's construction, and the
original mosaics that survive, might be viewed as the pope's public decla-
ration of Christianity's triumph over pagan and Jewish heresies alike.[23]

Unlike its Roman counterparts, Santa Maria Maggiore did not limit
pictorial displays to the apse area but contained rows of mosaics along the
nave itself. These mosaics displayed in built form the once-prophesied
and then fulfilled Christian theology. The basilica's upper nave originally contained forty-two mosaics depicting various scenes from the Old
Testament lives of Abraham, Jacob, Moses, and Joshua, among others.[24]
As worshipers walked through this holy space, they witnessed the most
important themes of salvation history: promise and sacrifice.[25] Old Testament figures either prophesied or signified the most pivotal moment
in human history—the coming of the Messiah. The arch showed this
promise fulfilled with illustrations of Christ's nativity, including the Annunciation and various events in the God-Man's childhood. These images operated not only as a perspective into human history, reminding
the viewer that all human experience culminated in Christ, but also as an
affective visual devise transporting the viewer from fifth-century Rome

to biblical Palestine.[26] The images, in a sense, created their own holy place (*loca sancta*) to review the biblical moments of Mary's obedience and Christ's conception.

These nave images, largely limited to Abraham, Moses, and Joshua, demonstrated the Old Testament's prefiguring of New Testament events. In one mosaic Melchizedek extends bread and wine to Abraham as an ancient symbol of the Eucharist;[27] there stands a chalice in front of Melchizedek to emphasize the sublime analogy (fig. 2). Another image introduces the ark of the covenant, a seemingly heavy burden borne by Jews. This image might prefigure the God-Man held within Mary's womb; the ark, like Mary's container-womb, contains the Manna and Law for humanity (fig. 3).

The nave led to the apse where, no longer extant, Mary probably sat on a throne holding Christ on her lap, surrounded by angels, martyrs, and Pope Sixtus himself.[28] Santa Maria Maggiore celebrated Mary's participation in Christ's miraculous birth, successfully translating early Christian theology about Mary into visual, built form.

Merovingian artistic and architectural references to Mary are more difficult to trace as few survive. According to hagiographic accounts, many abbesses enhanced and even justified their authority by aligning themselves with the Virgin Mary in heaven. They built churches dedicated to Mary; they advertised personal miracles that Mary performed for them in the holy spaces they constructed; and they contended for the prize burial positions nearest the front altars usually dedicated to Mary and the apostles.

Several Merovingian queens and abbesses abandoned their worldly stations to construct churches and monasteries where they planned to govern as spiritual mothers in imitation of Mary. Eustadiola of Bourges (c. 594–684) converted all of her homes to Marian basilicas and then built a monastery for herself and her maids. At the churches she offered great riches: gold and silver vessels, chalices, beautiful crosses and candelabra. In her own monastic house, God's handmaid attracted several followers and became a "mother of the monastery."[29] In the poetic description of her maternal sacrifices, Eustadiola resembled a new Mary, actively governing her spiritual family in imitation of her heavenly prototype.

Many other Merovingian queens constructed Marian edifices and then boasted personal miracles performed by the Holy Mother. Saint

Figure 2. Abraham and Melchizedek. Santa Maria Maggiore, Rome.
Photo courtesy of Art Resource.

Figure 3. The Ark of the Covenant being carried across the Jordan. Santa Maria Maggiore, Rome. Photo courtesy of Art Resource.

Clothild commissioned a Marian church to be built on the Seine where many miracles occurred;[30] Radegund finally gained her freedom from King Clothar at an oratory dedicated to Mary;[31] and Rusticula was buried in Saint Mary's Basilica, to the altar's right hand.[32] In all these instances, holy women sought association with Marian edifices where miracles immediately followed. Because of that alliance both the Marian cult and the holy women themselves gained spiritual prestige.

Spiritual authority did not simply end at death, however. According to her hagiographers, immediately after her death Rusticula's soul ascended to Christ's right hand, although her corpse remained at the right side of Mary's altar in a Marian basilica. Rusticula had finally joined the heavenly "chorus of virgins in which the Blessed Virgin Mary holds first place."[33] Yet Rusticula was not absent from her community; even from heaven she guarded her flock as a pious mother. In many of her postmortem miracles, she cured the sick "handmaids of Christ" at her convent. Her hagiographer noted that even after death this holy mother (Rusticula, not the Virgin Mary) "exercised the same care and solicitude as when she was living in the body."[34]

Glodesind, abbess at Metz, also governed her convent from beyond the grave. Her biographer recognized that the abbess, after her body's interment at a Marian church, "still rules though she rests in her grave."[35] Monastic families were thus seldom separated; earthly virgins identified with the chorus of heavenly virgins singing at the throne of God while their spiritual mothers sat by Mary's right hand. Marian altars and basilicas were visual reminders of her sublime position, as well as her authority, an authority that could sometimes be lent to prominent abbesses who governed in her name.

Many abbesses were not satisfied with sitting at Mary's right hand in heaven; they also wanted their bodies to rest near the high altars of their churches. This sometimes required miraculous intervention because the male clergy, as altar servants, ultimately controlled the altar and its surrounding sacred space. The clergy's authority only multiplied as the attention to relics and dead body parts proliferated throughout Merovingian Gaul.

As saint veneration became more popular in the early Middle Ages, church architecture had to change. Late antique church styles had limited the number of people who could directly encounter the holy relics; but by the fifth century more people wanted greater access to the holy. Church councils soon encouraged all altars to include relics of a saintly bishop or martyr; the Fifth Council of Carthage in 401 even declared that altars without dead body parts should be destroyed.[36] Pious congregations also required that saints' relics be visible and accessible: Christians desired admittance to the relics in order to kiss, touch, or bow to them. The Church of Mary's Tomb in Gethsemane provided a series of slots so that pilgrims could insert their hands and feel the sarcophagus.[37] Close proximity to the holy was indeed a prized treasure, and early Medieval architectural innovations had to allow some direct access (however limited).

Merovingian architects had to contend first with the issue of space. The earliest church altars had restricted any direct contact between petitioners and holy relics because they were constructed over the lower levels of catacombs. Priests conducted mass over the small crypts, but only small groups of people entered the modest space. As the saints' popularity grew, architects incorporated shafts that reached from the altar on the main level to the tombs below.[38] Pious petitioners could communicate with the saints down the shafts or lower items to touch the holy crypts (thus creating contact relics).[39] With the Merovingians, church builders moved the tombs to the main levels and displayed the holy relics in the church's holy space. Hagiographers often characterized the saint's presence as a celestial light permeating the room; and, they claimed, this radiance touched not only the heart but also the soul. Gregory of Tours described Mary's relics as a "radiating light" from the altar at Clermont.[40] Everyone in the vast space then had virtual proximity to the holy.

The clergy, however, did not surrender control of the relic itself. Either in a barricaded oratory or through an enclosed shaft, the church tightened its regulation of the saint cults (thereby further mystifying the holy). This trend only accelerated. Whereas Merovingian hagiography encouraged its audience to kiss and touch holy items, Carolingian authors betrayed the impossibility of such proximity. By the late eighth century, Carolingian hagiographers enjoined their audience to gaze upon the holy wonders and glittering spectacles of the distant sarcophagi.[41]

In this hierarchical schema, with the most holy on display to the most pious, prominent bishops, abbots, and holy figures competed for eternal rest beside the high altar. Beginning in the sixth century, holy men and women might be interred within the church walls, but after miraculous signs their bodies could advance toward the high altar. This prestigious spot was of course the place of great honor, and several saints expressed their desire to be promoted through miraculous visions. After proper exhumation, the saintly bodies (usually churchmen and abbesses from royal stock) could be moved down the aisle symbolically closer to Christ.[42] Saint Germanus of Paris (d. 576), for example, appeared to a pious woman two hundred years after his first burial and requested better accommodations behind the main altar.[43]

Glodesind of Metz also ordered (posthumously) that a church be erected to the Blessed Virgin Mary near her convent. After the church's construction, the abbess's body was disinterred and moved to its second resting place within the Marian church's walls (ca. seventh century). Later, in 830, the bishop of Metz noticed that Glodesind's tomb emerged from the earth. He reckoned this portent signaled Glodesind's desire to move yet again. After much prayer the priests moved the holy corpse to a third and final resting place "in the monastery's older church behind the altar which had been built and consecrated in praise of the Holy Mother of God, Mary, and Saint Peter, the Prince of the Apostles."[44] After this final translation, Glodesind worked many miracles that attracted many pilgrims and enjoyed an even more revered status among her family's dead.[45] By the seventh century holy bodies such as Glodesind's could be moved at will to illustrate their celestial status but only after the approval of the male episcopacy.

Fatima and the ahl al-bayt in Built Form

Muslim artists neither decked walls with Fatima mosaics nor constructed statues in her likeness; yet Shi`ite material culture certainly realized her sublime station as mother and intercessor. One of the most poignant displays of Fatima's sublime authority is present in the mosque itself. Some Shi`ite exegetes correlate Fatima with the mosque's prayer niche, or *mihrab*. This architectural design might signify for a Shi`ite audience a visual metaphor for Fatima's intercessory powers.

The *mihrab* is one among many architectural designs that delineate and adorn the mosque as sacred space. The boundaries of that sacred space often shifted, however; the medieval mosque functioned equally as a civic structure. Caliphs and local political authorities made public speeches from its stages; in the daytime it sometimes hosted trade shows; and at night it provided a shelter for the local homeless.[46] The mosque did maintain one distinct spiritual function: it offered a place of prayer (*masjid*, a place of prostration).[47]

As a sacred place of prayer, the mosque exhibited Qur'anic verses and prayers inscribed in Arabic calligraphy, a medieval art form in its own right.[48] This calligraphy was intended not only as decoration but also as a focus of meditation. The mosque also contained architectural styles that distinguished its spiritual function. The imam, or prayer leader (distinct from the Shi`ite Imams, descendants of `Ali and Fatima), usually stood at a pulpit (*minbar*) to deliver his Friday sermon; ablution pools conferred ritual purity; and the Qur'an rested upon a chair (*kursi*) in high honor. All these elements might have contained elaborate calligraphic or even geometric ornamentation, or they might have remained quite plain. One of the true focal areas of the mosque was the *mihrab*, which functioned as a pointer of sorts; it oriented the worshiper toward Mecca for obligatory prayers.

The *mihrab* has a complicated history. Its basic design, ascertained from both textual description and archaeological evidence, contains an arch, supporting columns, and the empty space between them.[49] Most scholars agree that in pre-Islamic Arabia the *mihrab* designated a place of royal ascendancy or a place of honor in palaces.[50] In religious contexts the *mihrab* referred to a sanctuary or holy place that probably housed cultic images. In ancient Semitic cultures it was probably portable; Bedouin tribes used it to transport their gods and, for early Jewish tribes, to orient themselves toward Jerusalem.[51] The *mihrab* in its religious function symbolized a doorway from the mundane to the sacred, from this world to the next.

Shi`ite hagiographers assimilate Fatima to this doorway, this empty space. In one hadith mentioned above, Fatima stands illuminating the Muslim community with her sublime light at times of obligatory prayer. Her father, Muhammad, commands his community to orient themselves toward her. She becomes the *mihrab*, pointing her people toward Mecca.[52] Traditional mosque design places a hanging lamp within that *mihrab* and engraves either on the lamp itself or somewhere nearby the very pertinent Qur'anic Light Verse (24.35):[53]

Allah is the Light of the heavens and earth. The parable of His Light
is as if there were a niche and within it a lamp: the lamp enclosed in
glass: the glass as it were a brilliant star.

The *mihrab*'s design, as a visual metaphor, correlates the hanging lamp
with Fatima, who contains within herself the light of the Imams (often
associated with the star). Just as Mary provided an empty space for God
to dwell, Fatima's body enclosed the *nur* of the Imams. Residing in the
symbolic portal between heaven and earth, Fatima offers the hope of
intercession and prayer on behalf of her adopted kin.

All Muslims, Sunni and Shi`i, associate the *mihrab* as a prayer portal
pointing toward Mecca; but for Shi`ite viewers, the *mihrab* lamp might
also signify Fatima's intercessory station. Often Shi`ite artists chose
to present the entire holy family rather than the holy mother alone.
Throughout Iran and Iraq, for example, five hanging lamps often adorn
a central *mihrab* symbolizing the five members of the *ahl al-bayt*.[54] Calligraphic inscriptions of the Twelve Imams' names and their miracles
might also outline the *mihrab*, further identifying its Shi`ite audience.[55]

The association between Fatima and the *mihrab*, however symbolic,
also resonates with Islamic traditions about Mary and her own *mihrab*.[56]
According to the Qur'an, Zechariah (John the Baptist's father) cared for
Mary after her parents dedicated her to the Temple. Each time Zechariah
would visit his charge in her *mihrab*, he found her miraculously supplied
with food (Qur'an 3.36–37). Muslim exegetes as early as the eighth century
linked Mary's *mihrab* with the Bayt al-Maqdis, a mosque in Jerusalem.[57]
Mary was believed to have lived in the mosque's inner sanctum and there
received food from Allah. By the eleventh century, pilgrimage guides combined Mary's *mihrab* with `Isa's (Jesus') cradle, both located on the Tem-
ple platform.[58] Ottoman Turks later engraved the verse describing Mary's
mihrab above their own mosques' *mihrab*s. Mary, along with Fatima in
Shi`ite tradition, remained closely linked with this prayer portal.

Until recently most art historians have failed to appreciate fully the
distinctions between Sunni and Shi`ite material culture. They have in-
stead marginalized Shi`ism as a heterodoxy and categorized its styles as
exceptional. Yet there is evidence that many forms of Islamic architecture
held different meanings for Shi`ite communities and their Sunni counter-
parts. Mausoleums constructed for the Imams and their families, for

example, played an important part in defining holy space. When Sunni Muslims conquered Shi`ite areas, they usually first sacked the shrines as a symbol of Shi`ite defeat, both physical and theological. While Shi`ite architects constructed and transformed mausoleums in a variety of patterns, they also built some with twelve sides representing the Twelve Imams. Distinctively Shi`ite interpretation of Islamic art and architecture has yet to be fully explored.

One current study has attempted to fill that scholarly lacuna by examining the mosque/mausoleum Gunbad-i `Alawiyan at Hamadan, Iran.[59] Through comparative analysis, the work isolated some basic Shi`ite architectural and commemorative patterns. First, at the Hamadan mosque twelve arches line the interior lower division; this might refer to the Twelve Imams. Each of the corner towers contain a series of five arched units that might signify the *ahl al-bayt*.[60] Second, the interior and exterior walls incorporate popular Qur'anic verses among Shi`ite mosques.[61] Qur'an 5.55, for example, explains:[62]

> Your [real] friends are [no less than] Allah, His Messenger, and the Believers—those who establish regular prayers and pay zakat [or tithes] and they bow down humbly [in worship].

At first this verse appears rather nonsectarian: it repeats the basic formulation of the faith (*shahada*) by reaffirming Allah and his messenger, Muhammad; and it introduces some of the basic tenets of ritual praxis (prayer, tithing, etc.). According to the twelfth-century Shi`ite exegete al-Fadl ibn al-Hasan al-Tabarsi, this passage discloses an esoteric message commending `Ali and the *ahl al-bayt*.[63] The "believers," says al-Tabarsi, should be read in the singular, and that singular believer refers to `Ali: "Your (real) friends are (no less than) Allah and His messenger *and `Ali*." According to this interpretation, Allah ordained `Ali (and his implied family) as his intercessor just as the prophet Muhammad. The Shi`ite exegete and the calligraphic inscription reminds the viewer of the family's exalted status.

Finally, the Hamadan mosque/mausoleum incorporates a *mihrab* adorned in a Shi`ite pattern. Like most other prayer niches, even those of Sunni persuasion, this *mihrab* includes the Throne Verse (Qur'an 2.255):

He knows what (appears to His creatures as) before or after or behind them. Nor shall they compass aught of His knowledge except as He wills. His Throne does extend over the heavens and the earth, and He feels no fatigue in guarding and preserving them.

For a non-Shi`ite Muslim, this verse confirms Allah's expansive power; his throne symbolizes the beginning and end of all creation and the cosmos. Shi`ite viewers (especially those in the medieval period), however, might associate the throne with the Imams as well: they existed, engraved on the throne of God, since before created time.[64] The verse thus links the Imams' authority directly with Allah's celestial realm.

Other art historians have suggested that Islamic art and architecture might reveal a sectarian split in subtler ways, particularly during the eleventh- and twelfth-century Sunni revival. During these centuries, Sunni (particularly Seljuk Turk) authorities encouraged a more uniform Islam not only through legal and theological argument but also through material culture. Calligraphic inscriptions at mosques and madrasas (theological colleges) emphasized Sunni, particularly Ash`ari, ideals with increasingly standardized forms.[65] Calligraphic script, for example, shifted from the largely illegible Kufic style to a legible cursive. This script subtly challenged the Shi`ite recognition of both esoteric (*batin*, or hidden) and exoteric (*zahir*, or external) truth; with the new script, only one reading and one interpretation prevailed.[66]

The Safavid regime, in contrast, devoted considerable means to building pilgrimage sites and shrines to the Imams and their families, demonstrating their Shi`ite identity. Safavid royal women in particular endowed the shrine of Fatima al-Ma`suma, the eighth Imam `Ali b. Musa al-Reza's sister, in Qum. Shi`ite Safavids widely recognized Fatima al-Ma`suma as the principal intercessor for women. According to tradition, she arrived in Qum in 817 on her way to visit her brother-Imam, but she became ill and requested burial there in the cemetery gardens. The shrine built at her tomb became a popular pilgrimage site by the ninth and tenth centuries.[67] Several Safavid women identified themselves with Fatima al-Ma`suma and her namesake, Fatima (Muhammad's daughter). Histories and hagiographies alike celebrated their reputations as pious mothers, daughters, and brides.

With the contributions of Safavid queens and royalty, Fatima al-Ma`suma's dome was rebuilt and calligraphic inscriptions adorned the courtyard and inner tomb chamber. These inscriptions included hadith that threatened with hellfire anyone who opposed the *ahl al-bayt* and likened the holy family to Noah's ark. The inscriptions also awarded the Safavid donors epithets similar to their heavenly prototype, Fatima al-Batul (the Virgin) and Fatima al-Zahra (the Radiant).[68]

The holy family's fame extends beyond the mosque, madrasa, and shrines into many homes as artists inscribe the names of the *ahl al-bayt* and the Twelve Imams as a type of magical formula on wall hangings or even domestic items.[69] Scholars typically sanction such practices as long as the articles refer to Allah and Muhammad's family, although religious authorities strictly forbid any illustration that appeals to alternate powers such as the *jinn*, demons, or false gods. Among Shi`ite communities, amulets and sacred artifacts usually entreat the holy family to intervene against the evil eye. The most common symbol of this sacred mediation is the human hand.[70] Because it recalls Allah and the Imams as authorities, it remains licit for most Shi`ite communities (fig. 4).[71]

The hand amulet as it is used in various cultures also seems to challenge traditional gender expectations. Most good luck talismans throughout the Middle East and Africa appeal to masculine, phallic imagery.[72] The hand amulet, however, alludes to a mother and her family, and it is equally popular among both genders, in both public and private space. While women often wear the symbol as jewelry, men invoke its powers as symbolic stamp or insignia: it is used in official business transactions, on modes of transportation (camels or automobiles), and on entrances to homes and offices. The holy family's authority, with Fatima at its nexus, supersedes traditional gender designations and promises active intercession available through a mother, bride, and daughter.

Despite the disparate theologies surrounding images and pictorial displays, both Christian and Shi`ite artists managed to reveal Mary's and Fatima's sublime authority in built form. Artists and architects situated both women's imagery in sacred space: Mary was both prefigured and depicted in Santa Maria Maggiore's mosaic cycle, and later priests associated her with the high altar. Fatima's authority might be symbolized in mosque lamps as well as the *mihrab* itself. In both traditions, these

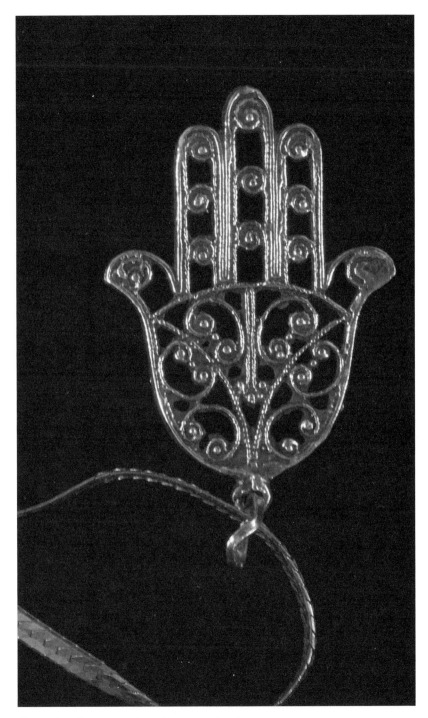

Figure 4.   Khamsa pendant. Courtesy of author.

holy women symbolically if not literally illuminated their communities. Mary's relics emanated light from the altar at Clermont, and Fatima's *nur* pointed pious Muslims toward Mecca. The holy mothers' presence allowed pious petitioners to gain access to the throne of God and the mercies of Allah.

Marian imagery flourished in early Christianity: third-century catacombs bore a Madonna and Child; church mosaics celebrated her participation in Christ's birth; and Merovingian holy women commissioned countless edifices and altars dedicated to their holy mother. Such artifacts emphasized Mary's role as intercessor and sublime matriarch; Merovingian women sought to share in her authority by affiliating themselves with her sacred spaces.

Shi`ite Muslims also promoted Fatima's intercessory position between heaven and earth and her pivotal role in the *ahl al-bayt*. Mosque lamps and Qur'anic verses attested to the family's divine light (*nur*) and perhaps their primordial existence on God's throne. Mosques and shrines alike included symbols of the family's authority either through architectural innovation or through calligraphy. Amulets of the human hand allowed Shi`ites continual access to the family for supplication and protection against evil.

Both religious systems enshrined their holy women in built form without seriously compromising conservative gender designations. A male hierarchy continued to arrogate to itself the authority of Christian sacred space; only male priests serve as altar servants in churches. Fatima remained inextricably tied to her male counterparts: she served as intercessor not only to Allah but also to her father, husband, and sons.

Conclusion

According to early medieval Christian and Shi`ite tradition, God chose Mary and Fatima as vessels for his sublime progeny. Mary, an obedient maiden, gave birth to the God-Man Jesus; Fatima, sharing in the divine *nur*, held the Imamate within her womb. The attention to two female figures did not stop with theological concerns; hagiographers also chose Mary and Fatima *to think about* matters of political and sectarian identity. The sacred narratives and hagiographies produced by these authors, most of whom were men, offer historians windows into theology, gender expectations, and notions of the holy. If we read these texts with a critical eye to rhetorical design and cultural context, they reveal a complex construction of feminine images intended for a variety of purposes and audiences.

A careful comparison of Mary and Fatima depends on problematic sources. Late antique and early medieval authors proliferated images of Mary and Fatima at times of social, political, and religious change. Christian authors from roughly 200 to 750, for example, employed Mary as a symbol of the orthodox or right church as well as to bolster their Christology. Shi`ite authors used the image of Fatima in a similar way; however, their texts originate from a different time and space. Shi`ite hadith transmitters stressed Fatima's role in the Imamate, the Prophet

119

Muhammad's lineage that held true religious authority among Muslims. Such texts, dating to the eighth and ninth centuries, allowed various Shi`ite groups to express their differences (e.g., on the Imams' identities) as well as the emerging distinction between Sunni and Shi`ite. Both Christian and Shi`ite texts thus reveal a process of self-identification wherein male authors rely on feminine ideals as markers of community.

Theologians clearly relied on Mary and Fatima to articulate and expand their respective orthodoxies and notions of rightness. By defining first their pure and immaculate nature, authors transformed Mary's and Fatima's bodies into sacred containers. Early church fathers such as Ambrose and Jerome explained Jesus' own miraculous composition as both human and divine by scrutinizing Mary's body, miraculously pure and intact. In developing their Mariology, theologians developed their Christology. Ambrose transformed Mary into a new Hebrew temple, sealed to all except the High Priest, or God himself. Fatima also served as a sacred vessel, holding the Imam's *nur* within her while simultaneously sharing it. Fatima al-Zahra existed as the only female member of the holy family and, like her father, husband, and sons, remained immaculate and infallible. Both Shi`ite and Christian authors also likened their holy women to an ancient container, Noah's ark; the women's wombs carried humanity's true salvation.

Mary and Fatima served equally important functions in political and sectarian discourse. With such a rhetorical agenda in mind, hagiographers accented Mary's and Fatima's maternal roles. These holy women, as mothers, effectively defined the limits of community and sectarian division. By symbolically adopting believers to their maternal care, Mary and Fatima damned unbelievers to hell. Hagiographers advertised their holy mothers by describing their homey miracles and domestic skill. Both women experienced superhuman parturitions, multiplied food, and interceded for their spiritual offspring.

In the early medieval West, Mother Mary identified Franks as orthodox and anointed by God. When the Merovingians converted to Christianity, Mary defended her children against Arian and Jewish contamination. Merovingian priests, bishops, queens, and holy women sometimes defined themselves through Mary: bishops boasted of her relics; queens dedicated their families and Gallo-Roman populations to her care; and holy women nurtured their communities as pious mothers.

Shi`ite authors articulated the Imamate's divine authority as the community's leaders by advertising Fatima's motherhood in much the same way. Fatima gave birth free from pollutants and simultaneously shared in the preexistent *nur* from which Allah crafted the *ahl al-bayt*. Shi`ite authors declared their sectarian identity by proclaiming Fatima's numinous status as the Prophet's daughter, `Ali's wife, and the Imams' mother. She provided the uterine connection, the bloodline, that authorized the Imams' station as the Shi`ite community's infallible leaders. The identification with Fatima's family granted considerable prestige in the struggle between Sunni and Shi`ite sovereignty as well as clerical responsibility in Shi`ite communities. The Shi`a demonstrated its blessed status by describing Fatima's abasement of `A'isha and distinction as the Prophet's daughter. For the majority of Shi`ites (or Twelvers), the Imamate's authority shifted with the twelfth Imam's occultation in the tenth century. When the last Imam remains in hiding, the Shi`ite community's clerics or scholars rule in his stead. By fortifying the link between Fatima and the Imams, these scholars secured their own authority within Shi`ism.

Mary's and Fatima's chosen status reveals much about gender designations in medieval Christianity and Islam. Both traditions labeled women as spiritually depraved descendants of Eve especially susceptible to temptation and sin. To transform Mary and Fatima into worthy vessels, God first redeemed them from the physical burdens borne by the rest of their sex. Mary remained physically intact and Fatima remained ritually pure while performing miraculous deeds. These divergent religions provide radically different idealized female bodies: Mary as virgin remains impenetrable; the heavenly Fatima and houris retain their virginity while engaging men with unusual sexual stamina.

It is clear that ordinary women could never achieve the same emancipation as their holy models and thus appear as the ideal female form, yet they still operated in the same patriarchal systems that both feared and sought to contain female sexuality and pollution. By appropriating the image of Mary and Fatima to their own circumstance, it seems many women succeeded in gaining some amount of spiritual authority. As mothers and brides, Merovingian queens and abbesses converted their families, wielded royal might, and (effectively) ruled monasteries. While not the focus of this study, it seems that Shi`ite royal women such as those in the Safavid dynasty, self-styled in Fatima's image, endowed shrines from their own estates.

Both Mary and Fatima, in a sense, draw their spiritual authority from the family and domestic sphere. Early church fathers explained that Mary never left home and remained under the protection of male priests and her husband, Joseph, while at the same time she intercedes for humanity and reigns in heaven as Christ's mother and bride. Fatima, the mystical nexus of the holy family, rewards her adoptive kin who weep for her slain son, Husayn, and escorts women into paradise on judgment day. Because these women are both powerful in their own right yet intimately connected to domestic (private) space, they can be employed by authors for a variety of purposes. Mary and Fatima can signify both female independence and agency and submission and chastity. The tendency to imbue Mary and Fatima with such symbolic meaning for a specific political purpose is not unique to the medieval period.

Contemporary Catholic Christians have attributed a plethora of meanings and interpretations to the Blessed Virgin Mary.[1] When Mary appeared to three children in Fatima, Portugal, in 1917, the church explained that she promised Communism's demise if believers would live pious lives and pray to her. The Polish Pope John Paul II later credited Mary with Communism's defeat in the late 1980s and encouraged the church to continue its Marian piety.[2] Mary, champion of democracy, vanquished Russia's secular regime. Yet Mary provides more than political identity; many inner-city gangs in the United States use Mary as a symbol of their (usually ethic) communities. Gang members, usually Latino, often have Mary of Guadalupe, a sixteenth-century visionary icon, tattooed on their backs to demonstrate their gang allegiance.[3]

The more conservative elements within Catholicism certainly have a vested interest in limiting Mary to traditional ideals. These forces advance Mary as the feminine model in the twenty-first century to counteract what they deem rampant sexual promiscuity. Mary, as Virgin, provides young women with a path of life—virginity through abstinence, which leads to marriage and procreation. More important, Mary provides a model of submission, denying her (and women) a priestly role. More liberal, feminist elements within the church demand that Mary be reimagined. For these groups, historical interrogation and biblical scholarship leads to a more complex view of Mary; in this reconstruction, Mary resembles an independent woman, free to choose her future.[4] Many feminist Catholics want to emphasize the medieval Marian epithets Co-Redeemer and Mediatrix to revitalize women's roles in the church.[5]

Similarly, modern Muslim authors appeal to Fatima in support of their political and religious causes. Shi'ite adoration of Fatima continues today, most prominently in *taziya* ceremonies that re-create Husayn's death and suffering. These passion narratives appear in the Buyid period (tenth century) in recitation form and became actual dramatizations by the Safavid era. One nineteenth-century observation of an Iranian *taziya* describes Fatima in much the same language as her medieval hagiographers: the author defines her as one of the "best of the women of the world"; she is called *al-batul*, the virgin, and *al-zahra*, the radiant; and he commends her perpetual virginity as the "Mary of this people."[6]

More recent ethnographies describe Fatima's miraculous appearance during celebrations related to the Karbala massacre. Fatima joins the faithful group of women while they recount her many miracles and acts of humility, strength, and piety.[7] According to some practitioners, Fatima miraculously attends the various ceremonies that re-create Husayn's martyrdom and notes who participates in her son's suffering. She observes the *matam* rituals wherein believers beat their breasts or inflict bleeding wounds on their bodies to share in Husayn's pain. By her presence, Fatima creates a sacred space and time in which the believers' suffering joins with the *ahl al-bayt*'s at Karbala. She then returns to paradise, pleased with her community's loyalty.[8]

Iranian leaders put Fatima to more rhetorical use during the Iranian Revolution in the 1970s. Ideologues such as 'Ali Shariati presented Fatima as a critique of Western women who are merely pawns of capitalism and materialism. Shariati encouraged young Iranian women to first imitate Fatima as a protector of Islamic law and justice but then to return to home and family after the revolutionary struggle.[9] Most revolutionaries described Zaynab, Fatima's daughter, as the paradigm for political action. Zaynab was present at Husayn's martyrdom at Karbala and denounced the caliph's humiliation of her brother's body. Women should imitate Zaynab in their political resurgence, but, according to Shariati, they should follow Fatima as an example of political responsibility followed by domestic quietude. Zaynab might be used for revolutions and reform, but Fatima provides the idealized woman for more typical times.

Whether in the seventh century or the twenty-first, Mary's and Fatima's charisma affords scholars and religious alike an important symbol of community and religiosity that may be manipulated in various ways. The holy women's attendance within the home subtly stresses the male householders' presence and dominance. In the end, however, Mary and Fatima—chosen by God as holy vessels and chosen by men as didactic models—manage to provide moral exemplars for women, promote standards of sanctity and faith, and chastise religious and political heresy. Within such legacies the domestic indeed complements public (masculine) authority and gains a place for feminine sanctity not easily ignored.

Genealogies

The Muslim Caliphs

*The Four Rashidun
or, The Four Rightly Guided Caliphs*

Abu Bakr, 632–34
`Umar ibn `Abd al-Khattab, 634–44
`Uthman ibn `Affan, 644–56
`Ali ibn Abi Talib, 656–61

The Umayyad Dynasty

Mu`awiya ibn Abi Sufyan I, 661–80
Yazid I, 680–83
Mu`awiya II, 683–84
Marwan I, 684–85
`Abd al-Malik, 685–705
`Al-Walid I, 705–15

Sulayman, 715–17

`Umar ibn `Abd al-`Aziz, 717–20

Yazid II, 720–24

Hisham, 724–43

Al-Walid II, 743–44

Yazid III, 744

Ibrahim, 744

Marwan II, 744–50

Establishment of `Abbasid Dynasty, 750

The Shi`i Imams

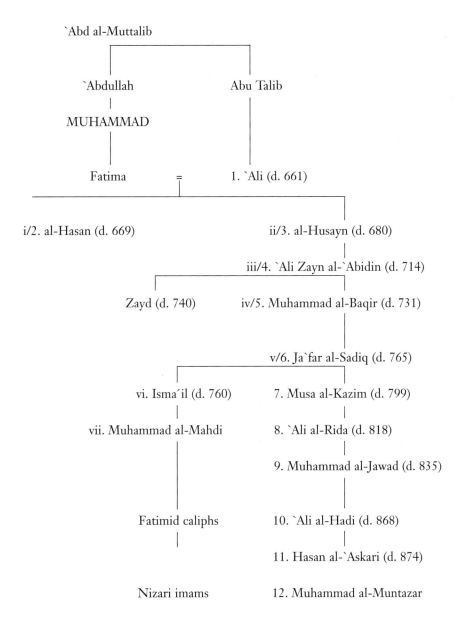

'Abd al-Muttalib

'Abdullah   Abu Talib

MUHAMMAD

Fatima   =   1. `Ali (d. 661)

i/2. al-Hasan (d. 669)   ii/3. al-Husayn (d. 680)

iii/4. `Ali Zayn al-`Abidin (d. 714)

Zayd (d. 740)   iv/5. Muhammad al-Baqir (d. 731)

v/6. Ja`far al-Sadiq (d. 765)

vi. Isma´il (d. 760)   7. Musa al-Kazim (d. 799)

vii. Muhammad al-Mahdi   8. `Ali al-Rida (d. 818)

9. Muhammad al-Jawad (d. 835)

Fatimid caliphs   10. `Ali al-Hadi (d. 868)

11. Hasan al-`Askari (d. 874)

Nizari imams   12. Muhammad al-Muntazar

Arabic numerals indicate the line of succession recognized by the Twelver Shi`ites.
Roman numerals indicate the line recognized by the Isma`ilis.
Adapted from Albert Hourani, *A History of the Arab Peoples* (Belknap Press, 2003).

The Family of the Prophet

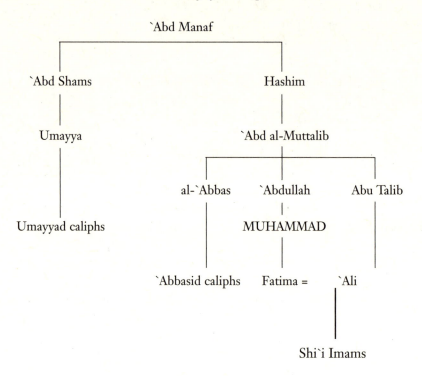

Glossary of Arabic Terms

ahl al-bayt: people of the house. In Shi`ite tradition, refers to the Prophet Muhammad and his family: Fatima, `Ali, Hasan, and Husayn.

ahl al-kisa´: people of the cloak. Refers to a Shi`ite tradition wherein the Prophet Muhammad designates his family—Fatima, `Ali, Hasan, and Husayn—as his chosen successors by wrapping them in his cloak.

*`aql:* reason. Shi`ites contend that reason is the primary source of most basic theological principles.

batin: internal or esoteric meaning; opposite of *zahir.*

al-batul: virgin. An epithet often applied to Mary and Fatima.

bayt al-ahzan: house of suffering. Refers particularly to the suffering of the *ahl al-bayt.*

ghayba: occultation, or concealment. Used to describe the current state of the twelfth Imam.

ghulat: extremists. Early groups of Shi`ites that held "extreme" views, for example, that one or more of the Imams were, in fact, divine.

ghusl: full ablution. Purity ritual that involves a full bath.

haram: forbidden.

huriyat: pl. of *hur,* or virgin of paradise.

129

ijtihad: Independent legal reason used in Islamic law, practiced by a *mujtahid.*

'ilm: knowledge or science. Those who possess religious knowledge are called *'ulama'.*

'isma: infallible. In Shi`ite tradition the *ahl al-bayt* and the Imams are considered *ma'sumin,* or the infallible ones.

isnad: the chain of transmitters in hadith.

Ithna-'ashariyya: the Twelvers, the largest sect of Shi`ism. The name refers to the recognition of twelve Imams.

madrasa: school.

matn: the text or "story" of hadith.

mihrab: the niche in a mosque's qibla wall, indicating the direction of Mecca for prayer.

minbar: pulpit. The raised pulpit in a mosque from which the imam delivers the Friday sermon.

mi`raj: ascension. Refers specifically to Muhammad's night journey to paradise where he met Allah.

mubahala: ritual cursing. According to Shi`ite tradition, the Qur'anic *mubahala* verse (3.61) was revealed at the occasion when Muhammad, `Ali, Hasan, and Husayn became known as the *ahl al-kisa'.*

mut`a: temporary marriage.

nass: the formal designation of an Imam's successor.

nur: light. According to Shi`ite tradition, the primordial Muhammad and Imams existed as "light" on Allah's throne.

Rashidun: The rightly-guided caliphs that succeeded the Prophet.

sahaba: companions.

salat: ritual prayer.

shi`at `Ali: party of `Ali.

shirk: association. Considered one of the most grievous sins when one associates others with Allah.

sunna: custom or way of acting. The customs of the Prophet are especially valued and transmitted in hadith.

takbir: The uttering of "Allahu Akbar."

tafsir: Qur'anic exegesis.

tawhid: Maintaining the unity of Allah.

*ta`ziya:* consolation. In Shi`ite tradition the *ta`ziya* is the passion drama commemorating Imam Husayn's death at Karbala.

`ulama`: the class of learned religious scholars.

umma: community.

wali: friend or protector. Can also refer to Muslim saints (pl. *awliya*).

wilaya: legal guardianship.

wudu`: lesser ablutions performed before prayer and reading the Qur'an.

zahir: external or obvious meaning; opposite of *batin*.

ziyara: visitation. Pilgrimage to a holy place or shrine.

Abbreviations

AS	*Acta Sanctorum.* Brussels: Impression Anastaltique Culture et Civilisation, 1970.
al-Bukhārī	*Ṣaḥīḥ.* Edited by L. Krehl and W. Juynboll. Leiden, 1862–1908.
CC	*Corpus Christianorum. Series Latina.* Turnholt: Brepolis Editores Pontificii, 1956.
CSEL	*Corpus Scriptorum Ecclesiasticorum Latinorum.* New York and London: Johnson Reprint, 1963.
EI¹; EI²	*Encyclopedia of Islam,* 1st and 2d eds. Leiden: E. J. Brill.
GC	Gregory of Tours, *Liber in gloria confessorum.* Edited by B. Krusch. *MGH SRM* 1.2.
GM	Gregory of Tours. *Liber in gloria martyrum.* Edited by B. Krusch. *MGH SRM* 1.2.
IJMES	*International Journal of Middle East Studies.* London: Cambridge University Press.
LH	Gregory of Tours, *Decem Libri Historiarum.* Edited by B. Krusch and W. Levison. *MGH SRM* 1.1.
al-Majlisī	*Biḥār al-anwār.* Tehran-Qum, 1376–92/1956–72.

MGH	*Monumenta Germaniae Historica.* Societas Aperiendis Fontibus Rerum Germanicarum.
AA	*Auctores Antiquissimi.*
EPP	*Epistolae.*
SCR	*Scriptorum.*
SRM	*Scriptores Rerum Merovingicarum.*
PG	J. P. Migne, ed., *Patrologia Graeca.* Paris, 1886.
PL	J. P. Migne, ed., *Patrologia Latina.* Paris, 1886.
SC	*Sources Chrétiennes.* Paris: Editions du Cerf, 1943– .
VP	Gregory of Tours, *Liber de vitae partum.* Edited by B. Krusch. *MGH SRM* 1.2.

Notes

Introduction

1. al-Majlisī, v. 43.3, p. 24.

2. Important sources on the Franks are Patrick Geary, *Before France and Germany: The Creation and Transformation of the Merovingian World* (Oxford: Oxford University Press, 1988); Janet L. Nelson, *The Frankish World, 750–900* (Rio Grande: Hambledon Press, 1996); and, of course, J. M. Wallace-Hadrill's leading works, including *Barbarian West, A.D. 400–1000* (New York: Harper & Row, 1962), and *The Long-Haired Kings* (New York: Barnes & Noble, 1962).

3. Ralph W. Mathisen provides an important look at Arian Germanic churches and hierarchy in "Barbarian Bishops and the Churches '*in barbaricis gentibus*' during Late Antiquity," *Speculum* 72.3 (1997): 664–97.

4. *GM* 8, 10.

5. Throughout the eighth and ninth centuries, these identities were still evolving. Sectarian divisions centered particularly on supporters of 'Ali and his descendants versus the supporters of the caliphs. For clarity, I shall distinguish the groups as Shī'ite and Sunni Muslims which, of course, conveys a doctrinal distinction that took centuries to fully solidify.

6. For 'Arwa, see Farhad Daftary's "Sayyida Hurra: The Ismā'īlī Ṣulayḥid Queen of Yemen," in *Women in the Medieval Islamic World*, ed. Gavin R. G. Hambly (New York: St. Martin's Press, 1998), 117–30; and Fatima Mernissi's *The Forgotten Queens of Islam*, trans. M. J. Lakeland (Cambridge: Polity Press, 1993); also see Kishwar Rizvi's "Gendered Patronage: Women and Benevolence during the Early Safavid Empire," in *Women, Patronage, and Self-Representation in Islamic Societies*, ed. D. Fairchild Ruggles (New York: State University of New York Press, 2000), 123–53.

7. Rivzi, "Gendered Patronage," 126.

8. Averil Cameron provides an important discussion of paradoxical imagery in Christian discourse in *Christianity and the Rhetoric of Empire: The Development*

of a Christian Discourse (Berkeley: University of California Press, 1991). She examines the Virgin Mary in chap. 5, 155–88.

9. Theologians formally recognized Mary as God's "container" only after extended debates. Mary received the appellation Theotokos, or God-bearer, at the highly controversial Council of Ephesus in 431 CE.

10. For secondary sources on early female virgins (including their imitation of Mary), see Virginia Burrus, "Word and Flesh: The Bodies and Sexuality of Ascetic Women in Christian Antiquity," *Journal of Feminist Studies in Religion* 10 (1994): 27–51; Averil Cameron, "Virginity as Metaphor: Women and the Rhetoric of Early Christianity," in *History as Text: The Writing of Ancient History*, ed. Averil Cameron (London: Duckworth, 1988), 181–205; Gillian Clark, *Women in Late Antiquity* (Oxford: Oxford University Press, 1993); Mary Foskett, *A Virgin Conceived: Mary and Classical Representations of Virginity* (Bloomington: Indiana University Press, 2002).

11. See the arguments of Lynda L. Coon, *Sacred Fictions: Holy Women and Hagiography in Late Antiquity* (Philadelphia: University of Pennsylvania Press, 1997).

12. According to some classical authors, Muhammad paralleled *shayāṭīn* and wives, including Eve's temptation of Adam. M. J. Kister quotes al-Munāwī, al-Suyūṭī, and al-Daylāmī in "Legends in *tafsīr* and *ḥadīth* Literature: The Creation of Adam and Related Stories," in *Approaches to the History of the Interpretation of the Qur'an*, ed. Andrew Rippin (New York: Oxford University Press, 1988), 93.

13. See Annemarie Schimmel's introduction to feminine imagery in Sufi literature, *My Soul Is a Woman: The Feminine in Islam*, trans. Susan H. Ray (New York: Continuum, 1997), 20.

14. There are a number of secondary sources devoted to Shi`ite cosmology and the Imams in particular. Two basic works are Mahmoud Ayoub, *Redemptive Suffering in Islam: A Study of the Devotional Aspects of `Ashūrā in Twelver Shi`ism* (The Hague: Mouton, 1978); and Mohammad Ali Amir-Moezzi, *The Divine Guide in Early Shi`ism: The Sources of Esotericism in Islam*, trans. David Streight (New York: State University of New York Press, 1994).

15. See Giselle de Nie's "Consciousness Fecund through God: From Male Fighter to Spiritual Bride-Mother in Late Antique Female Sanctity," in *Sanctity and Motherhood: Essays on Holy Mothers in the Middle Ages*, ed. Anneke B. Mulder-Bakker (New York: Garland, 1995).

16. Vernon K. Robbins explains the rhetorical nature of certain images in historical, social, cultural, and political works. He defines these as "patterns of intertexture," or the ways in which texts stand in relation to other texts and interpretations. See *The Tapestry of Early Christian Discourse: Rhetoric, Society, and Ideology* (New York: Routledge, 1996).

17. al-Majlisī, v. 43.2, p. 18.

18. For important methodological discussions of material culture, gender, and theology, see Robin Margaret Jensen, *Understanding Early Christian Art* (New York: Routledge, 2000); Roberta Gilchrist, *Gender and Material Culture: The Archaeology of Female Monastic Houses* (London: Routledge, 1994); Moira Donald and Linda Hurcombe, eds., *Gender and Material Culture in Historical Perspective* (New York: St. Martin's Press, 1999).

19. See recent discussions of poststructuralist theory and the implications for early Christian studies in Coon's *Sacred Fictions*, introd.; Mary Ann Tolbert, "Social, Sociological, and Anthropological Methods," in *Searching the Scriptures: A Feminist Introduction*, ed. Elisabeth Schüssler Fiorenza (New York: Crossroad, 1993); Gillian Cloke, *This Female Man of God: Women and Spiritual Power in the Patristic Ages, 350–450* (London: Routledge, 1995); Thomas Laqueur, *Making Sex: Body and Gender from the Greeks to Freud* (Cambridge, Mass.: Harvard University Press, 1990); and, of course, Judith Butler's groundbreaking work on gender performance, *Gender Trouble: Feminism and the Subversion of Identity* (New York: Routledge, 1990).

20. For a review of feminist hermeneutics in the 1970s, see Elisabeth Schüssler Fiorenza, *In Memory of Her: A Feminist Theological Reconstruction of Christian Origins* (New York: Crossroad, 1983), chap. 1, "Toward a Feminist Critical Hermeneutics."

21. See, for example, Rosemary Radford Ruether and Eleanor McLaughlin, eds., *Women of Spirit: Female Leadership in the Jewish and Christian Traditions* (New York: Simon and Schuster, 1979). Schüssler Fiorenza articulates a "hermeneutics of suspicion" that questions male authors' misogynistic imagery and a "hermeneutics of remembrance" to reconstruct the "reality" of the early church; see *In Memory of Her*.

22. Many authors have reviewed the historical circumstances of women in Islam to argue for contemporary political change and to revive a pristine Qur'anic gender ideal free from patriarchal interference. See Leila Ahmed, *Women and Gender in Islam: Historical Roots of a Modern Debate* (New Haven: Yale University Press, 1992); Fatima Mernissi, *Beyond the Veil: Male-Female Dynamics in Modern Muslim Society* (Bloomington: Indiana University Press, 1987); Lila Abu-Lughod, *Remaking Women: Feminism and Modernity in the Middle East* (Princeton: Princeton University Press, 1998); Miriam Cooke, *Women Claim Islam: Creating Islamic Feminism through Literature* (New York: Routledge, 2001); and Asma Barlas, *"Believing Women" in Islam: Unreading Patriarchal Interpretations of the Qur'an* (Austin: University of Texas Press, 2002).

23. Most authors either contest Fatima's historical authenticity (see the articles in *EI*[1] and *EI*[2]) or consider her an exemplary model in contemporary political debates. See, for example, `Ali Shari`ati, *Shari`ati on Shari`ati and the Muslim Woman* (Chicago: Kazi Publications, 1996); Fatima Mernissi, *Women's*

Rebellion and Islamic Memory (Atlantic Highlands, N.J.: Zed Books, 1996). As a notable exception, Denise Spellberg considers in passing Fatima's role in historical rhetoric in her *Politics, Gender and the Islamic Past: The Legacy of `A'isha bint Abu Bakr* (New York: Columbia University Press, 1994).

24. See the important works by Mary Clanton, *The Cult of the Virgin Mary in Anglo-Saxon England* (New York: Cambridge University Press, 1990) and *Apocryphal Gospels of Mary in Anglo-Saxon England* (New York: Cambridge University Press, 1998).

25. Bede, *Historia Ecclesiastica*, I.29. See Alan Thacker's article regarding Rome's influence on English piety, "In Search of Saints: The English Church and the Cult of Roman Apostles and Martyrs in the Seventh and Eighth Centuries," in *Early Medieval Rome and the Christian West: Essays in Honour of Donald A. Bullough*, ed. Julia Smith (Leiden: E. J. Brill, 2000), 247–77.

26. See Peter O'Dwyer, *Mary: A History of Devotion in Ireland* (Dublin: Four Courts Press, 1988). O'Dwyer examines the "Old Irish Life of S. Brigid" as well as "Adamnān's Law Code" in discussing Marian imagery in the early seventh century.

Chapter One.   *Holy Women in Context*

1. Denise Spellberg uses this approach in her *Politics, Gender, and the Islamic Past*. She carefully distinguishes the difference between `A'isha's "life" and "legacy" within the Sunni community.

2. Another controversial element (besides the Christological debate) was Mary's own lack of sin. Popular piety throughout late antiquity and the early Middle Ages equated the Virgin Mary with the Song of Song's woman "without spot" (4.7). It follows that should Mary provide the flesh for the God-Man, it must indeed be "sinless." Yet theologians debated the point (i.e., how could redemption occur before the Crucifixion?), and the Immaculate Conception only became dogma in 1854. Another question remains, however: if Mary was indeed "without stain," did she inherit the physical marks of Eve's sin, i.e., menstruation? The *Protevangelium of James* had promoted the notion that Mary could "pollute" the temple; and, according to medieval conceptions of anatomy and physiology, menstrual blood transformed into milk, thus allowing Mary to lactate (a popular image in the late Middle Ages). Theology retained the incongruity that Mary remained free from sin, yet bore some of the burdens of the flesh (just as Christ did). See Charles T. Wood's "The Doctors' Dilemma: Sin, Salvation, and the Menstrual Cycle in Medieval Thought," *Speculum* 56.4 (1981): 710–27.

3. For Cyril's refutations, see *Acta Conciliorum Oecumenicorum*, *PG*, v. 77.

4. See Gillian Clark's discussion in *Early Church as Patrons: Christianity and Roman Society* (Cambridge: Cambridge University Press, 2004), esp. chap. 6.

5. There is a significant debate about ethnic designations in the early Middle Ages. As Lawrence Nees points out, many historians argue that ethnic distinctions between the "barbarians" and the Gallo-Romans only supports the Roman propaganda that distinguished their "pure" culture from the barbaric ones. See his introduction in *Speculum* 72.4 (1997): 959–69. Yet other historians contend that ethnic distinctions are useful; see James Russell, *The Germanization of Early Medieval Christianity: A Sociohistorical Approach to Religious Transformation* (New York: Oxford University Press, 1994); and Walter Pohl and Helmut Reimetz, eds, *Strategies of Distinction: The Construction of Ethnic Communities, 300–800* (Leiden: E. J. Brill, 1998). Gerd Althoff considers ethnic distinctions important as well; he suggests that Roman senatorial families largely inherited church authority (in the cities) while Frankish aristocratic families assumed more local control in rural areas; see *Family, Friends and Followers: Political and Social Bonds in Early Medieval Europe*, trans. Christopher Carroll (Cambridge: Cambridge University Press, 2004).

6. See E. Weig, "Volkstum und Volksbewusstsein in Frankenreich des 7. Jahrhunderts," *Caratteri del Secolo VII in Occidente* (Spoleto: Settimane di Studio del Centro italiano di studi sull) *Alto Medioevo* 5 (1958): 587–648; and Raymond Van Dam, *Leadership and Community in Late Antique Gaul* (Berkeley: University of California Press, 1985), 180–81.

7. Political overtones remained because the Visigoths and some other tribes were still Arian, which set them apart theologically from the Franks. Yet it is important to note that these differences were expressed as theological instead of only political.

8. Historians have argued that the level of "literacy" in the Merovingian period has been underestimated. See, for example, Yitzhak Hen, *Culture and Religion in Merovingian Gaul, A.D. 481–751* (Leiden: E. J. Brill, 1995), 21–42; M. van Uytfanghe, "L'Hagiographie et son publique à l'époque mérovingienne," *Studia Patristica* 16 (1985): 54-62; and Katrien Henne, "Merovingian and Carolingian Hagiography: Continuity and Change in Public and Aims?" *Analecta Bollandiana* 107 (1989): 415–28.

9. Many works have examined the status and proliferation of saint cults from late antiquity to Merovingian and Carolingian Gaul. See, for example, the excellent introduction to Thomas F. X. Noble and Thomas Head, eds., *Soldiers of Christ: Saints and Saints' Lives from Late Antiquity and the Early Middle Ages* (University Park: Pennsylvania State University Press, 1995); Alan Thacker and Richard Sharpe, eds., *Local Saints and Local Churches in the Early Medieval West* (Oxford: Oxford University Press, 2002); and Raymond Van Dam, *Saints and Their Miracles in Late Antique Gaul* (Princeton: Princeton University Press, 1993).

10. See Van Dam's discussion, drawing on the works of the cultural anthropologist Clifford Geertz, in *Leadership and Community*, 188.

11. See Janet T. Nelson's discussion of Carolingian rhetoric, which recasts the Franks as the "new Israel," in "Kingship and Empire in the Carolingian World," in *Carolingian Culture: Emulation and Innovation*, ed. Rosamond McKitterick (Cambridge: Cambridge University Press, 1994), 52–87. See also R. G. Heath's "Western Schism of the Franks and the Filioque," *Journal of Ecclesiastical History* 23 (April 1972): 97–113.

12. Van Dam discusses Gregory of Tours's assimilation of Frankish history to an Old Testament model in *Leadership and Community*, 196–97.

13. See the insightful discussion of Merovingian hagiography in J. M. Wallace-Hadrill's *The Frankish Church* (Oxford: Clarendon Press, 1960), 37–54. Carolingian historians later completed this identification and pronounced the Franks as the new Chosen People claiming their Promised Land.

14. See Louise P. M. Batstone's "Doctrinal and Theological Themes in the Prayers of the Bobbio Missal," in *The Bobbio Missal: Liturgy and Religious Culture in Merovingian Gaul*, ed. Yitzhak Hen and Rob Meens (Cambridge: Cambridge University Press, 2004), 168–86.

15. Ibid., 179; quoting *Bobbio* 70, 128.

16. See Yitzhak Hen's "The Liturgy of the Bobbio Missal," in *The Bobbio Missal*, 140–53. The Feast of the Assumption was celebrated on 18 January in Gaul (see Hen's note, p. 144).

17. See the discussion of ritual and meaning in Clifford Geertz's "Ethos, World View and the Analysis of Sacred Symbols," in *The Interpretation of Cultures* (New York: Basic Books, 1973), 126–41.

18. Gregory of Tours provides one important example of Saint Gallus, a bishop from an aristocratic family (and also Gregory's paternal uncle), who left the "terrestrial possessions which [he] despised" and turned to "celestial matters"; see *VP* 5.1. Althoff also notes that ecclesiastical appointments were largely awarded to family members, thus establishing kin groups with specific loyalties throughout Gaul; see *Family, Friends and Followers*, 23–25.

19. Bishops did in fact found their own saint cults. Gregory's great-grandfather, Gregorius, discovered a martyr-saint at Dijon after a miraculous dream; see *GM* 50. Van Dam also discusses this miracle in *Leadership and Community*, 208–9.

20. Gregory of Tours's appointment, for example, was influenced by Queen Brunhild's approval and favor.

21. Balthild's hagiographer discusses her kindness to monasteries and bishops alike in *Vita Sanctae Balthildis* 9–10. Janet T. Nelson also notes Brunhild's and Balthild's support of saint cults, "Queens as Jezebels," 40, 69–70. She points

out that Balthild was possibly responsible for gaining Saint Martin's cloak for the royal collection and Saint Denis's arm for the palace oratory. See also *LHF*, cap. 44, p. 316.

22. Gregory describes Mary's assumption into heaven in *GM* 4. It is important to note, too, that this description immediately follows Gregory's explication of Christ's own resurrection and ascension (*GM* 3). This identification of Mary's experience with Christ's sets her apart from the other saints, in a sense, as she was escorted to paradise to sit beside her Son.

23. *GM* 8.

24. *GM* 18.

25. *GM* 10; *MGH SRM* 1.2.45: Tunc extractam a pectore crucem elevo contra ignem; mox in aspectu sanctarum reliquiarum ita cunctus ignis obstipuit, acsi non fuisset accensus.

26. Gregory, for example, describes the construction of Mary's church in Jerusalem by Constantine (as discussed above) and then immediately explains that Clermont itself claims many Marian relics. He also states that he has seen for himself their miraculous power; see *GM* 8.

27. Gregory advertised the tombs and relics of many saints along with Mary's, especially those of Saints Martin and Julian. Gregory even boasts that Gaul is the spiritual equal of Rome because of Saint Martin's tomb; see *Sermo in laudem S. Martini* 4, also discussed in Van Dam, *Leadership and Community*, 244.

28. The Khārijites (literally, "those who go out") were radically opposed to any arbitration because they fiercely accepted the notion of divine justice. For the Khārijites, the forces of Mu'āwiya, as the kinsmen of 'Uthmān, had committed grave sins and deserved divine punishment. 'Ali should not have compromised in any way. The Khārijites later crafted a theory that the community's leadership should be based on righteousness instead of kin relationship or inheritance.

29. According to Shi'ite tradition, Mu'āwiya bribed Hasan to abdicate any claims to the caliphate by promising peace and protection for the *shi'at 'Ali*. Later Mu'āwiya bribed one of Hasan's wives to poison him so as to ensure his own son's succession. See Arzina R. Lalani's discussion, *Early Shī'ī Thought: The Teachings of Imām Muḥammad al-Bāqir* (London: I. B. Tauris, 2000), 28–29.

30. See Moshe Sharon, *Black Banners from the East: The Establishment of the 'Abbasid State—Incubation of a Revolt* (Leiden: Magnes Press, 1983).

31. See Wilfred Madelung, "The Hāshimiyyāt of al-Kumayt and Hāshimī Shi'ism," *Studia Islamica* 70 (1989): 5–26; Patricia Crone, "On the Meaning of the 'Abbasid Call to *al-Riḍā*," in *Islamic World from Classical to Modern Times*, ed. C. E. Bosworth, Charles Issaw, Roger Savory, and A. L. Udovitch (Princeton: Darwin Press, 1989), 95–111.

32. See Louis Massignon's discussion of the Mubāhala event in "La Mubāhala de Médine et l'hyperdulie de Fāṭima," in *Opera Minora*, v. 1 (Beirut: Dār al-Maʿārif, 1963). Also see "Mubāhala," in *EI²*, 264.

33. The rationale and practice of mutual cursing is set out in Sura 3.61, or the "Mubāhala verse": "If any one disputes in this matter with you, now after knowledge has come to you, say: 'Come! Let us gather together, our sons and your sons, our women and your women, ourselves and yourselves; then let us earnestly pray. And invoke the curse of Allah on those who lie!'"

34. See Denise Louise Soufi's review of these traditions included in Ibn Ḥanbal's *Faḍā'il*, 2.632, and al-Ṭabarī's *Jāmiʿ al-bayān*, 22.7, in "The Image of Fatima in Classical Muslim Thought" (Ph.D. diss., Princeton University, 1997).

35. The proclamation of Muhammad ibn al-Ḥanafiyya as Mahdī has tremendous impact on the formation of Imami theology. Under Mukhtār the concepts of divine guide (or Mahdī) and occultation and return are first articulated. These theories are later, of course, applied to the twelfth Imam, Muhammad al-Mahdī. See Moojan Momen's discussion in *An Introduction to Shiʿi Islam: The History and Doctrines of Twelver Shiʿism* (New Haven: Yale University Press, 1985).

36. Al-Ṭabarī, *Ta'rīkh al-Rasūl wa-l-mulūk*, III, 213; as quoted in Sharon, *Black Banners*, 91.

37. Anti-Shiʿite sentiment is also apparent in the controversy over the ʿashīra verse, Qur'an 26.214: "And admonish your nearest kinsmen . . ." Traditions from the *musannaf* collections related this revelation to the last days and explained that Muhammad was intimating his inability to intercede for his family; the *ahl al-bayt*, in effect, held no special status and was responsible for their own deeds. See Uri Rubin's discussion in *The Eye of the Beholder: The Life of Muhammad as Viewed by the Early Muslims, a Textual Analysis*, Studies in Late Antiquity and Islam 5 (Princeton: Darwin Press, 1995).

38. Balādhurī, *Ansāb al-ashrāf*, III (ed. Dūrī) (Beirut, 1398/1978); as quoted in Moshe Sharon, "*Ahl al-Bayt*: People of the House," *Jerusalem Studies in Arabic and Islam* 8 (1986): 177.

39. As Sharon points out, many of the earliest Sunni scholars acknowledged the *ahl al-bayt* as the Prophet's immediate family and recognized them as special and beloved members of Muhammad's household. Yet as Shiʿite piety evolved and became more defined, later scholars rejected the exclusivity of such a definition. See Sharon, "*Ahl al-Bayt*," 172 ff.

40. The ʿAbbasid line met these arguments with their own accusations. For example, the ʿAbbasids refused to recognize Abū Ṭālib's supremacy because he never accepted Islam. See, for example, Sharon's argument in *Black Banners*, 97.

41. See Sharon's argument in "*Ahl al-Bayt*," 178.

42. See esp. Amir-Moezzi's *The Divine Guide in Early Shiʿism*.

43. Amir-Moezzi includes the tenth-century works of Ibn Bābawayh, Shaykh Ibn Abī Zaynab al-Nu`mānī, al-Kulaynī, and al-Shaykh al-Saffār al-Qummī among his early sources.

44. See an overview of these dynasties in Momen, *An Introduction to Shi`i Islam.* For separate works see, among other important works, Joel Kraemer, *Humanism in the Renaissance of Islam: The Cultural Revival during the Buyid Age* (Leiden: E. J. Brill, 1986); Paul Walker, *Exploring and Islamic Empire: Fatimid History and Its Sources* (New York: I. B. Tauris, 2002); Farhad Daftary, *Medieval Isma`ili History and Thought* (New York: Cambridge University Press, 1996); and Renato Traini, *Sources biographiques des Zaidites* (Paris: Centre National de la Recherche Scientifique, 1977).

Chapter Two.   Holy Women in Holy Texts

1. The comparativist Jonathon Z. Smith emphasizes the importance of looking for the "new" among categories of comparison instead of merely listing sameness and difference. See, for example, his argument in *Drudgery Divine: On the Comparison of Early Christianities and the Religions of Late Antiquity* (Chicago: University of Chicago Press, 1990), esp. 46–53.

2. Robert D. Baird discusses different types of categories available to scholars using a functional definition of religion; see his *Category Formation and the History of Religions* (The Hague: Mouton, 1971).

3. For some of the essential studies of hagiography and the various ways it should be approached, see Hippolyte Delehaye, *The Legends of the Saints*, trans. Donald Attwater (New York: Fordham University Press, 1962); René Aigrain, *L'Hagiographie: Ses sources, ses méthodes, son histoire* (Paris: Bloud et Gay, 1953); Baudoin de Gaiffier, *Recueil d'hagiographie*, Subsidia Hagiographica 61 (Brussels: Société des Bollandistes, 1977), and *Recherches d'hagiographie Latine*, Subsidia Hagiographica 52 (Brussels: Société des Bollandistes, 1971); Pierre Delehaye, *Les légendes hagiographiques* (Brussels: Société des Bollandistes, 1955); and C. G. Loomis, *White Magic: An Introduction to the Folklore of Christian Legends* (Cambridge, Mass.: Mediaeval Academy of America, 1948). More recent works include Rudolph Bell, *Holy Anorexia* (Chicago: University of Chicago Press, 1985); Stephen Wilson, ed., *Saints and Their Cults: Studies in Religious Sociology, Folklore and History* (New York: Columbia University Press, 1983); Thomas Heffernan, *Sacred Biography: Saints and Their Biographers in the Middle Ages* (Oxford: Oxford University Press, 1988); Peter Brown, *Cult of the Saints: Its Rise and Function in Latin Christianity* (Chicago: University of Chicago Press, 1981); and Richard Kieckhefer and George D. Bond, eds., *Sainthood: Its Manifestations in World Religions* (Berkeley: University of California Press, 1988). Also, a more recent article by Felice Lifshitz

explains how dangerous the term "hagiography" has become and suggests that we understand it as modern creation, void of meaning in the Middle Ages because it reflects only a political agenda; see "Beyond Positivism and Genre: 'Hagiographical' Texts as Historical Narrative," *Viator* 25 (1994): 94–113.

4. E. Catherine Dunn has suggested that recitation of hagiographies actually resembled theatrical performances; see *The Gallican Saint's Life and the Late Roman Dramatic Tradition* (Washington, D.C.: Catholic University Press, 1989).

5. Saint Helena, Constantine's mother, popularized the Holy Land for Western audiences and, according to tradition, first located bits of the True Cross. Eusebius includes the narrative of Helena's discovery and other pious attributes in his *Vita Constantini*, *PG* 20.905–1230. Also, see the important secondary works Robert L. Wilken, *The Land Called Holy: Palestine in Christian Literature and Thought* (New Haven: Yale University Press, 1992); Jan Willem Drijvers, *Helena Augusta: The Mother of Constantine the Great and the Legend of Her Finding of the True Cross* (Leiden: E. J. Brill, 1992); and P. W. L. Walker, *Holy City, Holy Places* (Oxford: Clarendon Press, 1990).

6. See Caroline Williams's arguments concerning the political use of shrine pilgrimage in "The Cult of `Alid Saints in the Fatimid Monument of Cairo, Part 1: The Mosque of al-Aqmar," *Muqarnas* 1 (1985): 37–52.

7. *VP*, incipit, *MGH SRM* 1.2.212: "cum sit diversitas meritorum virtutumque, una tamen omnes vita corporis alit in mundo." See also James's translation, 28.

8. See, for example, M. van Uytfanghe, "Modèles bibliques dans l'hagiographie," in *Le Moyen Âge et la Bible*, ed. Pierre Riché and Guy Lobrichon (Paris: Éditions Beauchesne, 1984).

9. One particularly important genre to arise out of Egypt and Syria was the collection of "sayings" from desert fathers (and mothers). See the *Apophthegmata Patrum*, *PG* 65.71–440; also see the translation by Benedicta Ward, *The Desert Christian: Sayings of the Desert Fathers, the Alphabetical Collection* (New York: Macmillan, 1975).

10. R. A. Markus, for example, provides an important discussion of ascetic deeds as new manifestations of, or perhaps new alternatives to, physical martyrdom. He also interprets desert theology in relation to its neo-Platonic heritage. See his *The End of Ancient Christianity* (Cambridge: Cambridge University Press, 1982).

11. See *Vita Antonii*, *PG* 26.835–976; also see the English translation by Robert C. Gregg, *The Life of Antony and the Letter to Marcellinus*, Classics of Western Spirituality (New York: Paulist Press, 1980).

12. Athanasius details Anthony's miraculous talents after his transformation in the cave, all in *imitatio Christi*. See, for example, *Vita Antonii* 14, 38.

13. For an overview of missionary efforts in the West, see Richard Sullivan, "The Papacy and Missionary Activity in the Early Middle Ages," in *Christian Missionary Activity in the Early Middle Ages*, Variorum Collected Studies (Aldershot: Variorum, Ashgate 1994), III, 46–104.

14. Saint Jerome is famous for his female entourage that supported him and his missionary exploits. See, for example, his *Epitaphium Sanctae Paulae, CSEL* 55(2).306–51, for his idealized female *patrona*, Paula.

15. Sulpicius Severus, *Vita S. Martini, SC* 133; also see the English translation by F. R. Hoare, "The Life of Saint Martin of Tours," in *Soldiers of Christ*.

16. Coon provides an important view of the "pastoral bishop" in light of Hebrew, Christian, and Roman virtues; see *Sacred Fictions*, 23–36.

17. Henne, "Merovingian and Carolingian Hagiography," 415–28.

18. See, for example, *VP* 19.4. Herein Gregory describes the various cures that accompanied oil that Monegund had blessed before her death. One such miracle involved a group of nuns applying the oil to a deacon's swollen foot, which was immediately cured. Gregory also lamented the frequent visits of pious petitioners who filed away parts of the saints' tombs. According to his account, Bishop Cassianus of Autun's tomb actually suffered structural damage after so much filing. See *GC* 73.

19. Katrien Henne, "Audire, legere, vulgo: An Attempt to Define Public Use and Comprehensibility of Carolingian Hagiography," in *Latin and the Romance Language in the Early Middle Ages*, ed. Roger Wright (New York: Routledge, 1991); and Julia Smith, "The Problem of Female Sanctity in Carolingian Europe, c. 780–920," *Past and Present* 146 (1995): 3–37.

20. For discussion of Hume and Gibbon, see Brown, *Cult of the Saints*, 13–22; and Patrick Geary, "Saints, Scholars, and Society," in *Living with the Dead* (Ithaca: Cornell University Press, 1994), 9–10.

21. See John Kitchens's discussion of Delehaye and Peter Brown in *Saints' Lives and the Rhetoric of Gender: Male and Female in Merovingian Hagiography* (New York: Oxford University Press, 1998), 3–22.

22. Peter Brown has greatly revolutionized the way hagiography is studied; see his *Cult of the Saints* and *The Body and Society: Men, Women and Sexual Renunciation in Early Christianity* (New York: Columbia University Press, 1988). Caroline Walker Bynum has also, of course, contributed greatly to the study of gender designations in hagiography; see Bynum, *Holy Feast and Holy Fast: The Religious Significance of Food to Medieval Women* (Berkeley: University of California Press, 1987); and Carolyn Walker Bynum, Stevan Harrel, and Paula Richman, eds., *Gender and Religion: On the Complexity of Symbols* (Boston: Beacon Press, 1986).

23. Among the earliest extant Shi`ite pilgrimage-literature to include all parts of the Islamic world was compiled by `Alī b. Abi Bakr al-Harāwi (d. 1215), *Kitāb al-isharāt ilā ma`rifāt al-zīyārāt*.

24. See Josef W. Meri's discussion in "The Etiquette of Devotion in the Islamic Cult of Saints," in *The Cult of Saints in Late Antiquity and the Middle Ages*, ed. James Howard-Johnston and Paul Antony Hayward (Oxford: Oxford University Press, 1999), 263–86.

25. There exists a distinct understanding of "sainthood" among many Muslim audiences, however. Many Sunni, Shi`ite, and especially Sufi Muslims recognize local saint figures, usually associated with gifts of healing. For reviews of sanctity in Islam, see Grace Martin Smith, ed., *Manifestations of Sainthood in Islam* (Istanbul: Isis Press, 1993); and Jan Knappert, *Islamic Legends: Histories of the Heroes, Saints, and Prophets of Islam* (Leiden: E. J. Brill, 1985). Also see the discussions of Sufi sanctity in the translated primary source of al-Hakīm al-Tirmidhī, *The Concept of Sainthood in early Islamic Mysticism: Two Works by al-Ḥakīm al-Tirmidhī*, trans. Bernd Radtke and John O'Kane (Concord, Mass.: Paul & Co., 1996); and Margaret Smith's description in *Rabi`a the Mystic and Her Fellow Saints in Islam* (Cambridge: University Press, 1928). The closest word in Arabic to the Latin *sanctus* is *walī*, which translates as "friend" (Qur'an 10.62). In early sources, *walī* designated a social and legal relationship; *friend* denoted a legal patron, benefactor, or simple companion. Later it assumed the meaning "friend of God" and thus became associated with sanctity. See *EI*[1], 1109–11; and Vincent J. Cornell, *Realm of the Saint: Power and Authority in Moroccan Sufism* (Austin: University of Texas Press, 1998).

26. See M. J. Kister's discussion of the controversies surrounding Jewish Haggadah and Christian saint stories' inclusion in early Muslim hadith transmission: *Studies in Jāhiliyya and Early Islam* (London: Variorum Reprints, 1980), chap. 15.

27. By the ninth century, miracle stories about the Prophet began to circulate in biographical and battlefield (*maghāzi*) accounts. Ibn Ishīq's *Sīra* (Biography) of the Prophet survives only in Ibn Hishām's (d. 834) recension, for example. See also Chase Robinson, "Prophecy and Holy Men in Early Islam," in Howard-Johnston and Hayward, eds., *The Cult of the Saints in Late Antiquity and the Middle Ages*, 241–62.

28. The Qur'an outlines virtues of the believers very much akin to Moses' Ten Commandments in 17.23–39. It also provides direction for ritual and laws for the community; for example, see the directives established for divorce, 2.228–33. And, finally, the Qur'an describes the events of the final judgment, which will include a book of deeds with the promise of hellfire and paradise; see, for example, 18.47–49.

29. The Qur'an commends the virtues of many of the same prophets as Jewish and Christian traditions, such as Adam, Noah, Moses, Joseph, and Jesus. See, for example, the Qur'anic description of Abraham as an upright Muslim because he bowed in submission (Islam) to Allah, 3.67.

30. For a good introduction to hadith literature, see R. Marston Speight, "The Function of Hadith as Commentary on the Qur'an, as Seen in the Six Authoritative Collections," in *Approaches to the History of the Interpretation of the Qur'an*, ed. Andrew Rippin (New York: Oxford University Press, 1988), 63–81.

31. Some of the most important works are al-Kulaynī, *al-Furū` min al-kāfī* (4 vols., Tehran, 1334/1956), and *al-Rawḍa min al-kāfī* (text and Persian trans. H. Rasūlī Maḥallāṭī, Tehran, 1389/1969); Ibn Bābawayh, *Kitāb man lā yaḥḍuruhū al-faqīh* (ed. al-Mūsawī al-Kharsān, 5th ed., 1390/1970); Ṭūsī, *Tahdhīb al-aḥkām* (ed. al-Kharsān, Najaf, 1375–76/1955–56), and *Kitab al-istibsār* (ed. Al-Kharsān, Najaf, 1375–76/1955–56).

32. Maher Jarrar provides an important survey of Imami authority in medieval communities in *"Sīrat ahl al-Kisā':* Early Shi`i Sources on the Biography of the Prophet," in *The Biography of Muhammad: The Issue of the Sources*, ed. Harald Motzki (Leiden: E. J. Brill, 2000), 98–129.

33. Ibn Bābawayh, *`Ilal al-sharā'i` wa l-aḥkām* (Najaf, 1385/1966), chap. 9, as quoted in Amir-Moezzi, *The Divine Guide*, 45.

34. This is, of course, one genre of Shi`ite hadith. Other collections differ very little from Sunni hadith, particularly those dealing with Islamic law (*fiqh*). These, for the most part, outline the same responsibilities of every Muslim, including prayer, fasting, and tithing. See Amir-Moezzi, *The Divine Guide*, 22–28.

35. Amir-Moezzi includes an important survey of early Shi`ite texts; see *The Divine Guide*, 19–22.

36. See Muhammad Mustafa Azami, *Studies in Early Hadith Literature, with a Critical Edition of Some Early Texts* (Beirut: al-Maktab al-Islamī, 1968), and his *On Schacht's Origins of Muhammad Jurisprudence* (Riyadh: King Saud University, 1985). Also see Nabia Abbott, *Studies in Arabic Literary Papyri*, v. 2, Oriental Institute Publications, no. 276 (Chicago: University of Chicago Press, 1967); and her *Arabic Literature to the End of the Umayyad Period*. Cambridge History of Arabic Literature (Cambridge: Cambridge University Press, 1983), 289–98.

37. See Ignaz Goldziher, *Introduction to Islamic Theology and Law*, trans. Andras Hamori and Ruth Hamori (Princeton: Princeton University Press, 1981); and Joseph Schacht, *An Introduction to Islamic Law* (Oxford: Clarendon Press, 1964).

38. G. H. A. Joynboll, *Studies on the Origins and Uses of Islamic Hadith* (Brookfield, Vt.: Variorum, 1996). Also see an important review of hadith historiography by Barbara Stowasser, "The Mothers of the Believers in the Hadith," *Muslim World* 82 (1992): 1–36.

39. Uri Rubin takes up a similar methodology in his important work, *The Eye of the Beholder*.

40. See Roger Savory's important work, *Iran under the Safavids* (Cambridge: Cambridge University Press, 1980).

41. Mahmoud Ayoub correlates many of al-Majlisī's hadith with earlier collections in *Redemptive Suffering*.

42. John Walbridge expressed this opinion, which is shared by many Islamicists, in conversation. Jarrar discusses many of the problems and benefits of using al-Majlisī as a source in *"Sīrat ahl al-kisā'"*, 99–100.

43. Al-Majlisī himself seems confounded by some of the mystical imagery. In one beautiful hadith, Allah is described as mixing light and spirit to form ʿAli and Muhammad; and then—from ʿAli, Muhammad, Hasan, and Husayn—Allah formed the heavens and the Sun and Moon. Fatima is described as a radiant lamp that Allah hung as an "earring" (*qurṭ*) from his throne. Al-Majlisī's only exegesis is that *al-qurṭ* designates an earring that hangs from the lobe of an ear (!); see v. 43.2, 18.

44. Rizvi puts forth a similar argument regarding Safavid authorities in general in "Gendered Patronage," 123–53.

45. For a basic introduction to early Christian theology and these particular theologians, see Eric Osborn, *The Emergence of Christian Theology* (Cambridge: Cambridge University Press, 1993); and Rowan Greer, *Broken Lights and Mended Lives: Theology and Common Life in the Early Church* (University Park: Pennsylvania State University Press, 1986).

46. The debate over Mary's Immaculate Conception is a long and circuitous one. Uniquely among most Marian traditions, this theology arose and won the most adherents in the West. Augustine and Ambrose championed Mary's existence free from sin (or mistakes), but the notion of original sin was itself still evolving. Many medieval theologians, such as Saint Bernard of Clairvoux, later warned against its acceptance. Augustine's most famous support of the theology came from his *De Natura et Gratia*, 36, 42; *CSEL*, 238–40. For secondary discussions, see Luigi Gambero, *Mary and the Fathers of the Church: The Blessed Virgin Mary in Patristic Thought*, trans. Thomas Buffer (San Francisco: Ignatius Press, 1999); Jaroslav Pelikan, *Mary through the Centuries: Her Place in the History of Culture* (New Haven: Yale University Press, 1996); and Marina Warner, *Alone of All Her Sex: The Myth and the Cult of the Virgin Mary* (New York: Vintage Books, 1983). The theology was only approved in 1854.

47. Pope Gregory illustrates the importance of hagiography as a genre when he writes his *De Vita et Miraculis Venerabilis Benedicti*. See Joan Peterson's discussion in *The Dialogues of Gregory the Great in Their Late Antique Cultural Background* (Toronto: Pontifical Institute of Mediaeval Studies, 1984).

48. See Giselle de Nie's discussion of Gregory in *Views from a Many-Windowed Tower: Studies of Imagination in the Works of Gregory of Tours* (Amsterdam: Rodopi, 1987). Also, Van Dam has provided several translations of Gregory's hagiographies as well as important discussions of his world in *Saints and Their Miracles*.

49. Fortunatus, *De Vita Sanctae Radegundis Liber I, MGH SRM* 2.364–77; Baudonivia, *De Vita Sanctae Radegundis Liber II, MGH SRM* 2.377–95.

50. See Rosamond McKitterick, "Frauen und Schriftlichkeit im Frühmittelalter," in *Weibliche Lebensgestaltung im Frühen Mittelalter*, ed. H. W. Goetz (Cologne: Böhlau, 1991), 65–118; and Jocelyn Wogan-Browne, "Saints' Lives and the Female Reader," *Forum for Modern Language Studies* 27 (1991): 314–32.

51. See, for example, Ahmad ʿAbd al-Rāziq, "Trois fondations féminines dans l'Égypte mamlouke," *Revue des Études Islamiques* 41 (1973): 96; and Carl Petry, "A Paradox of Patronage," *Muslim World* 73 (1983): 199–200. Two important works that recover women's economic and cultural contributions to society are Julia Bray's "Men, Women and Slaves in ʿAbbasid Society" and Nadia Maria El Cheikh's "Gender and Politics in the Harem of al-Muqtadir," both in Brubaker and Smith, eds., *Gender in the Early Medieval World*.

52. See Jonathan Berkey's important work, *The Transmission of Knowledge in Medieval Cairo: A Social History of Islamic Education* (Princeton: Princeton University Press, 1991), esp. 161–81.

53. See Muhammad Hishām Kabbānī and Laleh Bakhtiar, *Encyclopedia of Muhammad's Women Companions and the Traditions They Related* (Chicago: ABC International Group; distributed by Kazi Publications, 1998).

Chapter Three. **Virgins and Wombs**

1. Mary Douglas, *Purity and Danger: An Analysis of Concepts of Pollution and Taboo* (London: Routledge & Kegan Paul, 1966).

2. Ibid., 114–28.

3. See David Brakke, "The Problematization of Nocturnal Emissions in Early Christian Syria, Egypt, and Gaul," *Journal of Early Christian Studies* 3.4 (1995): 419–60; Burrus, "Word and Flesh"; and Brown, *The Body and Society*.

4. There are, however, hadith that describe Hasan's and Husayn's birth from Fatima's left thigh, suggesting Fatima's corporal integrity. Ibn ʿAbd al-Wahhāb, *ʿUyūn al-muʿjizāt*, 61–62, discussed in Spellberg, *Politics, Gender, and the Islamic Past*, 160.

5. Al-Majlisī, v. 11, p. 173. See Uri Rubin, "Pre-existence and Light: Aspects of the Concept of Nur Muhammad," *Israel Oriental Studies* 5 (1975): 62–117.

6. The light was threatened not only by impurities associated with the body but also by illicit sex in general, including forbidden relations or sex outside of Islamic marriage. Adam's son Seth posed a particular problem here because tradition taught that Adam's sons married their sisters, a relation forbidden by Islamic law. Thus other traditions postulated that Seth married a woman from

paradise (the houris of paradise, or *haurā'*) whom Allah sent to preserve the prophetic light. See Rubin, "Pre-existence and Light," 73–74.

7. Rubin, "Pre-existence and Light," 92.

8. Ibid., 93.

9. Al-Majlisī, v. 11, p. 173.

10. See Ruth Padel, "Women: Model for Possession by Greek Daemons," in *Images of Women in Antiquity*, ed. Averil Cameron and Amelie Kuhrt (Detroit: Wayne State University Press, 1983), 3–17.

11. See the fine discussion of menstrual contamination in Thomas Buckley and Alma Gottlieb, eds., *Blood Magic: the Anthropology of Menstruation* (Berkeley: University of California Press, 1988).

12. I am using *daemon* as it is used in Greek literature, i.e., devoid of any Christian association with evil. Instead, as in the Greek context, *daemon* could refer to any divine spirit, whether it resulted in benign possession or chaos.

13. See, for example, Janice Boddy's "Womb as Oasis: The Symbolic Context of Pharaonic Circumcision in Rural Northern Sudan," *American Ethnologist* 9 (1982): 682–98. Sondra Hale presents a nice description of male/female space in Islamic homes in "Women's Culture/Men's Culture: Gender, Separation, and Space in Africa and North America," *American Behavioral Scientist* 31 (1987): 115–34. See also Gholamhossein Memarian and Frank Edward Brown, "Climate, Culture, and Religion: Aspects of the Traditional Courtyard House in Iran," *Journal of Architectural and Planning Research* 20.3 (2003): 181–98.

14. Perhaps the most famous example of women being possessed by a divine presence in the Greek world is the oracle at Delphi. See Herodotus's *Histories* for a complete description of the Delphic practices. Also, Euripides describes the bacchanalia practices (and possession by Dionysus) in his *Bacchae*. Sophocles describes how such possession could also be a curse. According to his *Agamemnon*, Cassandra's gift of prophecy becomes a curse after she refuses Apollo's advances.

15. In the *Bacchae*, for example, Euripides explains that women possessed by Dionysus represent a potential threat to the social order: they cast aside their proscribed gender roles and behave chaotically, engaging in sexual frenzy and nursing wild animals at their breasts. Padel briefly explains the archetype of the possessed woman and her chaotic presence in male-ordered societies in "Women: Model for Possession by Greek Daemons," 6.

16. See Gary Anderson's discussion of Jewish exegesis on sexuality, procreation, and the Garden of Eden in "Celibacy or Consummation in the Garden? Reflections on Early Jewish and Christian Interpretations of the Garden of Eden," *Harvard Theological Review* 82.2 (1989): 121–48.

17. Scholars such as Rosemary Radford Ruether, Elizabeth Clark, Virginia Burrus, and Averil Cameron have devoted considerable attention to women in

the early church. Dyan Elliott surveys celibacy in patristic traditions in *Spiritual Marriage: Sexual Abstinence in Medieval Wedlock* (Princeton: Princeton University Press, 1993), 16–50. And, of course, see especially Elaine Pagels's discussion of virginal asceticism in *Adam, Eve, and the Serpent* (New York: Vintage Books, 1988), 3–31, 78–97.

18. *Acts of Paul and Thecla*, in *New Testament Apocrypha*, ed. and trans. E. Hennecke and W. Schneemelcher (Philadelphia: Westminster Press, 1965).

19. Clement, *Stromata* 3.58, in *Alexandrian Christianity*, trans. John Ernest, Leonard Oulton, and Henry Chadwick, Library of Christian Classics 2 (Philadelphia: Westminster Press, 1954). See Rom. 13.13–14.

20. See Pagels's argument in *Adam, Eve, and the Serpent*, 26–31. Pagels discusses, in particular, Irenaeus, *Against the Heresies* 3,22,4; and Clement's *Stromata* 3,94,103.

21. See David Brakke's discussion of Athanasius's ascetic program in *Athanasius and the Politics of Asceticism* (Oxford: Clarendon Press, 1995), 142–200; and Coon's description of Antony's *vita* in *Sacred Fictions*, 72–77.

22. See Gregg's translation, Athanasius, *Life of Antony*, esp. 37–39.

23. See Coon's discussion of harlot-saints in *Sacred Fictions*, 71-94; and Benedicta Ward's *Harlots of the Desert: A Study of Repentance in Early Monastic Sources*, Cistercian Studies 106 (Kalamazoo, Mich.: Cistercian Publications, 1987).

24. See Coon, *Sacred Fictions*, 76. Coon concludes, "tombs and cells of holy women, on the other hand, function as the fixed places of their piety and are symbolic of saintly women's inviolable chastity." The desert tombs, then, symbolize the impenetrable female form identified with the Virgin Mary. Mary of Egypt's *vita*, for example, proclaims the Virgin Mary as the impetus for the harlot's conversion and radical renunciation of the world and flesh. See *Vita S. Mariae Aegyptiacae, Meretricis*, 16 (*PL* 73.671–90).

25. *Odes of Solomon*, ed. and trans. James Charlesworth (Missoula, Mont.: Scholars Press, 1977), Ode 19, 82.

26. Also, in the apocalyptic text *The Ascension of Isaiah*, Mary's painless parturition occurred without the Virgin's knowledge. She simply glanced down and saw Jesus: "Mary . . . beheld with her eyes and saw a small child, and she was amazed." See *The Ascension of Isaiah*, 11, in *New Testament Apocrypha*, 374–88.

27. *Protevangelium of James*, 8.1.

28. See Mary Douglas's discussion of the tabernacle as body in *Leviticus as Literature* (Oxford: Oxford University Press, 1991), esp. chap. 4.

29. *Protevangelium of James*, 10.1.

30. Ibid., 11.1.

31. Ibid., 20.1–2.

32. Ambrose, *De virginibus, Liber II, 3.19:* Ergo Sancta Maria disciplinam vitae informet, Thecla doceat immolari. *PL* 16.211.

33. Ambrose, *De virginibus, Liber II*, 2.9–10: Prodire domo nescia, nisi cum ad Ecclesiam conveniret, et hoc ipsum cum parentibus, aut propinquis. Domestico operosa secreto, forensi stipata comitatu; nullo meliore tamen sui custode quam se ipsa: quae incessu affatuque venerabilis, non tam vestigium pedis tolleret, quam gradum virtutis attollerert . . . ingressus angeli inventa domi in penetralibus, sine comite, ne quis intentionem abrumperet, ne quis obstreperet; neque enim comites feminas desiderabat, quae bonas cogitationes comites habebat. *PL* 16.209–10; *Library of Nicene and Post-Nicene Fathers*, III.19, p. 375. Compare with the Greek works of Athanasius, *First Letter to Virgins*, 13: "For [Mary] desired good works, doing what is proper, . . . she did not desire to be seen by people. Nor did she have an eagerness to leave her house . . . ; rather, she remained in her house being calm, imitating the fly in honey. She virtuously spent the excess of her manual labour on the poor. . . . And she did not permit anyone near her body unless it was covered, and she controlled her anger. . . . She was not a braggart, but completely humble. . . . She forgot her good works and her merciful deeds: she did them secretly." Translated in Brakke, *Athanasius*, 278.

34. See, for example, Ambrose, *De institutione virginis, Liber I*, 60–61, *PL* 16.321; and Jerome, *Epistle 22, 25, PL* 22.411.

35. Ambrose, *De virginibus, Liber II*, 2.18: quotidie pro redemptione corporis Christus immolatur. *PL* 16.211; *Library of Nicene and Post-Nicene Fathers*, III.19, p. 376.

36. Ambrose, *De virginibus, Liber II*, 2.18: Beatae virgines, quae tam immortali spiratis gratia, ut horti floribus, ut templa religione, ut altaria sacerdote! *PL* 16.211; *Library of Nicene and Post-Nicene Fathers*, III.19, p. 376.

37. Ambrose, *De institutione virginis*, 52–53: Et infra dicit propheta vidisse se in monto alto nimis aedificationis civitatis cujus portae plurimae significantur; una tamen clausa describitur, de qua sic ait: Et convertime secundum viam portae sanctorum exterioris, quae respicit ad Orientem, et haec erat clausa. Et ait ad me Dominus: Porta haec clausa erit, et non aperietur, et nemo transibit per eam, quoniam Dominus Deus Israel transibit per eam. . . . Quae est haec porta, nisi Maria; ideo clausa, quia virgo? Porta igitur Maria, per quam Christus intravit in hunc mundum . . . quae clausa erat, et non aperiebatur. Transivit per eam Christus, sed non aperuit. *PL* 16.234.

38. Jerome, *Dialogus adversus Pelagianos, PL* 23.517–626.

39. Jerome, *Adversus Helvidium*: Definitiv sermo Dei, quid sit primogenitum, Omne, inquit, quod aperit vulvam. *PL* 23.202. In this treatise Jerome refuted Helvidius's claim that married life was just as sacred as celibate life. After all, Helvidius argued, Mary had more children after Jesus because the Gospels referred to him as the "first born." Jerome retorted that "first born" refers to "everything that opens the womb." Thus Jesus might have been the first born, but Mary assuredly remained a virgin afterward.

40. Cameron, "Virginity as Metaphor," alludes to the symbolic and practical applications of virginal imagery in late antiquity. She describes how male authors employed virginity as a metaphor for salvation, the paradox of Christianity, and power. She suggests: "Feminist theologians would do well to consider again the question why the cult of the Virgin became prominent just at the time when the strong Christian women whose memory they have successfully rehabilitated were at their most active" (198). For descriptions of late antique women's *vita activa*, see Cloke, *This Female Man of God*; and Jo Ann McNamara, "Muffled Voices: The Lives of Consecrated Women in the Fourth Century," in *Medieval Religious Women*, vol. 1: *Distant Echoes*, ed. John A. Nichols and Lillian Thomas Shank (Kalamazoo, Mich.: Cistercian Publications, 1984).

41. See Jerome, *Epistle 22*, *PL* 22.394–425.

42. This "elite" asceticism promoted by Jerome (*Epistle 22*) and other Western theologians appears almost ludicrous compared to the regimens practiced in the eastern deserts. Jerome directed ascetic women to refrain from eating sweets or "dainty dishes," drinking wine (the "first weapon used by demons against the young"), and wearing too much silk. Jerome's own regimen was one of ascetic snobbery or, as translated by Peter Brown, "holy arrogance" (*Epistle 22*, 1.16); see Brown, *The Body and Society*, 366–86.

43. Jerome, *Epistle* 108.15: Liberalitas sola excedebat modum. Et usuras tribuens, versuram quoque saepius faciebat, ut nulli stipem rogantium denegaret . . . testem invocans Deum, se pro illius nomine cuncta facere; hoc et habere voti, ut mendicans ipsa moreretur: ut unum nummum filiae non dimitteret, et in funere suo aliena sindone involveretur. *PL* 22.890–91; English translation in Ross S. Kraemer, ed., *Maenads, Martyrs, Matrons, Monastics: A Sourcebook on Women's Religions in the Greco-Roman World* (Philadelphia: Fortress Press, 1988), 127–68.

44. See Coon's eloquent description of Paula's relinquishment of traditional virtues for Christian charisma, *Sacred Fictions*, 103–9.

45. See especially de Nie's argument in "Consciousness Fecund through God," 151. De Nie traces the metaphor of spiritual fecundity from late antique authors such as Origen through early medieval figures such as Fortunatus's biography of Radegund. Also, Gregory of Tours describes the apostle Paul's deeds in terms of fecundity; Paul gave birth to believers and nourished them with spiritual milk. See *GM* 28: Paulus vero apostolus post revolutum anni circulum ipsa die, qua Petrus apostolus passus, apud urbem Romam gladio percussus occubit. Ex cuius sacro corpore lac defluit et aqua. Nec mirum, si lac eius manavit ex corpore, qui gentes incredulas et parturivit et peperit ac lacte spiritali nutritas ad cibum solidum Scripturarum Sanctarum opaca reserando perduxit.

46. Origen, *In Numeros Homilia*, 20.2, *PG* 17.728. Discussed in de Nie, "Consciousness Fecund through God," 102.

47. Augustine discusses the fecundity of the mind/soul in *Sermo* 15.8, ed. Germanus Morin, *Sancti Augustini Sermones post Maurinos Reperti* (Rome: Tipografia Polyglotta Vaticana, 1930): Ergo in mente pariant membra Christi, sicut Maria in ventre virgo peperit Christum; et sic eritis matres Christi.

48. Mary's obedient act, of course, earned her the appellation God's submissive "handmaid." Hagiographers constructed the lives of virgins and Merovingian queens in imitation of this virtue, labeling them the "ancillae Dei," or the little servants of God. See *Vita Radegundis*, I.4; *Vita Rusticulae*, 10.

49. Jerome, *Epistle 22*.24. Augustine, too, teaches that virgins may imitate Mary's conception (an exact type of spiritual fecundity) through their faith: "ipsae cum Maria matres Christi sunt, si Patris eius faciunt voluntatem." See Augustine's *De sancta virginitate* 5, *PL* 40.399.

50. Avitus, *Poematum* 6.65–66, *MGH AA* 6:2.277: Scriberis in thalamos ac magni foedera regis/Et cupit electam speciem sibi iungere Christus.

51. Avitus, *Poematum* 6.201–4, *MGH AA* 6:2.281: Tu Mariam sequeris, dono cui contigit alto/ virginis et matris gemina gaudere corona/ Conciperet cum carne deum caelique creator/ Intraret clausum reserans mysteria ventrem./ . . . sed nec tibi gloria tanti/ Defuerit facti, si Christum credula corde/ Concipiens operum parias pia germina caelo. See also the translation and erudite commentary by George W. Shea, *The Poems of Alcimus Ecdicius Avitus*, Medieval and Renaissance Texts and Studies, 172 (Tempe: Arizona State University, 1997), esp. 138–40.

52. Avitus, *Poematum* 6.280–81, *MGH AA* 6:2.283: animum potius quam vincere sexum. See also Shea's translation, 140.

53. Avitus, *Poematum* 6.413–14.

54. See de Nie's discussion of Eugenia in "Consciousness Fecund through God," 126.

55. See *Vita S. Eugenia*, *PL* 73.602–24; Avitus discusses Eugenia in Poem 6. See also Shea's insightful discussion of Avitus's choice and combination of hagiographies in bk. 6, 57–70.

56. Ceasarius of Arles, *Regula Virginum*, *SC* 345. An English translation is also available in Maria Caritas McCarthy, *The Rule for Nuns of Caesarius of Arles* (Washington, D.C.: Catholic University Press, 1960). Also see William E. Klingshirn, *Caesarius of Arles: The Making of a Christian Community in Late Antique Gaul* (Cambridge: Cambridge University Press, 1994), for a survey of Caesarius's cultural context.

57. *Vita Radegundis*, II.24.

58. *Vita Radegundis*, I.17–19, 22–26. Coon discusses the ascetic displays unique to Fortunatus's rendition as compared to Baudonivia's *vita* in *Sacred Fictions*, 126–35.

59. Fortunatus, *Carminum* 11.6, 9–14, *MGH AA* 4/1.260: ac si uno partu mater Radegundis utrosques/ visceribus castis progenuisset, eram/ et tamquam

pariter nos ubera cara beatae/ parissent uno lacte fluente duos. See also Judith George's translation in *Venantius Fortunatus: Personal and Political Poems*, Translated Texts for Historians, 23 (Liverpool: Liverpool University Press, 1995), 103–4. Fortunatus wrote this text, in part, to defend his relationship with Agnes against rumor and innuendo. Herein he identifies their love as that of spiritual siblings rather than physical lust.

60. It is important to note here that Merovingian hagiography and theology do not praise the virtues of virginity as enthusiastically as late antique texts. In many ways these texts provide the history of the Franks, i.e., their families, their networks often achieved through marital ties, and their Christianization.

61. Fortunatus, *Carminum* 6.5.237–44, *MGH AA* 4/1.142–43; see also George's translation, *Venantia Fortunatus*, 46–47. The passage reads: iungitur ergo toro regali culmine virgo/ et magno meruit plebis amore coli/ hos quoque muneribus permulcens, vocibus illos/ et lict ignotos sic facit esse suos/ utque fidelis ei sit gens armata, per arma/ iurat iure suo, se quoque lege ligat./ Regnabat placido conponens tramite vitam, pauperibus tribuens advena mater erat. As George points out, Fortunatus wrote his poem on Galswinth in commemoration of her very controversial death. Chilperic had presented a rather large *morgengabe* (morning gift) to his new bride, which his brother and sister-in-law, Brunhild (also Galswinth's sister), then disputed. Also, as rumor had it, Galswinth's death was orchestrated by Chilperic and his favored wife, Fredegund. See Gregory of Tours's account in *LH*, 4.28.

62. Fortunatus, *Carminum* 6.5.275–80. Gregory of Tours also records this miracle in *LH*, 4.28.

63. Fortunatus later confirms Galswinth's presence in heaven where she "applauds the Lord's glorious mother, Mary," and "serves under God." Fortunatus, *Carminum* 6.5.363–64.

64. Qur'an 4.57; see also 3.15, 198; 15.45–48; 36.55–58; 76.5–22; and 78.31–35 for other descriptions of paradise.

65. Al-Qādhi, *Daqā-iq al-akhbār al-kabīr fī ahikr al-janna wa l-nār*; Al-Suyūṭī, *Kitāb al-durar al-ḥisān fīl- ba`th wa ha`ā imi l-jinān*. Discussed in Abdelwahab Bouhdiba, *Sexuality in Islam*, trans. Alan Sheridan (Boston: Routledge & Kegan Paul, 1985).

66. See Bouhdiba's discussion of the houris in *Sexuality in Islam*, 73–76. Al-Suyūṭī describes in careful detail how the male sexual appetite increases: "each climax is extended and extended and lasts for twenty-four years"; noted in Bouhdiba, 75.

67. The Qur'an dictates that men may have as many as four wives as long as they are all treated equally and justly; see 4.3.

68. Bouhdiba even uses the term "infinite orgasm," 72–87.

69. For a general discussion of homoerotic imagery in Arabic poetry, see J. W. Wright Jr. and Everett K. Rowson, *Homoeroticism in Classical Arabic*

Literature (New York: Columbia University Press, 1997); also, for a specific discussion of homoerotic imagery in paradisiacal texts, see Aziz al-Azmeh, "Rhetoric for the Senses: A Consideration of Muslim Paradise Narratives," *Journal of Arabic Literature* 26 (1995): 215–31.

70. See Shahla Haeri, *Law of Desire: Temporary Marriage in Shiʿi Iran* (Syracuse: Syracuse University Press, 1989).

71. See Caroline Walker Bynum's discussion in *The Resurrection of the Body in Western Christianity, 200–1336* (New York: Columbia University Press, 1995), esp. chaps. 1, 2.

72. Ibid., 100.

73. See Qur'an 2.187: "approach your wives; they are your garments and you are their garments." Also, 4.1 suggests that men and women are created from the same soul; marriage thus returns the masculine and feminine elements to perfect unity. See Sachiko Murata, *The Tao of Islam: A Sourcebook on Gender Relationships in Islamic Thought* (Albany: State University of New York Press, 1992).

74. It is important to note, however, that purification is both spiritual and physical. Without the right "intent of the heart," the physical acts of ablution remain incomplete.

75. See Bouhdiba, *Sexuality in Islam*, 74–76.

76. Fatima's fashioning as al-Batūl and *Maryam al-kubrā* appears in early Shiʿite hadith collections such as al-Kulaynī, *Al-Uṣūl min al-kāfī*; and Ibn ʿAbd al-Wahhāb, *ʿUyūn al-muʿjizāt*; see Spellberg's discussion in *Politics, Gender, and the Islamic Past*, 156–61; and the important work of Jane Dammen McAuliffe, "Chosen of All Women: Mary and Fatima in Qur'anic Exegesis," *Islamochristiana* 7 (1981): 19–28.

77. Al-Majlisī, v. 43.1, p. 4: qāla al-nabī lammā ʿaraja bī ilā al-samā' akhadha bi-yadī jibra'īl fa-adkhalanī al-janna fa-nāwalanī min ruṭabihā fa-akaltuhū fa-taḥāwala dhālika nuṭfa fī ṣulbī fa-lammā habaṭtu ilā al-arḍ wa aqaʿatu khadīja fa-ḥamalat bi-fāṭima.

78. Ibid., v. 43.1, p. 5: fa-anā ashammu minhā rā'iḥat al-janna.

79. See al-Majlisī, v. 43, pp. 5, 15, 21, for his sources and variants of the traditions.

80. Al-Majlisī, v. 43.2, p. 15: allatī lam tara ḥumra qaṭṭu ay lam taḥid.

81. See al-Majlisī, v. 43, pp. 15–16, for variants of the traditions.

82. Al-Majlisī, v. 43.1, p. 3: dakhalat ʿalayhā arbaʿ niswa sumr ṭawāl ka-annahunna min nisā' banī hāshim fa-fazaʿat minhunna lammā rā'athunna fa-qālat iḥdāhunnā: lā taḥzanī yā khadīja fa-innā rusul rubbiki ilayki wa naḥnu akhawātuki anā sāra wa hādhihī āsiya bint mazāhim . . . wa hādhihī maryam bint ʿimrān wa hādhihī kulthūm ukht mūsa bin ʿimrān ān baʿathanā allāh ilayki . . . fa-jalasat wāḥida ʿan yamīnihā wa uḥrā ʿan yasārihā wa l-thālitha bayn yadayhā wa al-rābʿia min khalfiḥā fa-wadaʿat fāṭima ṭāhira muṭahhara.

83. As quoted in Rubin, "Pre-existence and Light," 73.

84. Al-Majlisī, v. 43.1, p. 2: yakhbarunī annahā unthā wa annahā al-nasla l-ṭāhira l-maymūna wa anna allāh tabāraka wa taʿālā sa-yajʿalu naslī minhā . . . wa yajʿaluhum khulafā'ahū fī arḍihi.

85. See al-Kulaynī, *Kitāb al-uṣūl min al-kāfī*, ed. Sayyid Jawād Mustafawī (Tehran: al-Maktabah al-ʿIlmīyya al-Islāmīyya, Haydurt Press, n.d.), 277–78. See also Ayoub's discussion of the Light Verse, *Redemptive Suffering*, 57–58.

86. Shiʿite tradition reveals how the ancient patriarchs both prefigure and ultimately participate in the holy family. Ayoub includes a discussion of the ancient prophets and explains how each joined in the House of Sorrows. Adam, for example, descended directly to Karbala when he was expelled from Paradise. There he felt saddened and then tripped, and blood gushed from his foot. He asked what sin he had committed, but God explained that he stood on the future location of his son Husayn's martyrdom. In a similar narrative Abraham is riding his horse one day and suddenly falls off. He, too, asks God what sin he has committed; God replies that he has just crossed the plain of Karbala. Thus both prophets not only recognize the *ahl al-bayt*'s authority but also participate in its suffering. See Ayoub, *Redemptive Suffering*, 27–36.

87. Muhibb al-Dīn al-Ṭabarī, *Dhakhā'ir al-ʿuqbah* (Beirut, 1973, 20); and Murtaḍā al-Ḥusaynī Fīrūzābādī, *Faḍā'il al-khamsa* (Beirut, 1393/1973), II, 56–59, 75–87; as quoted in Sharon, "*Ahl al-Bayt*," 169–84.

88. Saint Hildephonsus of Toledo (607–67), *Sermones*, PL 96.239–83.

89. See ʿAbdallāh al-Baḥrānī, *Maqtal al-ʿawālim* (Tabriz: Dār al-Ṭibāʿa, n.d.), 29; al-Majlisī, vol. 43, 241–42; both cited in Ayoub, *Redemptive Suffering*, 31–32.

90. See al-Majlisī, v. 43, p. 243; also, as cited in Ayoub, *Redemptive Suffering*, 32. Jaʿfar al-Tustarī, *Khaṣā'iṣ al-Ḥusayn wa-Mazāyā al-Mazlūm* (n.p., n.d., lithograph of manuscript, copied 1305/1887), 66.

Chapter Four.   *Mothers and Families*

1. Brown, *The Body and Society*, 153; my emphasis.
2. An approach similar to that employed in chapter 3.
3. Cameron, "Virginity as Metaphor."
4. Al-Majlisī, vol. 43.2, p. 19; v. 43.3, pp. 28–29; v. 43.3, p. 29.
5. See Jerome, *Against Jovinianus*, bk. 1.
6. Historians have recently noticed the iconic parallels between Mary and Jesus as bride/groom and Roman depictions of reigning empress/emperor. See Thomas Matthews, *The Clash of the Gods: A Reinterpretation of Early Christian Art* (Princeton: Princeton University Press, 1993).

7. See Bernard's *Cantica Canticarum, In Laud. V. Mar.*, and *In Assumptione Beatae Mariae Virginis* in *PL* 182–83; also see *Sancti Bernardi Opera Omnia*, 8 vols., ed. Jean Leclercq, Charles H. Talbot, and Henri-Marie Rochais (Rome, 1957–78). As Caroline Walker Bynum points out in *Jesus as Mother* (Berkeley: University of California Press, 1982), Bernard and other mystics also identified the bride as the individual soul or the community of monks as a whole.

8. Ambrose, *Exp. in Ps.* 118 1.16, *PL* 15.1206–7; discussed in H. Graef, *Mary: A History of Doctrine and Devotion*, vol. 1, *From the Beginnings to the Eve of the Reformation* (New York: Sheed and Ward, 1963), 85–89.

9. Ambrose, *De virginibus*, 65: et virgo concepit, virgo peperit bonum odorem, Dei Filium. *PL* 16.282; discussed in Graef, *Mary*, 85–89.

10. The student is usually identified as Quodvultdeus, *PL* 40.661; discussed in Graef, *Mary*, 131–32. Graef also points out that the Greek Oecumenius provided the most complete Marian interpretation of Revelation 12. He states that the vision "describes the Theotokos," quoted in Graef, 132.

11. See Ambrose, *Exposito in Evangelium Secundum Lucam*, 7.5, *PL* 15.1700.

12. See Augustine, *Sermones ad Populum, Classis II. de Tempore*, 181.1, *PL* 38.995; Ambrose, *Expositio Evangelium secundum Lucam*, 2.2, *PL* 15.1553.

13. Augustine, *Sermones ad Populum, Classis II. de Tempore*, 192.2: Ut quod egit uterus Mariae in carne Christi, agat cor vestrum in lege Christi. Quomodo autem non ad partum Virginis pertinetis, quando Christi membra estis? Caput vestrum peperit Maria, vos Ecclesia. Nam ipsa quoque et mater et virgo est: mater visceribus charitatis, virgo integritate fidei et pietatis. Populos parit, sed unius membra sunt, cuius ipsa est corpus et conjux, etiam in hoc similitudinem gerens illius virginis, quia et in multis mater est unitatis. *PL* 38.1012; *FC*, v. 17, 192.2, 33.

14. See also Augustine's "*Sermones ad Populum, Classis II. de Tempore*, 191.3(4): Nec propterea vos steriles deputetis, quia virgines permanetis. Nam et ipsa pia integritas carnis, ad fecunditatem pertinet mentis. . . . Sic in mentibus vestris et fecunditas exuberet, et virginitas perseveret. *PL* 38.1011.

15. Mary's obedience also accentuated her status as Eve's righteous counterpart. Whereas Eve's disobedience introduced corruption and death, Mary allowed for Christ's birth and hope of redemption. Irenaeus developed this Eve-Mary parallel in his *Against the Heresies*, 3, 22, 24.

16. Bouhdiba, *Sexuality in Islam*, 7–8; see also Murata's discussion of masculine and feminine completion in *The Tao of Islam*; and Umar R. Ehrenfels's "Weibliche elemente in der symbolik des Islam," in *Zeitschrift für Missionswissenschaft und Religionswissenshaft* (Meunster in Westfalen, 1950).

17. These, of course, are generalized expectations. Degrees of covering and modesty ultimately depend on independent cultural systems, local custom, and interpretation. For important works on veiling, including social and

cultural analyses, see Fatima Mernissi, *The Veil and the Male Elite: A Feminist Interpretation of Women's Rights in Islam*, trans. Mary Jo Lakeland (Reading, Mass.: Addison-Wesley, 1991); Arlene Elowe Macleod, *Accommodating Protest: Working Women, the New Veiling, and Change in Cairo* (New York: Columbia University Press, 1991); Nilufer Gole, *The Forbidden Modern: Civilization and Veiling* (Ann Arbor: University of Michigan Press, 1996); and Claudia Knieps, *Geschichte der Verschleierung der Frau im Islam* (Wurzburg: Ergon, 1993).

18. These expectations reflect traditional gender roles as described in hagiographic texts. Important historical works reveal that some social norms allowed for various types of gender performance, however. See Everett K. Rowson, "Gender Irregularity as Entertainment: Institutionalized Transvestism at the Caliphal Court in Medieval Baghdad," in *Gender and Difference in the Middle Ages*, ed. Sharon Farmer and Carol Braun Pasternack (Minneapolis: University of Minnesota Press, 2003); and his "The Effeminates of Early Medina," *Journal of the American Oriental Society* 111 (1991): 671–93.

19. Bouhdiba discusses these traditions in *Sexuality in Islam*, 217–18.

20. Al-Majlisī, vol. 43.3, p. 24 (I have pluralized the hadith in my quotation).

21. Al-Majlisī, vol. 43.2, p. 17.

22. Al-Balādhurī, *Ansāb al-ashrāf* 1.401; al-Dūlābī, *al-Dhurriyya al-ṭāhira* 91; al-Kulaynī, *al-Kāfī: al-uṣūl wa l-furū' wa l-rawḍa*, 8.340. Variant sources place the marriage contract earlier with the ceremony/consummation after the Battle of Badr, see Soufi, "The Image of Fatima," 33; *EI²*, "Fatima," 842–43.

23. See Lammens's discussion in *EI¹*, 85–88. His sometimes overly critical approach views the variant hadith regarding Fatima's age as proof of her insignificance and unattractiveness; that is, Muhammad had problems marrying off his daughter. He claims that Shi'ite hadith refute this image by listing Fatima's several proposals from other (very prominent) men.

24. See Soufi, "The Image of Fatima," 35–36. She quotes hadith from al-Balādhurī, Ibn Ḥanbal, Ibn Qutayba, and al-Dūlābī.

25. Al-Dūlābī 94, 95; Ibn Ḥanbal, *Kitāb faḍā'il al-ṣaḥāba*, 2.569, 632, 762; see discussion and variant sources in Soufi, "The Image of Fatima," 36; and *EI²*, "Fatima," 842–43.

26. See *EI²*, "Fatima," 842–43.

27. See explanations of early Islamic marriage in Gertrude H. Stern, *Marriage in Early Islam* (London: Royal Asiatic Society, 1939).

28. Rustam al-Ṭabarī (c. tenth century), *Dalā'il al-imāma*, 12; Ibn Shahrāshūb (c. twelfth century), *Manāqib Āl Abī Ṭālib*; discussed in *EI²*, "Fatima," 846.

29. See al-Majlisī, vol. 43, pp. 92–145, for variant traditions. According to some transmitters, 'Ali and Fatima were wed during Muhammad's night journey; and other sources measure Fatima's *mahr* at one-fifth or one-fourth of the earth.

Also see Soufi's discussion of the heavenly marriage in "The Image of Fatima," 38–45. Soufi points out that reports of the heavenly marriage also appear in some post-fourth/tenth-century Sunnī works.

30. The *ṭūbā* tree is described by various exegetes commenting on *ṭūbā*, mentioned in Qur'an 13.29: "For those who believe and work righteousness, is (every) blessedness (*ṭūbā*), and a beautiful place of (final) return." See Soufi, "The Image of Fatima," 40; and *EI²*, "Fatima," 846–47.

31. See the full description of Fatima's role on the day of resurrection and judgment below.

32. See *EI²*, "Fatima," 846–47.

33. See *EI²*, "Fatima," 846–47; Soufi, "The Image of Fatima," notes other practices modeled after ʿAli and Fatima's ceremony. She mentions Muhammad's supplication before the couple as he sprinkled their chests with water. This, she notes, is repeated at some modern ceremonies; see esp. 36–37.

34. Al-Ṭūsī, *Amālī 'l-shaykh al-ṭūsī*, 1.38; al-Kulaynī, *al-Kāfī*, 5.378; and al-Qummī, *Tafsīr al-qummī*, 2.336-338; discussed in Soufi, "The Image of Fatima," 44–45.

35. See Haeri, *Law of Desire*, 38–40. Opponents argue that Muhammad married ʿA'isha when she was only nine years old, and thus only parental approval was necessary.

36. See, for example, al-Mufīd, 2.5, 414; or, *EI²*, "Fatima," 846–47.

37. Al-Majlisī, vol. 43, p. 8: nādat udan li-uḥaddithuka bi-mā kāna wa bi-mā huwa kā'in wa bi-mā lam yakun ilā yawm al-qiyāma ḥīna taqūmu al-sāʿa.

38. The *ahl al-bayt* are collectively known as the *bayt al-aḥzān*, or house of sorrows, because of the abandonment, persecution, and poverty they experienced. See Ayoub's discussion in *Redemptive Suffering*, 23–52. Also see Louis Massignon's *Opera Minora*, ed. Y. Moubarac (Beirut: Dār al-Maʿārif, 1963), I.573 ff., on the importance of Fatima in the *bayt al-aḥzān*.

39. Al-Majlisī, vol. 43, p. 25; al-Mufīd, chap. 4, 133.

40. The inheritance of Fadak is an important theological point for Shiʿites. Fatima's claim to inherit land from her father would set precedent for inheritable position. Abū Bakr, however, claimed that the Prophet had said, "We the prophets neither inherit nor give inheritance." This intimated that the family of the Prophet held no privileged status above the faithful companions. See Ayoub, *Redemptive Suffering*, 49–50; Momen, *Introduction to Shiʿi Islam*, 20–21; and *EI²*, "Fadak," 725–27.

41. Jaʿfar b. Muḥammad b. Qawlawayh al-Qummī, *Kāmil al-zīyārāt*, ed. Mirzā ʿAbdallāh al-Ḥusayn al-Amīnī al-Tabrīzī (Najaf: Mutadawīyyah, 1356/1937), 82; as quoted in Ayoub, *Redemptive Suffering*, 144–45.

42. For discussions of gender and death rituals, see El-Sayed El-Aswad, "Death Rituals in Rural Egyptian Society: A Symbolic Study," *Urban Anthropology*

and Studies of Cultural Systems and World Economic Development 16 (1987): 205–41; and the more recent article by Lila Abu-Lughod, "Islam and the Gendered Discourses of Death," *IJMES* 25 (1993): 187–205.

43. See Nadia Abu-Zahra, "The Comparative Study of Muslim Societies and Islamic Rituals," *Arab Historical Review for Ottoman Studies* 3–4 (1991): 7–38. For examples of female saints who refuse to wail, see Abu-Lughod, "Islam and the Gendered Discourses of Death," 194–95.

44. See David Pinault's discussion of contemporary Muharram rituals that cast Fatima as the welcoming mother, rewarding those Shi`ites who mourn the death of Husayn, in *The Shi`ites: Ritual and Popular Piety in a Muslim Community* (New York: St. Martin's Press, 1992).

45. The preceding chapters discuss these theological treatises in greater detail, including the great debate over Mary's title Theotokos. I argue there that the third- and fourth-century eruption of Marian piety and texts relates more to theology than popular piety. In *Mary*, Graef provides one of the most concise yet well documented surveys of Marian theology in late antiquity and the Middle Ages.

46. *GM* 12, *MGH SRM* 1.2.46: patuitque evidenti ratione, contra iniquam et Deo odibilem Arrianam heresim, quae eo tempore pullulabat, haec acta. Agnitumque est, sanctam Trinitatem in una omnipotentiae aequalitate connexam, nullis garrulationibus posse disiungi. Also see Van Dam's translation, 32.

47. In another test of faith, a Catholic deacon thrust his hand into boiling water to no effect while the Arian hand suffered severe burns (*GM* 80).

48. *VP* XIX, *MGH SRM* 1.2.286: ad extremum semper virginis intactaeque Mariae dignatur utero suscipi, et praepotens inmortalisque Creator mortalis carnis patitur amictu vestiri. See also Van Dam's translation, 124.

49. *GM* 9. Peter Schäfer provides a fascinating survey of the furnace story in late antique and early Christian texts. He also looks at Jewish apocryphal tales that countered Mary's miraculous deeds along with Jesus' divine nature. See Peter Schäfer, *Mirror of His Beauty: Feminine Images of God from the Bible to the Early Kabbalah* (Princeton: Princeton University Press, 2002), 197–216.

50. *GM* 9; *MGH SRM* 1.2.44: ille Christo domino ac suis legibus inimicus.

51. *GM* 9; *MGH SRM* 1.2.44: quasi super plumas mollissimas.

52. Cf. Dan. 3.8–30.

53. *GM* 9; *MGH SRM* 1.2.44: mulier, quae in basilicam illam, ubi panem de mensa accepi, in cathedra resedens.

54. *GM* 9; *MGH SRM* 1.2.44: agnitam ergo infans fidem catholicam, credidit in nomine Patris et Filii et Spiritus sancti.

55. See Isabel Moreira, *Dreams, Visions, and Spiritual Authority in Merovingian Gaul* (Ithaca: Cornell University Press, 2000), 100–101.

56. Moreira, *Dreams*, 100–103; also, for a history of early medieval anti-Semitism, see Solomon Katz, *The Jews in the Visigothic and Frankish Kingdoms*

of Spain and Gaul (Cambridge, Mass.: Mediaeval Academy of America, 1937); and Ora Limor and Guy G. Stroumsa, eds., *Contra Iudaeos: Ancient and Medieval Polemics between Christians and Jews* (Tübingen: J. C. B. Mohr [Paul Siebeck], 1996).

57. See Paul Fouracre and Richard A. Gerberding's concise description of the Merovingian political milieu and family lineages in *Late Merovingian France.*

58. Janet T. Nelson discusses the importance of the royal household and domestic power and warns against relying on the traditional correlation between the public, political sphere with masculine space and the private, familial sphere with feminine space. See her "Queens as Jezebels," 31–77. She states: "A king might win or confirm his power on the battlefield, but he exercised it in the hall, and this we have seen to be the prime area of the queen's activity. Here in the royal *familia* the distribution of food, clothing, charity, the nurturing of the *iuvenes*, the maintenance of friendly relations between the *princeps*, the respectful reception of bishops and foreign visitors: all fell to the queen's responsibility. . . . All this explains why in the case of a queen, domestic power could mean political power," 74–75. See also W. Schlesinger, *Beiträge zur deutschen Verfassungsgeschichte des Mittelalters* (Göttingen: Vandenhoeck & Ruprecht, 1963).

59. See, among others, Ian Wood's discussion in *The Merovingian Kingdoms*, esp. chap. 8.

60. The Christianity that flourished in Merovingian Gaul revealed a unique blending of Gallo-Roman, Frankish, and Eastern piety. Ascetic traditions from Syria and Egypt entered Gaul through, in particular, John Cassian's (d. 435) reports of Eastern eremitism. (Major monastic centers influenced by Eastern ideals included the monasteries at Lérins, Arles, Tours, and Poitiers.) In his *Conferences*, Cassian magnified the self-abnegation and worldly rejection of holy men and women while tempering harsh asceticism with a *via media*. For example, he appointed the anchorite's life as an "ideal," but he favored the coenobitic (communal) life wherein monasticism could flourish. See John Cassian, *Conlationes*, *CSEL* 13, esp. bk. XIX. See also the discussion of Cassion's influence on Western spirituality in Markus, *The End of Ancient Christianity*, 181 ff. This ascetic model coupled with notions of Roman aristocracy and social order, along with a new Frankish ruling elite, resulted in a distinctive model of sanctity in Gaul.

61. McNamara discusses the proselytization efforts of women in Gaul in "Living Sermons: Consecrated Women and the Conversion of Gaul," in Nichols and Shank, eds., *Medieval Religious Women*, vol. 2, *Peaceweavers*, 19–37. Also, Schulenburg discusses the role of women in conversion throughout western Europe, including Gaul, Lombardy, Visigothic Spain, and Anglo-Saxon England, in *Forgetful of Their Sex*, esp. chap. 4, "Marriage and Domestic Proselytization," 177–209.

62. Gregory of Tours, *LH* II.30–31.

63. On the importance of Martin of Tours in the Christianization of Gaul, see Van Dam, *Leadership and Community*, 119–40. Also, Wallace-Hadrill provides an important description of Clovis's conversion in *The Frankish Church*, 17–36.

64. See Clothild's *vita*, *MGH SRM* 2.341–48; also, McNamara, *Sainted Women of the Dark Ages*, 38–50.

65. The Franks, unique among the Germanic invaders, converted to "orthodox" Christianity.

66. *Vita Genovefae*, *AS*, Jan. 3, 137–53; or see the later edition in *MGH SRM* 3.204–38; see also trans. in McNamara, *Sainted Women of the Dark Ages*, 17–37.

67. *Vita Chrothildis* 7, *MGH SRM* 2.344; or McNamara, *Sainted Women of the Dark Ages*, 44–45: veniente rege pagano ad baptismum, precederet sanctus Remigius vice Christi Iesu, et subsequeretur sancta regina Chrothildis vice ecclesie Deum interpellantis.

68. *Vita Chrothildis* 11, *MGH SRM* 2.346; or McNamara, *Sainted Women of the Dark Ages*, 47: corda gentis pagane et ferocissime . . . blanditiis emollivit et sanctis exortationibus et orationibus sedulis per beatum Remigium ad Deum convertit.

69. *Vita Chrothildis* 14, *MGH SRM* 2.347; or McNamara, *Sainted Women of the Dark Ages*, 49: His et aliis sanctis operibus referta sancta Chrothildis olim regina, tunc pauperum et servorum Dei famula, despiciens mundum et corde diligens Deum, consenuit in senectute bona, a Christo receptura premia sine fine mansura.

70. Al-Majlisī, v. 43.3, pp. 24–25: fāṭima bidʿa minnī wa hiya nūr ʿaynī wa thamara fuʾādī yasuʾunī mā sāʾahā wa yasurrunī mā sarrahā . . . fa-aḥsin ilayhā baʿdī wa ammā al-ḥasan wa al-ḥusayn fa-humā ibnāya wa rīḥānatayyā wa humā sayyidā shabāb ahl al-janna fa la-yakramā alayka ka-samʿuka wa baṣaruka.

71. See Rubin, "Pre-existence and Light," 99.

72. Al-Majlisī, v. 43.3, pp. 20–21: la-yaghdabu li-ghadabiki wa yarda li-radāʾiki.

73. Al-Majlisī, v. 43.3, pp. 25–26.

74. Al-Majlisī, v. 43.2, p. 18: summīyat fāṭima fī l-ard li-annahā fāṭimat shiʿatahā min al-nār.

75. Al-Mufīd, chap. 4; 126.

76. Al-Majlisī, vol. 43.3, p. 29.

77. These food replication miracles offer a striking comparison with the Mary and Martha dichotomy that evolves in the Christian tradition (Luke 10.38–42). In Christian exegesis Mary chooses to sit by Jesus' feet for instruction (the contemplative life) while Martha labors in the kitchen (the active life). In Shiʿite exegesis, however, Fatima performs the obligatory prayers and rituals while Allah provides for all the mundane chores.

78. Al-Majlisī, v. 43.3, p. 29.

79. See Jane Smith and Yvonne Haddad, "Eve: Islamic Image of Woman," in *Women and Islam*, ed. Azīzah al-Hibri (New York: Pergamon Press, 1982), 136. Note the comparison of Adam and Eve's culpability: in Qur'an 2.35, 7.19, both are allotted paradise and warned against the tree; 2.36, 7.20, Iblis's (Satan's) temptation of both; 2.121, both become aware of their nakedness; and 2.36, 20.123, 7.24, Allah expels them from the Garden.

80. See *al-Kisā'ī*, *The Tales of the Prophets*, trans. W. M. Thackston Jr. (Boston: Twayne, 1978), 31.

81. See Smith and Haddad, *Women and Islam*, 135–37.

82. See Barbara Freyer Stowasser's discussion of Hawwa' in *Women in the Qur'an, Traditions, and Interpretation* (New York: Oxford University Press, 1994), 25–38.

83. See Stowasser's discussion of al-Ṭabarī, *Women in the Qur'an, Traditions, and Interpretation*, 30.

84. According to one hadith, Muhammad himself acknowledges the potential danger of women as he compares the powers of one's personal *shayṭān* and one's wives: "My Satan was an unbeliever but God helped me against him and He converted to Islam; my wives were a help for me. Adam's Satan was an infidel and Adam's wife was an aid in his sin." Quoted from al-Munawī, al-Suyūṭī, and al-Daylāmī in Kister, "Legends in *tafsīr* and hadith Literature," 93. In al-Kisā'ī's *Tales of the Prophets*, 51, Satan even receives "woman" as his special, vulnerable prey.

85. See Ayoub, *Redemptive Suffering*, 62.

86. Al-Majlisī, v. 11, p. 164.

87. Al-Majlisī, v. 11, p. 165: wa tasallaṭa `alā hawwā' li-naẓarihā ilā fāṭima bi `ayn al-ḥasad ḥattā akalat min al-shajara ka-mā akala ādam fa-akhrajahumā āllah, `azza wa jalla, `an jannatihī, wa ahbaṭahumā `an jawārihī ilā l-arḍ.

88. *Umm al-Kitāb*, quoted by Louis Massignon, "L'hyperdulie de Fatima, ses Origines Historiques et Dogmatiques," in *La Mubahala de Medine et l'hyperdulie de Fatima* (Paris: Librairie Orientale et Americaine, 1955), 28.

89. Al-Kisā'ī, *Tales of the Prophets*, 41–42.

90. See 1 Kings 21–22.

91. On Brunhild's animosity toward Columbanus, see the *Vita Columbani, Liber I, MGH SRM* 4.65–112. Also see Fredegar's *Chronicle* for his descriptions of Brunhild's murderous plots, esp. *cap. 32*. The translation is available in J. M. Wallace-Hadrill, *The Fourth Book of the Chronicle of Fredegar, with Its Continuations* (London: Nelson 1960). Nelson also provides an important analysis of Brunhild's political ventures in "Queens as Jezebels."

92. Fouracre and Gerberding provide a good introduction to and translation of Balthild's *vita*; see *Late Merovingian France*, 97–132.

93. See *Vita Wilfridi, MGH SRM* 6.193–263. See also Nelson, "Queens as Jezebels," 65–66.

94. *Vita S. Balthildis*, 3.

95. *Vita S. Balthildis*, 4, *MGH SRM* 2.486: ut matrem, sacerdotibus ut filiam, iuvenibus sive adolescentibus ut piam nutricem.

96. *Vita S. Balthildis*, 4, *MGH SRM* 2.486: ministrans ipsa sacerdotibus et pauperibus, pascebat egenos et induebat vestibus nudos . . . dirigebat quoque per ipsum ad coenobia virorum ac sacrarum virginum auri vel argenti non modica munera.

97. Many Shi`ite hagiographers construct an antithesis to Fatima's virtue as well, both in Hawwa' (or Eve) and `A'isha, Muhammad's beloved wife.

98. See the *Protevangelium of James* and the *Odes of Solomon*, for example. These texts are discussed in greater detail in chap. 3.

99. See Daniel Boyarin's eloquent discussion of this fleshly hierarchy in "On the History of the Early Phallus," in *Gender and Difference in the Middle Ages*, Medieval Cultures 32, ed. Sharon Farmer and Carol Braun Pasternack (Minneapolis: University of Minneapolis Press, 2003), 7–8.

100. See de Nie's article, "Consciousness Fecund through God," 116–32, for an important analysis of Perpetua, Felicitas, and Eugenia.

101. There are many works available on transvestitism and transgendering in the early church. One article describes the Greco-Roman philosophical milieu in which this model evolved. See Elizabeth Castelli's "'I will make Mary male': Pieties of the Body and Gender Transformation of Christian Women in Late Antiquity," in *Body Guards: The Cultural Politics of Gender Ambiguity*, ed. Julia Epstein and Kristina Straub (New York: Routledge, 1991), 29–49.

102. Gregory of Tours, *GM* 9; *MGH SRM* 1.2.45: Nec enim potest fieri, ut deficiat triticum in eius monasterium, quae frugem vitae ex utero pereunti intulit mundo.

103. See, for example, Isabelle Réal's discussion in *Vies de saints, vie de famille: Représentation et système de la parenté dans le Royaume mérovingien (481–751) d'après les sources hagiographiques* (Brussels: Brepols, 2001).

104. For detailed discussion of property rites and toll exemptions, see Ian Wood, *The Merovingian Kingdoms, 450–751* (New York: Longman, 1994), esp. chaps. 11, 12; also see Jo Ann McNamara and Suzanne Wemple, "The Power of Women through the Family in Medieval Europe, 500–1100," in *Women and Power in the Middle Ages*, ed. Mary Erler and Maryanne Kowaleski (Athens: University of Georgia Press, 1983), 83–101; also see Janet L. Nelson's "The Wary Widow" and Paul Fouracre's "Eternal Light and Earthly Needs: Practical Aspects of the Development of Frankish Immunities," in *Property and Power in the Early Middle Ages*, ed. Wendy Davies and Paul Fouracre (Cambridge: Cambridge University Press, 1995). In *The Frankish Church*, Wallace-Hadrill discusses various

motivations for Merovingian investment in monastic houses. He includes the donors' desire for perpetual intercession provided by the "professional" monks and nuns; the localization of martyrs' and bishops' relics supervised by monastic houses; and the gaining of salvation through charitable gifts to monastic poverty (60–62).

105. In *Saints' Lives and the Rhetoric of Gender*, Kitchens argues that there are more continuities between male and female hagiography in the early Merovingian period than differences. He contends that charity, for example, is a constant virtue from the biblical period through the early Medieval era; and he does not see charity as a particularly female attribute. I disagree, however, as argued above.

106. See, for example, Athanasius, *Life of Antony*, 12. Coon also discusses the hagiographer Gerontius's subtle chastisement of Melania the Younger for flaunting her wealth around the Egyptian desert. According to the *vita*, Melania attempts to give some of the anchorites gold coins which they reject with disdain (see *Sacred Fictions*, 116–17).

107. See (among others) Matt. 5.3, 6.19; Mark 10.23–6; Matt. 21.12; Mark 11.15.

108. See Dominic Janes's discussion of late antique poverty and wealth in *God and Gold in Late Antiquity* (Cambridge: Cambridge University Press, 1998). She explains the ambiguities between textual exaltations of poverty and visual displays of wealth and grandeur in early churches and images. Ambrose and Augustine, for example, were careful to explain that the *desire* for wealth, not wealth itself, led to corruption and sin; see 154–55.

109. *Vita Melaniae*, 21 (*SC* 90), as quoted in Janes, *God and Gold*, 137.

110. Fortunatus, *Vita Radegundis* 13, *MGH SRM* 2.369: Mox indumentum nobile, quo celeberrima die solebat, pompa comitante, regina procedere, exuta ponit in altare et blattis, gemmis, ornamentis mensam divinae gloriae tot donis onerat per honorem. Cingulum auri ponderatum fractum dat opus in pauperum.

111. Fortunatus, *Vita Radegundis* 17, *MGH SRM* 2.370.

112. See Luke 10.40. In medieval exegesis Martha symbolizes the active life of charity, as opposed to the contemplative life of her sister Mary. Fortunatus calls Radegund the "new Martha" in *Vita Radegundis* 7.

113. The history of Ave Maria is, of course, complicated. The basic form of the prayer was established from the twelfth through the sixteenth centuries. The prayer borrowed from the biblical texts of Luke 1. 28 and 1.42, which recounted Gabriel's and Elizabeth's greetings to Mary. Most of the prayer, however, is present in the Western church's liturgy by the seventh century. Baudonivia's rendition of Mammezo's prayer resonates strongly with the structure of the Ave Maria: "Hail Mary, full of grace, the Lord is with you. Blessed are thou among women; blessed is the fruit of thy womb, Jesus. Holy Mary, Mother of God, pray for us

sinners now and at the hour of our death." See Anne Winston-Allen's history of the rosary in *Stories of the Rose: The Making of the Rosary in the Middle Ages* (University Park: Pennsylvania State University Press, 1997).

114. Baudonivia, *Vita Radegundis* 11, *MGH SRM* 2.385; or McNamara, *Sainted Women of the Dark Ages*, 94: Domina Radegundis, credo, te virtute Dei esse plenam, cuius voluntatem magis fecisti, quam hominum; domina bona, pietate plena, miserere mei, subveni infelice, ora pro me, ut mihi reddatur oculus, quia pro gravi crutiatu et dolore affligitur anima mea.

115. Baudonivia, *Vita Radegundis* 23. Gregory of Tours made this comment at Radegund's funeral; as he gazed upon Radegund he smelled lilies and roses that reminded him of the Holy Mother.

116. *Vita Rusticulae* 22, *MGH SRM* 4.348: omnes dominam, omnes piam matrem vocarent.

117. Ibn Sa`d, *Tabaqāt al-kubrā* (Bierut: Dar Sadir, 1957–58), 3.170; 8.64,66. Discussed in Spellberg, *Politics, Gender, and the Islamic Past*, 32–37.

118. Ibn Sa`d, *Tabaqāt al-kubrā*, 8.65,67; al-Tirmidhī, *Ṣaḥīḥ al-Tirmidhī*, 5.364–66; as discussed in Spellberg, *Politics, Gender, and the Islamic Past*, 33–34.

119. Spellberg cites traditions that explain that the Prophet's wives did not eat meat; therefore they were slender (!). See *Politics, Gender, and the Islamic Past*, 67–68.

120. Spellberg also cites, among others, Ibn Hishām's exegetical works that correlate the *hadith al-ifk* with the Qur'anic revelations; see *Kitāb sirat rasūl allāh*, vol. 1, pt. 2: 736; *Politics, Gender, and the Islamic Past*, 73–74.

121. The implications of this repudiation are far reaching in terms of Shi`ite historiography. As Etan Kohlberg points out, "It involves a rejection of the natural assumption that the earliest followers of true faith are also the best and the most virtuous of its practitioners; in Sunni Islam this principle is enshrined in the hadith, 'The most excellent people are my generation, then those following them, then those [who follow those] following them.'" Kohlberg goes on to explain that Shi`ite authors devoted their attention more to *rijāl* works concerning the Imams' followers than the biographers of the Companions. See "Some Imāmī Shī`i Views on the ṢAḤĀBA," *Jerusalem Studies in Arabic and Islam* 5 (1984): 149–50.

122. As Kohlberg points out, the tradition can be dated to traditionist `Alī b. Mujāhid al-Rāzī (d. 182/798) in his *Manāqib amīr al-mu'minīn wa mathālib al-munāfiqīn*. See Kohlberg's recension of the text in "Some Imāmī Shī`i Views on the ṢAḤĀBA," 152–56.

123. This hadith resonates with the miracle story of Numbers 22 wherein Balaam's donkey recognizes God's angel and diverts from its path.

124. See *Ṣaḥīḥ Bukhārī*, v. 7, 64.274.

125. See al-Majlisī, v. 43.3, pp. 28–29.

126. Caesarius, *Rule for Nuns*, 63, p. 191.

127. One of the most noted queens who escapes an unwanted marriage is Radegund; see *Vita Radegundis* 12. Also, Caesarius of Arles describes how virgins "unite to holy Mary" in the Mystical Body (i.e., the church) as the brides of Christ; see *Sermo VI*, p. 36. Also, McCarthy discusses this passage, along with the similarities with Augustine's *De sancta virginitate*, xix–xx, 252–54; xiv, 290–291; see McCarthy, *The Rule for Nuns*, 59.

128. See Donald Hochstetler, *A Conflict of Traditions: Women in Religion in the Early Middle Ages, 500–840* (Lanham, Md.: University Press of America, 1992). Hochstetler discusses the economic freedom of many abbesses and the question of community property on 16–24.

129. McNamara mentions this possibility in *The Ordeal of Community*, 12–13. Also, the rules of both Donatus and Caesarius remain clear about "testing" the young initiates for purity of purpose; Donatus, *Rule* 6; Caesarius, *Rule for Nuns*, 4.

130. See particularly Jane Tibbetts Schulenburg's discussion of family authority and royal patronage in *Forgetful of Their Sex*.

131. Donastus of Besançon, for example, notes in his *Rule* that no nun should act out of loyalty to another because of consanguinity. See McNamara and Halborg's translation in *The Ordeal of Community*, 74, p. 71. Also see McNamara's introduction, 12–13, which briefly summarizes some of the motivations for entering a convent in the early medieval period. Hochstetler provides a fine discussion of the "ideal" and actual inequalities in religious communities in *A Conflict of Traditions*, 119–26. Finally, note that Caesarius very clearly states that no nun, not even the abbess, should be permitted to have a personal maid.

132. Caesarius, *Rule for Nuns*, 25.

133. Ibid., 40.

134. See Caesarius, *Rule for Nuns*, 2, 59; also note Caesarius's comments in *Vereor* as discussed by McCarthy, *The Rule for Nuns*, 54: "She who desires to preserve religion in an immaculate heart and a pure body, ought never, or certainly only for great and unavoidable necessity, go out in public; familiar friendship with men, as much as possible should be rare." See *Vereor* 136–37.

135. See Schulenburg, *Forgetful of Their Sex*, 139–55.

136. *MGH Concilia* 1.12–13, p. 218. See Hochstetler's discussion of such church councils, 65–80.

137. *MGH Concilia* 1.17–18, 63; as quoted in Hochstetler, *A Conflict of Traditions*, 79–80.

138. There has been some debate over whether before the Council of Orléans deaconesses were allowed to participate in consecrating the Eucharist. If so, the delineation of a "proper" consecrated life further alienated women from roles of leadership. See, for example, Suzanne Wemple, *Women in Frankish Society*

(Philadelphia: University of Pennsylvania Press, 140); Hochstetler, *A Conflict of Traditions*, 76 ff.

139. See Hochstetler, *A Conflict of Traditions*, 16–19; Jane Tibbetts Schulenburg has done the most expansive studies on the topic of the decline of women's monasticism in the late Merovingian and Carolingian periods. See "Strict Active Enclosure and Its Effects on the Female Monastic Experience, ca. 500–1100," in Nichols and Thomas, eds., *Distant Echoes*, 51–86; and "Women's Monastic Communities, 500–1100: Patterns of Expansion and Decline," *Signs: Journal of Women in Culture and Society* 14.2 (1989): 261–92.

140. As already noted, there is no monastic tradition in Islam as there is in Christianity, so it is impossible to identify traditions of abbesses as mothers and familial rhetoric in ascetic communities to illustrate the power of domestic rhetoric. It is possible, however, to recognize some of the saint cults that arise in Shiʿite circles throughout the Middle Ages focusing on the sons and daughters (i.e., the extended families) of the Imams. In one of these cultic traditions in Egypt, for example, Sayyida Nafīsah bint al-Hasan is adored. In popular traditions, she is approached as "mother"; she is, in effect, imitating Fatima. See Devin J. Stewart, "Popular Shiʿism in Medieval Egypt: Vestiges of Islamic Sectarian Polemics in Egyptian Arabic," *Studia Islamica* 84.2 (1996): 35–66; Yusuf Ragib, "Al-Sayyida Nafīsa, sa légende, son culte et son cimetière," *Studia Islamica* 44 (1976): 61–86; and, for a comparative view with the Sufis, Valerie J. Hoffman-Ladd, "Devotion to the Prophet and His Family in Egyptian Sufism," *IJMES* 24 (1992): 615–37.

141. For discussions of Islamic scholars and their leadership in medieval communities, see Roy Mottahedeh, *Loyalty and Leadership in an Early Islamic Society* (Princeton: Princeton University Press, 1980); and Berkey, *The Transmission of Knowledge in Medieval Cairo*.

142. For an important discussion of the scholars' leadership of the Shiʿite community, see Momen's *An Introduction to Shîʿi Islam*, esp. 184–207.

Chapter Five.   **Sacred Art and Architecture**

1. See Henri Lefebvre, *The Production of Space*, trans. Donald Nicholson-Smith (Oxford: Blackwell, 1991), for a theoretical discussion of spatial practice.

2. See Jas Elsner, *Imperial Rome an Christian Triumph: The Art of the Roman Empire, AD 100–450* (Oxford: Oxford University Press, 1998). Elsner brilliantly discusses visual culture as a display of power and authority as he traces the changes from Roman to Christian material culture.

3. The cornerstone of Judeo-Christian monotheism, of course, resides in the Ten Commandments, Exod. 20.1–17. The Qurʾan 17.39 relates a similar set

of ethical imperatives, including the command to "take not, with Allah, another object of worship."

4. Matthews's work, *The Clash of Gods*, provides an important review of material culture and its function in late antiquity and the early Middle Ages. According to Matthews, for example, material culture was more than just a visual experience; it included sight, sound, and smells that overwhelmed the worshiper.

5. Many scholars (e.g., Elsner) have explained that the Jewish prohibitions against material displays in sacred space were indeed ideals. The synagogue at Dura Europas is a good example.

6. Al-Majlisī, v. 43.2, page 11.

7. See, for example, al-Kulaynī's discussion of Fatima as *nur* in *Kitāb al-uṣūl min al-kāfī*.

8. See Rizvi, "Gendered Patronage," 123–53.

9. The profound debate over material representation and figural images emerged in Christianity during the fifth and sixth centuries well before the iconoclast controversy in the Byzantine East. Popular opinion among the priests, bishops, and popes finally agreed that the church should employ images as didactic tools. See, for example, Pope Gregory the Great's *Letter to Bishop Serenus of Marseille*. Caecilia Davis-Weyer provides an excellent review of arguments for and against the use of images in worship (both public and private); see *Early Medieval Art, 300–1150: Sources and Documents* (Atlantic Highlands, N.J.: Prentice Hall, 1971). Gregory of Tours, for example, believed that pictures and ornaments made admirable instruments for educating the "rustics" (*rustici*) of Gaul. Gregory boasts of the images used in Saint Martin's *martyrium* in *HF* 10.31; 7.22. Also see Cynthia Hahn, "Seeing and Believing: The Construction of Sanctity in Early-Medieval Saints' Shrines," *Speculum* 72.4 (1997): 1095; Brown, *Society and the Holy*, 222–50. And in anti-Jewish polemic, Christian theologians further argued that God sanctioned the use of some images; indeed, he commanded Moses to mount cherubim on the Ark of the Covenant and Ezekiel to fill the Temple with figural effigies. See Charles Barber, "The Truth in Painting: Iconoclasm and Identity in Early-Medieval Art," *Speculum* 72.4 (1997): 1026–27. Barber discusses primarily Leontios of Neapolis, *Against the Jews*. For other texts, see Joan Branham, "Sacred Space under Erasure in Ancient Synagogues and Early Churches," *Art Bulletin* 74 (1992): 375–94.

10. In *The Formation of Islamic Art* (New Haven: Yale University Press, 1987), Oleg Grabar stresses that while this might be the rule of Islamic artistic display, there are certainly exceptions. He points out that different geographic locales were more permissive than others in allowing figural displays throughout history; and art and architecture intended for personal piety instead of public use often acceded to animals and sometimes people; see 72–73, 89. Also, Muhammad Issa argues as a Muslim that prohibitions against pictorial display served an

historical purpose only. He contends that Muhammad's injunctions served the earliest community to strengthen their nascent faith, but that need no longer exists. See his *Painting in Islam: Between Prohibition and Aversion* (Istanbul: Waqf for Research on Islamic History, Art, and Culture, 1996). See also Dominique Clevenot, *Splendors of Islam: Architecture, Decoration and Design* (New York: St. Martin's Press, 2000), esp. 126–33.

11. Robert Hillenbrand provides an important review of innovative styles of Umayyad and ʿAbbasid art forms; see *Islamic Art and Architecture* (London: Thames and Hudson, 1999).

12. I rely here on Grabar's foundational work, *The Formation of Islamic Art*. Also see Terry Allen, "Aniconism and Figural Representation in Islamic Art," in *Five Essays on Islamic Art* (Manchester, Mich.: Solipsist Press, 1988).

13. See Leslie Brubaker's important study, "Icons before Iconoclasm?" in *Morfologie sociali culturali in Europa fra tarda antichità e alto Medioevo* (Spoleto: Centro italiano di studi sull'alto Medioevo, 1998).

14. These hadith are both collected and quoted in Grabar, *The Formation of Islamic Art*, 82.

15. See Grabar, *The Formation of Islamic Art*, 81–83. This criticism is based on the Qur'anic verse 59.24. Also see Brown's "Dark Age Crisis" in *Society and the Holy*, 251–301.

16. See the important works on goddess imagery, including Ludy Goodison and Christine Morris, eds., *Ancient Goddess: The Myths and the Evidence* (Madison: University of Wisconsin Press, 1998); Merope Pavlides, "The Cult of Mary Compared with Ancient Mother Goddesses," in *Gender, Culture, and the Arts: Women, the Arts and Society*, ed. Ronald Dotterer and Susan Bowers (Selinsgrove, Pa.: Susquehanna University Press, 1993). Also, the works of Michael Carroll, psychohistorian, allude to ancient goddess worship as a prototype for Marian adoration; see, for example, *The Cult of the Virgin Mary: Psychological Origins* (Princeton: Princeton University Press, 1986).

17. See Christo Kovachevski's discussion of the ancient prototypes of Marian images in *The Madonna in Western Painting* (London: Cromwell Editions, 1991), 16–17; and Elsner, *Imperial Rome and Christian Triumph*, 220–28.

18. The Nestorians and other "heretical" groups rejected the images of Mary breast-feeding as well as any popular cult devoted to her milk. The Nestorians found it nothing less than disgusting to suggest that God actually fed at a woman's breast.

19. John Crook discusses the Virgin's milk in *The Architectural Setting of the Cult of the Saints in the Early Christian West, c. 300–1200* (New York: Oxford University Press, 2000), 7. It is ironic that this cult only gained some momentum in the twelfth century and then finally just before the Reformation. Erasmus condemned this popular adoration most virulently in many of his works,

including *Ten Colloquies*, English translation by Craig Thompson (New York: Macmillan, 1986).

20. Indeed, the T-shape model only triumphed among other variants during the eighth century. Richard Krautheimer, in "Carolingian Revival of Early Christian Architecture," in *Studies in Early Christian, Medieval, and Renaissance Art* (New York: New York University Press, 1969), 203–6, argues that Saint Denis was the first construction to follow the basic T-model since the fifth century. See also Krautheimer's article in the same volume, "The Beginning of Early Christian Architecture," 1–20.

21. Eric Fletcher presents the basic argument among art historians regarding the categories "Late Roman" and "Merovingian or Early Medieval" in "The Influence of Merovingian Gaul on Northumbria in the Seventh Century," *Medieval Archaeology* 24 (1980): 69–86. This important point, however, is beyond the scope of my argument; I am looking primarily at the evolution of Marian imagery, not the distinctive schools of art. Fletcher also, quite rightly, points out the problems associated with retrieving data on Merovingian architecture and art forms because of later Romanesque and Gothic additions.

22. *Liber Pontificalis*, 46; trans. Raymond Davis in *The Book of Pontiffs: The Ancient Biographies of the First Ninety Roman Bishops to AD 710* (Liverpool: Liverpool University Press, 1989).

23. See Margaret R. Miles, "Santa Maria Maggiore's Fifth-Century Mosaics: Triumphal Christianity and the Jews," *Harvard Theological Review* 86.2 (1993): 155–75. Miles emphasizes the mosaics' anti-Semitic message.

24. See André Grabar and Carl Nordenfalk, "Early Medieval Painting, from the Fourth to the Eleventh Century," in *The Great Centuries of Painting* (New York: Skira, 1957). Also see Henry N. Claman's description of Santa Maria Maggiore in *Jewish Images in the Christian Church: Art as the Mirror of the Jewish-Christian Conflict, 200–1250 C.E.* (Macon, Ga.: Mercer University Press, 2000), esp. 86–92; and John Lowden, *Early Christian and Byzantine Art* (London: Phaidon Press, 1997), 50–55.

25. See Suzanne Spain, "'The Promised Blessing': The Iconography of the Mosaics of S. Maria Maggiore," *Art Bulletin* 61 (1979): 518–40.

26. See, for example, William Loerke's discussion in "'Real Presence' in Early Christian Art," in *Monasticism and the Arts*, ed. Timothy Verdon (Syracuse: Syracuse University Press, 1984), 29–51. Loerke explains that pictorial cycles were intended not just to reference written texts but also to cause the observer to "emotionally inhabit them" (40–41).

27. Gen. 14.17–24.

28. Spain, "The Promised Blessing," 534–35.

29. *De S. Eustadiola, Abbatissa Bituricensi in Gallia, AS*, June 8, 132.

30. *Vita Chrothildis reginae francorum*, 11–12.

31. *Vita Radegundis*, 2.7.

32. *Vita Rusticulae*, 25.

33. Ibid.

34. Ibid., 28.

35. *Vita S. Glodesindae*, 18.

36. *Fifth Council of Carthage, CC*, 149.204. Crook discusses this and other relevant councils in *The Architectural Setting of the Cult of the Saints*, 13. Crook points out that although many areas agreed with this tradition, Merovingian Francia was slow to place such emphasis on the incorporation of relics. For one reason, other churches encouraged the deposition of entire bodies in the altar; Merovingian Gaul, on the whole, had fewer "intact" saints and relied more on contact relics; see 13–16.

37. Crook discusses Mary's tomb at Gethsemane in *The Architectural Setting of the Cult of the Saints*, 257. Also see B. Bagatti, M. Piccirillo, and A. Prodomo, *New Discoveries at the Tomb of Virgin Mary in Gethsemane*, Studium Biblicum Franciscanum, Collectio Minor, 17 (Jerusalem: Franciscan Printing Press, 1975).

38. Hahn describes a similar structure at Saint Thecla's tomb in Seleucia. According to her, access to Thecla's grotto was allowed through two holes in the ground. "Now the faithful could create relic-like mementos by lowering objects on string into the grotto or perhaps also peer or speak prayers into her residence chamber." See "Seeing and Believing" (1087).

39. Crook, *The Architectural Setting of the Cult of the Saints*, 63, discusses Gregory of Tours's description of a petitioner speaking into the tombs. See *GC* 36. Crook also compares the shaft construction to Roman libation holes that allowed offerings to be passed down to Roman coffins (63 ff.).

40. *GM* 8.

41. See Hahn's argument for the increasing clerical control of sacred space in "Seeing and Believing." She also points out that the "glittering spectacles" were intended to attract not only the petitioner's attention but also the saint himself/herself. Einhard, for example, constructs a spectacular shrine to "lure" two prominent saints, but they decline and go elsewhere (1083).

42. See Crook, *The Architectural Setting of the Cult of the Saints*, 69–74.

43. See *Translatio S. Germani Vetustissima, MGH SRM* 7.423–24. Werner Jacobsen discusses this miraculous translation in "Saints' Tombs in Frankish Church Architecture," *Speculum* 74.4 (1997): 1132–33.

44. *Vita Antiquior, De S. Glodesinde Virgine, AS*, July 25, 206: in eodem monasterio in ecclesia seniori post altare, quod constructum est atque sacratum in laude et honore sanctae Dei Genitricis Mariae, ac beati Petri principis Apostolorum. See also McNamara, *Sainted Women of the Dark Ages*, 148.

45. Glodesind's hagiographer claimed that she had been Bishop Arnulf's wife, a very important Carolingian saintly figure; her spiritual prowess expressed

from a high altar lent power to the blossoming Arnulfing line and the blossoming Carolingian claims to rule. McNamara argues that the anonymous author of the *vita* wrote his redaction in the ninth century, but he relied on a version that circulated much earlier. The later biographer emphasized Glodesind's connection to Arnulf; this supposition explains the late advent of her popular cult. See McNamara, *Sainted Women of the Dark Ages*, 137. Also, this trend in corpse shifting reveals how far the ninth century stands from the earlier period: Emperor Theodosius, for example, issued a fifth-century decree regulating the movement, dismemberment, and profit of the relic trade. See *Codex Theodosiani*, 9.17, "De Supulchri Violati," in *Theodosian Libri XVI*, 2 vols., ed. T. Mommsen and P. M. Meyer (Berlin, 1905). Crook, *The Architectural Setting of the Cult of the Saints*, discusses Theodosius and Gregory the Great, 69–74. He points out that Gregory had great reservations about dividing and moving holy relics and encouraged instead the use of contact relics. Gregory, for example, refused to send the Byzantine empress Constantina a relic of Saint Paul. Gregory informed the empress that contact relics were just as sublime, and he sent filings from Saint Paul's chains of captivity. As Crook also points out, Gregory's motivations may have been more political than theological.

46. Robert Irwin discusses some of the civic functions of local mosques in *Islamic Art in Context: Art, Architecture and the Literary World* (New York: Harry N. Abrams, 1997), 57–77.

47. The mosque's spiritual function is often identified by a calligraphic inscription from Qur'an 5.55, usually on the outer door: "Your (real) friends are (no less than) Allah, His Messenger, and the Believers—those who establish regular prayers and pay *zakāt* and they bow down humbly (in worship)."

48. See the important works on Arabic calligraphy, including Yousif Mahmud Ghulum, *The Art of Arabic Calligraphy* (Lafayette, Calif.: Y. M. Ghulam, 1982); George Atiyeh, ed., *The Book in the Islamic World: The Written Word and Communication in the Middle East* (Albany: State University of New York Press, 1995); and Nabih F. Safwat, *The Art of the Pen: Calligraphy of the 14th to 20th Centuries* (London: Nour Foundation, 1996).

49. *EI²*, "*miḥrāb*," 7.

50. See Grabar, *The Formation of Islamic Art*, chap. 5, 99–131.

51. *EI²*, "*miḥrāb*," 8.

52. Al-Majlisī, v. 43.2, p. 11.

53. For the structure of prayer niches complete with hanging lamps, see Nuha N. N. Khoury, "The *Miḥrab* Image: Commemorative Themes in Medieval Islamic Architecture," *Muqarnas*, no. 9 (1992): 11–28. Assadullah Souren Melikian-Chirvani also provides an excellent explanation of the assimilation of Persian-Zoroastrian symbols in an Islamic cultural system. She explains how the imagery of the *miḥrāb*'s light corresponded with Zoroastrian views of the divine

fire. See "The Light of Heaven and Earth: From the Chahār-tāq to the Miḥrāb," *Bulletin of the Asia Institute* 4 (1990): 95–131. Also, Sheila S. Blair and Jonathan B. Bloom, eds., *Images of Paradise in Islamic Art* (Hanover, N.H.: Hood Museum of Art, Dartmouth College, 1991), 36–40, discuss the mosque lamp as a symbol of Paradise, sometimes surrounded by images of heavenly gardens and flora.

54. Khoury, "The *Miḥrab* Image," 13–14.

55. Ibid. Khoury discusses the *miḥrāb* of Punja ʿAli at Mosul (1287–88); he describes the *miḥrāb*'s adornment along with two references to Imam ʿAli hand imprints and the hoof of his horse (contact relics).

56. See Priscilla Soucek's insightful article, "The Temple after Solomon: the Role of Maryam bint Imran and Her Mihrab," *Jewish Art* 23–24 (1997–98): 34–41.

57. See the *Tafsīr* Muqātil ibn Sulaymān, as discussed in Soucek, "The Temple after Solomon," 35.

58. Soucek, "The Temple after Solomon," 36. Muslims visited Jesus' cradle in commemoration of the Qur'anic miracle described in 19.30–33 wherein Jesus (as an infant in a cradle) defends his mother's virtue.

59. Raya Shani, *A Monumental Manifestation of the Shiʿite Faith in Late Twelfth-Century Iran: The Case of the Gunbad-i ʿAlawiyān, Hamadān* (Oxford: Oxford University Press, 1996).

60. Ibid., 141.

61. Shani, *A Monumental Manifestation*, includes a broader discussion of verses which appear on primarily Shiʿite architecture: Qur'an 5.55-56; 76.1–9; and 53.1–30.

62. Shani, *A Monumental Manifestation*, discusses this verse, 126–27.

63. Al-Ṭabarsī, *Majmaʿ al-bayān fī tafsīr al-qur'ān* (Tehran, Beyrouth, 1274/1900); as discussed in Shani, *A Monumental Manifestation*, 126.

64. See, for example, al-Majlisī, vol. 11, pp. 164–65.

65. Al-Ashʿari, the great tenth-century theologian, articulated a theology widely considered orthodox by Sunni Muslims.

66. See the innovative work of Yasser Tabbaa, *The Transformation of Islamic Art during the Sunni Revival* (Seattle: University of Washington Press, 2001).

67. Rizvi, "Gendered Patronage," 134.

68. Ibid., 134–40.

69. See Francis Romeril Maddison, *Science, Tools, and Magic* (London: Nour Foundation, 1997). Maddison discusses magical bowls inscribed with the names of the Twelve Imams found in India and China, 72–104.

70. For a full history of this symbol, see Dominique Champault and A. R. Verbrugge, *Le Main: Ses figurations au Maghreb et au Levant* (Paris: Musée de l'Homme, 1965); and Richard Bachinger and Helga Exler, *Die Hand: Schutz und*

Schmuch in Nordafrika: Katalog zur Ausstellung der Galerie Exler & Co., vom. 1-30, (Frankfurt am Main: Die Galerie, 1981).

71. Other works that contain discussions of the hand amulet specific to Islam include Sandor Fodor, *Amulets from the Islamic World: Catalogue of the Exhibition Held in Budapest in 1988* (Budapest: Eotvos Lorand University, 1988); Peter W. Schienerl, *Schmuck und Amulett in Antike und Islam* (Aachen: Alano, 1988); and Rudolf Kriss and Hubert Kriss-Heinrich, *Volksglaube im Bereich des Islam, Bd. 2: Amulette, Zauberformein, und Beschwoerungen* (Wiesbaden: O. Harrassowitz, 1962). Doris Jean Austin and Martin Simmons, eds., *Streetlights: Illuminating Tales of the Urban Black Experience* (New York: Penguin Books, 1996), include the hand amulet in their work on Islam and the urban black experience in the United States. Irene Markoff discusses specific Sufi representations of the hand in "Music, Saints, and Ritual: Sama` and the Alevis of Turkey," in *Manifestations of Sainthood in Islam,* ed. Grace Smith and Carl W. Ernst (Istanbul: Isis Press, 1993), 102.

72. Champault and Verbrugge, *Le Main,* 18–20.

Conclusion

1. See the overview of Marian imagery in Catholic Christianity in Maurice Hamington, *Hail Mary? The Struggle for Ultimate Womanhood in Catholicism* (New York: Routledge, 1995); and Charles E. Curran, Margaret A. Farley, and Richard A. McCormick, eds., *Feminist Ethics and the Catholic Moral Tradition* (New York: Paulist Press, 1996).

2. See the Catholic Church's account of the Marian apparition in Fatima, Portugal, in William Thomas Walsh, *Our Lady of Fatima* (New York: Doubleday, 1954).

3. See Melissa R. Katz, Robert Orsi, and Davis Museum and Cultural Center, *Divine Mirrors: The Virgin Mary in Visual Arts* (Oxford: Oxford University Press, 2001); and Kristy Nabhan-Warren, *The Virgin of El Barrio: Marian Apparitions, Catholic Evangelizing, and Mexican American Activism* (New York: New York University Press, 2005).

4. Such historical inquiries have been forwarded by Rosemary Radford Ruether, Elisabeth Schüssler Fiorenza, Mary Daly, and Elizabeth Johnson.

5. See Charlene Spretnak, *Missing Mary: The Queen of Heaven and Her Re-Emergence in the Modern World* (London: Palgrave Macmillan, 2004).

6. See Colonel Sir Lewis Pelly, *The Miracle Play of Hasan and Husain* (London: Wm. H. Allen and Co., 1879), esp. scenes 1–4. In scene 4, p. 57, Muhammad refers to Fatima "the Mary of this people."

7. See Vernon James Schubel, *Religious Performance in Contemporary Islam: Shiʿi Devotional Rituals in South Asia* (Columbia: University of South Carolina Press, 1993), 35–43.

8. See David Pinault, *The Shiʿites: Ritual and Popular Piety in a Muslim Community* (New York: St. Martin's Press, 1992); also Pinault, "Zaynab bint ʿAli and theʿPlace of Women in the Households of the First Imams in Shiʿite Devotional Literature," in *Women in the Medieval Islamic World*, ed. Gavin R. G. Hambly (New York: St. Martin's Press, 1998).

9. See ʿAli Shariʿati, *Fatima Is Fatima* (Tehran: Shariʿati Foundation, 1981); William R. Darrow's discussion of Shariʿati in "Women's Place and the Place of Women in the Iranian Revolution," in *Women, Religion, and Social Change*, ed. Yvonne Haddad and Ellison Banks Findly (New York: State University of New York Press, 1985), 307–19; and Marcia Hermansen, "Fatimeh as a Role Model in the Works of Ali Shariʿati," in *Women and Revolution in Iran*, ed. Guity Nashat (Boulder, Colo.: Westview Press, 1983).

Bibliography

Primary Sources

Acts of Paul and Thecla. English translation in *New Testament Apocrypha*. Edited and translated by E. Hennecke and W. Schneemelcher. Philadelphia: Westminster Press, 1965.

Ambrose. *De institutione virginis. PL* 16.319–47.

———. *De obitu Valentiniani consolatio. PL* 16.

———. *De virginibus. PL* 16.197–243.

———. *Exposito in Evangelium Secundum Lucam. PL* 15.1603–1945. Edited by M. Adriaen. *Corpus Christianorum, Series Latina* 14. Turnhout: Brepols, 1957.

———. *Exposito in Ps. CXVIII. PL* 15.1257–1603. Edited by M. Petschenig, *CSEL* 62. Vienna: F. Tempsky, 1913.

Apophthegmata Patrum. PG 65.71–440. English translation by Benedicta Ward. *The Desert Christian: Sayings of the Desert Fathers, the Alphabetical Collection.* New York: Macmillan, 1975.

Ascension of Isaiah. English translation in *New Testament Apocrypha*. Edited and translated by E. Hennecke and W. Schneemelcher. Philadelphia: Westminster Press, 1965.

Athanasius of Alexandria. *Vita Antonii. PG* 26.835–976. English translation by Robert C. Gregg, *The Life of Antony and the Letter to Marcellinus.* Classics of Western Spirituality. New York: Paulist Press, 1980.

Augustine. *De Natura et Gratia. CSEL* 238–40.

———. *De sancta virginitate. PL* 40.397–428.

———. *Sancti Augustin: Sermones post Maurinos Reperti.* Edited by Germanus Morin. Rome: Tipografia Polyglotta Vaticana, 1930.

———. *Sermones. PL* 38, 39.

Avitus of Vienne. *Poematum liber sextus de virginitate. MGH AA* 6:275–94; *PL* 59:369–82. English translation by George W. Shea, *The Poems of Alcimus*

Ecdicius Avitus. Medieval and Renaissance Texts and Studies, vol. 172. Tempe: Arizona State University, 1997.

Baudonivia. *De Vita Sanctae Radegundis Liber II.* Edited by Bruno Krusch. *MGH SRM* 2.377–95.

al-Bukhārī. *Ṣaḥīḥ.* Edited by L. Krehl and W. Juynboll. Leiden, 1862–1908. English translation by Muhammad Muhsin Khan, *The Translation of the Meanings of Ṣaḥīḥ al-Bukhari.* Medina: Dar al-Fikr, 1981.

Caesarius of Arles. *Regula Virginum.* Latin text with French translation by Adalbert de Vogüé and Joel Courreau. *SC* 345. English translation available in Maria Caritas McCarthy, *The Rule for Nuns of Caesarius of Arles.* Washington, D.C.: Catholic University Press, 1960.

Clement of Alexandria. *Stromata.* English translation in *Alexandrian Christianity,* translated by John Ernest, Leonard Oulton, and Henry Chadwick. Library of Christian Classics, vol. 2. Philadelphia: Westminster Press, 1954.

Codex Theodosiana 9.17. *Theodosian Libri XVI.* 2 vols. Edited by T. Mommsen and P. M. Meyer. Berlin, 1905.

Donatus of Besançon. *Regula ad virgines.* PL 87.273–98. English translation by Jo Ann McNamara and John Halborg, *The Ordeal of Community.* Toronto: Peregrina, 1993.

Fortunatus, Venantius. *De Vita Sanctae Radegundis Liber I.* Edited by Bruno Krusch. *MGH SRM* 2.364–77.

———. *Carminum. MGH AA* 4/1. English translation by Judith George, *Venantius Fortunatus: Personal and Political Poems.* Translated Texts for Historians Latin Series 23. Liverpool: Liverpool University Press, 1995.

Gregory of Tours. *Decem libri historiarum.* Edited by Bruno Krusch and William Levison. *MGH SRM* 1.1.

———. *Gloria Confessorum.* Edited by Bruno Krusch. *MGH SRM* 1.2. English translation by Raymond Van Dam, *Gregory of Tours, Glory of the Confessors.* Translated Texts for Historians Latin Series 4. Liverpool: Liverpool University Press, 1988.

———. *In Gloria Martyrum.* Edited by Bruno Krusch. *MGH SRM* 1.2. English translation by Raymond Van Dam, *Gregory of Tours, Glory of the Martyrs.* Translated Texts for Historians Latin Series 3. Liverpool: Liverpool University Press, 1988.

———. *Liber vitae patrum.* Edited by Bruno Krusch. *MGH SRM* 1.2. English translation by Edward James, *Gregory of Tours, Lives of the Fathers.* Translated Texts for Historians Latin Series 1. Liverpool: Liverpool University Press, 1986.

Ibn Bābawayh. *Kitāb man lā yaḥḍuruhu al-faqīh.* Edited by al-Mūsawī al-Kharsān, 5th ed., 1390/1970.

———. *`Ilal al-sharā'i` wa l-aḥkām.* Najaf, 1385/1966.

Ibn Hishām. *Al-Sīrat al-nabawiyya*. Edited by Suhayl Zakār. Dār al-fikr. Beirut, 1992. English translation in *The Life of Muhammad: A Translation of Ishāq's sīrat rasūl allah* with introduction and notes by A. Guillaume. New York: Oxford University Press, 1997.

Jerome. *Adversus Helvidium. PL* 23.

———. *Adversus Jovinianum. PL* 23.221–352.

———. *Dialogus adversus Pelagianos. PL* 23.517–626.

———. *Epistle XXII. PL* 22.394–425; *Epistolae. CSEL* 54–56.

———. *Epitaphium Sanctae Paulae. CSEL* 55(2).306–51.

Kabbani, Muhammad Hisham, and Laleh Bakhtiar, eds. *Encyclopedia of Muhammad's Women Companions and the Traditions They Related.* Chicago: ABC International Group. Distributed by Kazi Publications, 1998.

al-Kisā'ī. *The Tales of the Prophets.* English translation by W. M. Thackston Jr. Boston: Twayne, 1978.

al-Kulaynī. *Al-Kāfī: al-uṣūl wa 'l-furū` wa 'l-rawḍa.* Edited by `Ali Akbar al-Ghaffārī. Dār al-kutub al-islāmiyya. Tehran, 1391/1973.

———. *Kitāb al-uṣūl min al-kāfī.* Edited by Sayyid Jawād Mustafawī. Tehran: al-Maktabah al-`Ilmīyya, Haydurt Press, n.d.

Liber Pontificalis. English translation by Raymond Davis in *The Book of Pontiffs: the Ancient Biographies of the First Ninety Roman Bishops to AD 710.* Liverpool: Liverpool University Press, 1989.

al-Majlisī, Muḥammad Bāqir. *Biḥār al-anwār.* Tehran-Qum, 1376–92/1956–72.

McNamara, Jo Ann, and John E. Halborg, with E. Gordon Whatley. *Sainted Women of the Dark Ages.* Durham, N.C.: Duke University Press, 1992.

al-Mufīd, Shaykh. *Kitāb al-Irshād: The Book of Guidance into the Lives of the Twelve Imams.* Translated by I. K. A. Howard. New York: Tahrike Tarsile Qur'an, 1981.

Odes of Solomon. Edited and translated by James Charlesworth. Missoula, Mont.: Scholars Press, 1977.

Origen. *In Numeros Homilia. PG* 12.

Protevangelium of James. English translation in *New Testament Apocrypha*, edited and translated by E. Hennecke and W. Schneemelcher. Philadelphia: Westminster Press, 1965.

al-Qummī. *Kāmil al-zīyārāt.* Edited by Mirzā `Abdallāh al-Husayn al-Amīnī al-Tabrīzī. Najaf: Mutadawīyyah, 1356/1937.

Sulpicius Severus. *Vita S. Martini.* Latin text with French translation by Jacques Fontaine. *SC* 133. English translation by F. R. Hoare, "The Life of Saint Martin of Tours." In *Soldiers of Christ: Saints and Saints' Lives from Late Antiquity and the Early Middle Ages*, edited by Thomas F. X. Noble and Thomas Head. University Park: Pennsylvania State University Press, 1995.

al-Tirmidhī, al-Hakīm. *The Concept of Sainthood in Early Islamic Mysticism: Two Works by al-Hakīm al-Tirmidhī.* Translated by Bernd Radtke and John O'Kane. Concord: Paul & Co., 1996.

al-Ṭūsī. *Tahdhīb al-aḥkām.* Edited by al-Kharsān. Najaf, 1375–76/1958–62.

———. *Kitāb al-Istibṣār.* Edited by al-Kharsān. Najaf, 1375–76/1955–56.

Vita Columbani abbatis discipulorumque eius libri duo auctore Iona. MGH SRM 4.61–108.

Vita S. Balthildis. MGH SRM 2.482–508.

Vita S. Chrothildis reginae francorum. MGH SRM 2.341–48.

Vita S. Eustadiolae viduae. AS (June): 131–33.

Vita S. Eugenia. PL 73.602–24.

Vita S. Genovefae. MGH SRM 3.204–38.

Vita S. Glodesindae. AS (July): 25.198–224.

Vita S. Mariae Aegyptiacae, Meretricis. PL 73.665–90. English translation by Benedicta Ward, *Harlots of the Desert: A Study of Repentance in Early Monastic Sources.* Cistercian Studies, 106. Kalamazoo, Mich.: Cistercian Publications, 1987.

Vita S. Rusticulae. MGH SRM 4.337–51.

Vita Wilfridi. MGH SRM 6.193–263.

Secondary Sources

Abbott, Nabia. *Arabic Literature to the End of the Umayyad Period.* Cambridge History of Arabic Literature. Cambridge: Cambridge University Press, 1983.

———. *Studies in Arabic Literary Papyri.* Vol. 2. Oriental Institute Publications, no. 276. Chicago: University of Chicago Press, 1967.

ʿAbd al-Rāziq, Ahmad. "Trois fondations féminines dans l'Egypte mamlouke." *Revue des Études Islamiques* 41 (1973): 96.

Abu-Lughod, Lila. "Islam and the Gendered Discourses of Death." *IJMES* 25 (1993): 187–205.

———. *Remaking Women: Feminism and Modernity in the Middle East.* Princeton: Princeton University Press, 1998.

Abu-Zahra, Nadia. "The Comparative Study of Muslim Societies and Islamic Rituals." *Arab Historical Review for Ottoman Studies* 3–4 (1991): 7–38.

Ahmed, Leila. *Women and Gender in Islam: Historical Roots of a Modern Debate.* New Haven: Yale University Press, 1992.

Aigrain, René. *L'Hagiographie: Ses sources, ses méthodes, son histoire.* Paris: Bloud et Gay, 1953.

Allen, Terry. "Aniconism and Figural Representation in Islamic Art." In *Five Essays on Islamic Art.* Manchester, Mich.: Solipsist Press, 1988.

Althoff, Gerd. *Family, Friends and Followers: Political and Social Bonds in Early Medieval Europe.* Translated by Christopher Carroll. Cambridge: Cambridge University Press, 2004.

Amir-Moezzi, Mohammad Ali. *The Divine Guide in Early Shī'ism: The Sources of Esotericism in Islam.* Translated by David Streight. New York: State University of New York Press, 1994.

Anderson, Gary. "Celibacy or Consummation in the Garden? Reflections on Early Jewish and Christian Interpretations of the Garden of Eden." *Harvard Theological Review* 82.2 (1989): 121–48.

Atiyeh, George, ed. *The Book in the Islamic World: The Written Word and Communication in the Middle East.* Albany: State University of New York Press, 1995.

Ayoub, Mahmoud. *Redemptive Suffering in Islam: A Study of the Devotional Aspects of `Ashurā in Twelver Shī'ism.* The Hague: Mouton, 1978.

Azami, Mustafa. *On Schacht's Origins of Muhammad Jurisprudence.* Riyadh: King Saud University, 1985.

———. *Studies in Early Hadith Literature, with a Critical Edition of Some Early Texts.* Beirut: al-Maktab al-Islamī, 1968.

al-Azmeh, Aziz. "Rhetoric for the Senses: A Consideration of Muslim Paradise Narratives." *Journal of Arabic Literature* 26 (1995): 215–31.

Bachinger, Richard, and Helga Exler. *Die Hand: Schutz und Schmuck in Nordafrika: Katalog zur Ausstellung der Galerie Exler & Co., vom. 1–30.* Frankfurt am Main: Die Galerie, 1981.

Bagatti, B., M. Piccirillo, and A. Prodomo. *New Discoveries at the Tomb of Virgin Mary in Gethsemane.* Studium Biblicum Franciscanum, Collectio Minor, 17. Jerusalem: Franciscan Printing Press, 1975.

Baird, Robert D. *Category Formation and the History of Religions.* The Hague: Mouton, 1971.

Barber, Charles. "The Truth in Painting: Iconoclasm and Identity in Early-Medieval Art." *Speculum* 72.4 (1997): 1019–36.

Barlas, Asma. *"Believing Women" in Islam: Unreading Patriarchal Interpretations of the Qur'an.* Austin: University of Texas Press, 2002.

Batstone, Louise P. M. "Doctrinal and Theological Themes in the Prayers of the Bobbio Missal." In *The Bobbio Missal: Liturgy and Religious Culture in Merovingian Gaul,* edited by Yitzhak Hen and Rob Meens. Cambridge: Cambridge University Press, 2004.

Bell, Rudolph. *Holy Anorexia.* Chicago: University of Chicago Press, 1985.

Berkey, Jonathan. *The Transmission of Knowledge in Medieval Cairo: A Social History of Islamic Education.* Princeton: Princeton University Press, 1991.

Blair, Sheila S., and Jonathan B. Bloom, eds. *Images of Paradise in Islamic Art.* Hanover, N.H.: Hood Museum of Art, Dartmouth College, 1991.

Boddy, Janice. "Womb as Oasis: The Symbolic Context of Pharaonic Circumcision in Rural Northern Sudan." *American Ethnologist* 9 (1982): 682–98.

Boudhiba, Abdelwahab. *Sexuality in Islam.* Translated by Alan Sheridan. Boston: Routledge & Kegan Paul, 1985.

Boyarin, Daniel. "On the History of the Early Phallus." In *Gender and Difference in the Middle Ages,* edited by Sharon Farmer and Carol Braun Pasternack. Medieval Cultures 32. Minneapolis: University of Minnesota Press, 2003.

Brakke, David. *Athanasius and the Politics of Asceticism.* Oxford: Clarendon Press, 1995.

———. "The Problematization of Nocturnal Emissions in Early Christian Syria, Egypt, and Gaul." *Journal of Early Christian Studies* 3.4 (1995): 419–60.

Branham, Joan. "Sacred Space under Erasure in Ancient Synagogues and Early Churches." *Art Bulletin* 74 (1992): 375–94.

Bray, Julia. "Men, Women and Slaves in `Abbasid Society." In *Gender in the Early Medieval World, East and West, 300–900,* edited by Leslie Brubaker and Julia M. H. Smith. Cambridge: Cambridge University Press, 2004.

Brown, Peter. *The Body and Society: Men, Women and Sexual Renunciation in Early Christianity.* New York: Columbia University Press, 1988.

———. *Cult of the Saints: Its Rise and Function in Latin Christianity.* Chicago: University of Chicago Press, 1981.

Brubaker, Leslie. "Icons before Iconoclasm?" In *Morfologie sociali e culturali Europa fra tarda antichità e alto Medioevo.* Spoleto: Centro italiano di studi sull'alto Medioevo, 1988.

Buckley, Thomas, and Alma Gottlieb, eds. *Blood Magic: The Anthropology of Menstruation.* Berkeley: University of California Press, 1988.

Burrus, Virginia. "Word and Flesh: the Bodies and Sexuality of Ascetic Women in Christian Antiquity." *Journal of Feminist Studies in Religion* 10 (1994): 27–51.

Butler, Judith. *Gender Trouble: Feminism and the Subversion of Identity.* New York: Routledge, 1990.

Bynum, Caroline Walker. *Holy Feast and Holy Fast: The Religious Significance of Food to Medieval Women.* Berkeley: University of California Press, 1987.

———. *Jesus as Mother.* Berkeley: University of California Press, 1982.

———. *The Resurrection of the Body in Western Christianity, 200–1336.* New York: Columbia University Press, 1995.

Bynum, Carolyn Walker, Stevan Harrel, and Paula Richman, eds. *Gender and Religion: On the Complexity of Symbols.* Boston: Beacon Press, 1986.

Cameron, Averil. *Christianity and the Rhetoric of Empire: The Development of a Christian Discourse.* Berkeley: University of California Press, 1991.

———. "The Language of Images: The Rise of Icons and Christian Representation." In *The Church and the Arts*, vol. 28, edited by Diana Wood. Oxford: Blackwell Publishers, 1992.

———. "Virginity as Metaphor: Women and the Rhetoric of Early Christianity," In *History as Text: The Writing of Ancient History*, edited by Averil Cameron. London: Duckworth, 1988.

Carroll, Michael. *The Cult of the Virgin Mary: Psychological Origins*. Princeton: Princeton University Press, 1986.

Castelli, Elizabeth. "'I will make Mary male': Pieties of the Body and Gender Transformation of Christian Women in Late Antiquity." In *Body Guards: The Cultural Politics of Gender Ambiguity*, edited by Julia Epstein and Kristina Straub. New York: Routledge: 1991.

Champault, Dominique, and A. R. Verbrugge. *Le Main: Ses figurations au Maghreb et au Levant*. Paris: Musée de l'Homme, 1965.

Chishti, Saadia Khawar Khan. "Female Spirituality in Islam." In *Islamic Spirituality*, edited by Seyyed Hossein Nasr. World Spirituality: An Encyclopedic History of the Religious Quest, 17. New York: Crossroad, 1997.

Claman, Henry N. *Jewish Images in the Christian Church: Art as the Mirror of the Jewish-Christian Conflict, 200–1250 CE*. Macon, Ga.: Mercer University Press, 2000.

Clanton, Mary. *Apocryphal Gospels of Mary in Anglo-Saxon England*. New York: Cambridge University Press, 1998.

———. *The Cult of the Virgin Mary in Anglo-Saxon England*. New York: Cambridge University Press, 1990.

Clark, Gillian. *Early Church as Patrons: Christianity and Roman Society*. Cambridge: Cambridge University Press, 2004.

———. *Women in Late Antiquity*. Oxford: Oxford University Press, 1993.

Clevenot, Dominique. *Splendors of Islam: Architecture, Decoration, and Design*. New York: St. Martin's Press, 2000.

Cloke, Gillian. *Female Man of God: Women and Spiritual Power in the Patristic Age, 350–450*. London: Routledge, 1995.

Cooke, Miriam. *Women Claim Islam: Creating Islamic Feminism through Literature*. New York: Routledge, 2001.

Coon, Lynda L. *Sacred Fictions: Holy Women and Hagiography in Late Antiquity*. Philadelphia: University of Pennsylvania Press, 1997.

———. "'What is the Word if not Semen?' Priestly Bodies in Carolingian Exegesis." In *Gender in the Early Medieval World, East and West, 300–900*, edited by Leslie Brubaker and Julia M. H. Smith. Cambridge: Cambridge University Press, 2004.

Cooper, Kate. *The Virgin and the Bride: Idealized Womanhood in Late Antiquity*. Cambridge, Mass.: Harvard University Press, 1996.

Cornell, Vincent J. *Realm of the Saint: Power and Authority in Moroccan Sufism.* Austin: University of Texas Press, 1998.

Crone, Patricia. "On the Meaning of the ʿAbbasid Call to *al-Riḍā*." In *Islamic World from Classical to Modern Times*, edited by C. E. Bosworth, Charles Issaw, Roger Savory, and A. L. Udovitch. Princeton: The Darwin Press, 1989.

Crook, John. *The Architectural Setting of the Cult of the Saints in the Early Christian West, c. 300–1200.* New York: Oxford University Press, 2000.

Curran, Charles E., Margaret A. Farley, and Richard A. McCormick. *Feminist Ethics and the Catholic Moral Traditions.* New York: Paulist Press, 1996.

Daftary, Farhad. "Sayyida Hurra: The Ismāʿīlī Ṣulayḥid Queen of Yemen." In *Women in the Medieval Islamic World*, edited by Gavin R. G. Hambly. New York: St. Martin's Press, 1998.

———, ed. *Medieval Ismaʿili History and Thought.* New York: Cambridge University Press, 1996.

Darrow, William R. "Women's Place and the Place of Women in the Iranian Revolution." In *Women, Religion, and Social Change*, edited by Yvonne Haddad and Ellison Banks Findly. New York: State University of New York Press, 1985.

Davies, Wendy, and Paul Fouracre, eds. *Property and Power in the Early Middle Ages.* Cambridge: Cambridge University Press, 1995.

Davis-Weyer, Caecilia. *Early Medieval Art, 300–1150: Sources and Documents.* Atlantic Highlands, N.J.: Prentice Hall, 1971.

Delehaye, Hippolyte. *The Legends of the Saints.* Translated by Donald Attwater. New York: Fordham University Press, 1962.

Delehaye, Pierre. *Les légendes hagiographiques.* Brussels: Société des Bollandistes, 1955.

Donald, Moira, and Linda Hurcombe, eds. *Gender and Material Culture in Historical Perspective.* New York: St. Martin's Press, 1999.

Douglas, Mary. *Leviticus as Literature.* Oxford: Oxford University Press, 1999.

———. *Purity and Danger: An Analysis of Concepts of Pollution and Taboo.* London: Routledge & Kegan Paul, 1966.

Drijvers, Jan Willem. *Helena Augusta: The Mother of Constantine the Great and the Legend of Her Finding of the True Cross.* Leiden: E. J. Brill, 1992.

Dunn, E. Catherine. *The Gallican Saint's Life and the Late Roman Dramatic Tradition.* Washington, D.C.: Catholic University Press, 1989.

Dunn, Marilyn. *The Emergence of Monasticism: From the Desert Fathers to the Early Middle Ages.* Oxford: Blackwell, 2000.

Ehrenfels, Umar R. "Weibliche elemente in der symbolik des Islam." In *Zeitschrift für Missionswissenschaft und Religionswissenschaft.* Meunster in Westfalen, 1950.

El-Aswad, El-Sayed. "Death Rituals in Rural Egyptian Society: A Symbolic Study." *Urban Anthropology and Studies of Cultural Systems and World Economic Development* 16 (1987): 205–41.

El Cheikh, Nadia Maria. "Gender and Politics in the Harem of al-Muqtadir." In *Gender in the Early Medieval World, East and West, 300–900*, edited by Leslie Brubaker and Julia M. H. Smith. Cambridge: Cambridge University Press, 2004.

Elliott, Dyan. *Spiritual Marriage: Sexual Abstinence in Medieval Wedlock.* Princeton: Princeton University Press, 1993.

Elsner, Jas. *Imperial Rome and Christian Triumph: The Art of the Roman Empire, AD 100–450.* Oxford: Oxford University Press, 1998.

Erler, Mary, and Maryanne Kowaleski, eds. *Women and Power in the Middle Ages.* Athens: University of Georgia Press, 1983.

Fletcher, Eric. "The Influence of Merovingian Gaul on Northumbria in the Seventh Century." *Medieval Archaeology* 24 (1980): 69–86.

Fodor, Sandor. *Amulets from the Islamic World: Catalogue of the Exhibition Held in Budapest in 1988.* Budapest: Eotvos Lorand University, 1988.

Foskett, Mary. *A Virgin Conceived: Mary and Classical Representations of Virginity.* Bloomington: Indiana University Press, 2002.

Fouracre, Paul. "Eternal Light and Earthly Needs: Practical Aspects of the Development of Frankish Immunities." In *Property and Power in the Early Middle Ages*, edited by Wendy Davies and Paul Fouracre. Cambridge: Cambridge University Press, 1995.

Fouracre, Paul, and Richard A. Gerberding, eds. *Late Merovingian France: History and Hagiography, 640–720.* Manchester: Manchester University Press, 1996.

de Gaiffier, Baudoin. *Recherches d'hagiographie Latine.* Subsidia Hagiographica 52. Brussels: Société des Bollandistes, 1971.

———. *Recueil d'hagiographie.* Subsidia Hagiographica 61. Brussels: Société des Bollandistes, 1977.

Gambero, Luigi. *Mary and the Fathers of the Church: The Blessed Virgin Mary in Patristic Thought.* Translated by Thomas Buffer. San Francisco: Ignatius Press, 1999.

Geary, Patrick. *Before France and Germany: The Creation and Transformation of the Merovingian World.* Oxford: Oxford University Press, 1988.

———. *Living with the Dead.* Ithaca: Cornell University Press, 1994.

Geertz, Clifford. *The Interpretation of Cultures.* New York: Basic Books, 1973.

George, Judith. *Venantius Fortunatus: Personal and Political Poems.* Translated Texts for Historians, 23. Liverpool: Liverpool University Press, 1995.

Ghulam, Yousif Mahmud. *The Art of Arabic Calligraphy.* Lafayette, Calif.: Y. M. Ghulam, 1982.

Gilchrist, Roberta. *Gender and Material Culture: The Archaeology of Female Monastic Houses*. London: Routledge, 1994.

Goetz, H. W., ed. *Weibliche Lebensgestaltung im Frühen Mittelalter*. Cologne: Böhlau, 1991.

Gold, Penny Schine. *The Lady and the Virgin: Image, Attitude and Experience in Twelfth-Century France*. Chicago: University of Chicago Press, 1987.

Goldziher, Ignaz. *Introduction to Islamic Theology and Law*. Translated by Andras Hamori and Ruth Hamori. Princeton: Princeton University Press, 1981.

Gole, Nilufer. *The Forbidden Modern: Civilization and Veiling*. Ann Arbor: University of Michigan Press, 1996.

Goodison, Ludy, and Christine Morris, eds. *Ancient Goddess: The Myths and the Evidence*. Madison: University of Wisconsin Press, 1998.

Grabar, André, and Carl Nordenfalk. "Early Medieval Painting, from the Fourth to the Eleventh Century." In *The Great Centuries of Painting*. New York: Skira, 1957.

Grabar, Oleg. *The Formation of Islamic Art*. New Haven: Yale University Press, 1987.

Graef, H. *Mary: A History of Doctrine and Devotion*. Vol. 1, *From the Beginnings to the Eve of the Reformation*. New York: Sheed and Ward, 1963.

Greer, Rowan. *Broken Lights and Mended Lives: Theology and Common Life in the Early Church*. University Park: Pennsylvania State University Press, 1986.

Haeri, Shahla. *Law of Desire: Temporary Marriage in Shi`i Iran*. New York: Syracuse University Press, 1989.

Hale, Sondra. "Women's Culture/Men's Culture: Gender, Separation, and Space in Africa and North America." *American Behavioral Scientist* 31 (1987): 115–34.

Hahn, Cynthia. "Seeing and Believing: The Construction of Sanctity in Early-Medieval Saints' Shrines." *Speculum* 72.4 (1997): 1079–1106.

Hamington, Maurice. *Hail Mary? The Struggle for Ultimate Womanhood in Catholicism*. New York: Routledge, 1995.

Heath, R. G. "Western Schism of the Franks and the Filioque." *Journal of Ecclesiastical History* 23 (April 1972): 97–113.

Heffernan, Thomas. *Sacred Biography: Saints and Their Biographers in the Middle Ages*. Oxford: Oxford University Press, 1988.

Heinzelmann, Martin. *Gregory of Tours: History and Society in the Sixth Century*. Translated by Christopher Carroll. Cambridge: Cambridge University Press, 2001.

Hen, Yitzhak. *Culture and Religion in Merovingian Gaul, A.D. 481–751*. Leiden: E. J. Brill, 1995.

————. "Gender and Patronage of Culture in Merovingian Gaul." In *Gender in the Early Medieval World, East and West, 300–900*, edited by Leslie Brubaker and Julia M. H. Smith. Cambridge: Cambridge University Press, 2004.

————. "The Liturgy of the Bobbio Missal." In *The Bobbio Missal: Liturgy and Religious Culture in Merovingian Gaul*, edited by Yitzhak Hen and Rob Meens. Cambridge: Cambridge University Press, 2004.

Henne, Katrien. "Audire, legere, vulgo: An Attempt to Define Public Use and Comprehensibility of Carolingian Hagiography." In *Latin and the Romance Language in the Early Middle Ages*, edited by Roger Wright. New York: Routledge, 1991.

————. "Merovingian and Carolingian Hagiography: Continuity or Change in Public and Aims?" *Analecta Bollandiana* 107 (1989): 415–28.

Hermansen, Marcia. "Fatimeh as a Role Model in the Works of Ali Shari'ati." In *Women and Revolution in Iran*, edited by Guity Nashat. Boulder, Colo.: Westview Press, 1983.

al-Hibri, Azizah, ed. *Women and Islam*. New York: Pergamon Press, 1982.

Hillenbrand, Robert. *Islamic Architecture: Form, Function, and Meaning*. New York: Columbia University Press, 1994.

————. *Islamic Art and Architecture*. London: Thames and Hudson, 1999.

Hirn, Yrjö. *The Sacred Shrine: A Study of the Poetry and Art of the Catholic Church*. Translated from the Swedish edition of 1909, 2d English ed. Boston, 1957.

Hochstetler, Donald. *A Conflict of Traditions: Women in Religion in the Early Middle Ages, 500–840*. Lanham, Md.: University Press of America, 1992.

Hoffman-Ladd, Valerie J. "Devotion to the Prophet and His Family in Egyptian Sufism." *IJMES* 24 (1992): 615–37.

Irwin, Robert. *Islamic Art in Context: Art, Architecture and the Literary World*. New York: Harry N. Abrams, 1997.

Issa, Muhammad. *Painting in Islam: Between Prohibition and Aversion*. Istanbul: Waqf for Research on Islamic History, Art, and Culture, 1996.

Jacobsen, Werner. "Saints' Tombs in Frankish Church Architecture." *Speculum* 74.4 (1997): 1107–43.

Janes, Dominic. *God and Gold in Late Antiquity*. Cambridge: Cambridge University Press, 1998.

Jarrar, Maher. "*Sirāt ahl al-Kisā'*: Early Shi'i Sources on the Biography of the Prophet." In *The Biography of Muhammad: The Issue of the Sources*, edited by Harald Motzki. Leiden: E. J. Brill, 2000.

Jensen, Robin Margaret. *Understanding Early Christian Art*. New York: Routledge, 2000.

Joynboll, G. H. A. *Studies on the Origins and Uses of Islamic Hadith*. Brookfield, Vt.: Variorum, 1996.

Jussen, Bernhard. *Spiritual Kinship as Social Practice: Godparenthood and Adoption in the Early Middle Ages.* Newark: University of Delaware Press, 2000.

Kabbāni, Hishām, and Laleh Bakhtiar. *Encyclopedia of Muhammad's Women Companions and the Traditions They Related.* Chicago: ABC International Group. Distributed by Kazi Publications, 1998.

Katz, Melissa R., Robert Orsi, and Davis Museum and Cultural Center. *Divine Mirrors: The Virgin Mary in Visual Arts.* Oxford: Oxford University Press, 2001.

Katz, Solomon. *The Jews in the Visigothic and Frankish Kingdoms of Spain and Gaul.* Cambridge, Mass.: Mediaeval Academy of America, 1937.

Khoury, Nuha N. N. "The *Mihrab* Image: Commemorative Themes in Medieval Islamic Architecture." *Muqarnas,* no. 9 (1992): 11–28.

Kieckhefer, Richard, and George D. Bond, eds. *Sainthood: Its Manifestations in World Religions.* Berkeley: University of California Press, 1988.

Kister, M. J. "Legends in *tafsir* and *hadith* Literature: The Creation of Adam and Related Stories." In *Approaches to the History of the Interpretation of the Qur'an,* edited by Andrew Rippin. New York: Oxford University Press, 1988.

———. *Studies in Jāhiliyya and Early Islam.* London: Variorum Reprints, 1980.

Kitchens, John. *Saints' Lives and the Rhetoric of Gender: Male and Female in Merovingian Hagiography.* New York: Oxford University Press, 1998.

Klingshirn, William E. *Caesarius of Arles: The Making of a Christian Community in Late Antique Gaul.* Cambridge: Cambridge University Press, 1994.

Knappert, Jan. *Islamic Legends: Histories of the Heroes, Saints, and Prophets of Islam.* Leiden: E. J. Brill, 1985.

Knieps, Claudia. *Geschichte der Verschleierung der Frau im Islam.* Wurzburg: Ergon, 1993.

Kohlberg, Etan. "Some Imāmī Shī'ī Views on the ṢAḤĀBA." *Jerusalem Studies in Arabic and Islam* 5 (1984): 143–75.

Kovachevski, Christo. *The Madonna in Western Painting.* London: Cromwell Editions, 1991.

Kraemer, Joel. *Humanism in the Renaissance of Islam: The Cultural Revival during the Buyid Age.* Leiden: E. J. Brill, 1986.

Kraemer, Ross S. *Maenads, Martyrs, Matrons, Monastics: A Sourcebook on Women's Religions in the Greco-Roman World.* Philadelphia: Fortress Press, 1988.

Krautheimer, Richard. "Carolingian Revival of Early Christian Architecture." In *Studies in Early Christian, Medieval, and Renaissance Art.* New York: New York University Press, 1969.

Kriss, Rudolf, and Hubert Kriss-Heinrich. *Volksglaube im Bereich des Islam, Bd. 2. Amulette, Zauberformein, und Beschwoerungen.* Wiesbaden: O. Harrassowitz, 1962.

Lalani, Arzina R. *Early Shīʿī Thought: The Teachings of Imām Muḥammad al-Bāqir*. London: I. B. Tauris, 2000.

Lammens, Henri. *Fatima et les filles de mahomet*. Sumptibus Pontifici Instituti Biblici. Rome, 1912.

Lane, Barbara G. *The Altar and the Altarpiece: Sacramental Themes in Early Netherlandish Painting*. New York: Harper & Row, 1984.

Laqueur, Thomas. *Making Sex: Body and Gender from the Greeks to Freud*. Cambridge, Mass.: Harvard University Press, 1990.

Lefebvre, Henri. *The Production of Space*. Translated by Donald Nicholson-Smith. Oxford: Blackwell, 1991.

Lifshitz, Felice. "Beyond Positivism and Genre: 'Hagiographical' Texts as Historical Narrative." *Viator* 25 (1994): 94–113.

Limberis, Vasiliki. *Divine Heiress: The Virgin Mary and the Creation of Christian Constantinople*. New York: Routledge, 1994.

Limor, Ora, and Guy G. Stroumsa, eds. *Contra Iudaeos: Ancient and Medieval Polemics between Christians and Jews*. Tübingen: J. C. B. Mohr [Paul Siebeck], 1996.

Loerke, William. "'Real Presence' in Early Christian Art." In *Monasticism and the Arts*, edited by Timothy Verdon. Syracuse: Syracuse University Press, 1984.

Loomis, C. G. *White Magic: An Introduction to the Folklore of Christian Legends*. Cambridge, Mass.: Mediaeval Academy of America, 1948.

Lowden, John. *Early Christian and Byzantine Art*. London: Phaidon Press, 1997.

Macleod, Arlene Elowe. *Accommodating Protest: Working Women, the New Veiling, and Change in Cairo*. New York: Columbia University Press, 1991.

Maddison, Francis Romeril. *Science, Tools, and Magic*. London: Nour Foundation, 1997.

Madelung, Wilfred. *Der Islam al-Qasim ibn Ibrahim und die Glaubenslehre der Zaiditen*. Berlin: de Gruyter, 1965.

———. "The Hāshimiyyāt of al-Kumayt and Hāshimī Shiʿism." *Studia Islamica* 70 (1989): 5–26.

Markoff, Irene. "Music, Saints, and Ritual: Samaʿ and the Alevis of Turkey." In *Manifestations of Sainthood in Islam*, edited by Grace Smith and Carl W. Ernst. Istanbul: Isis Press, 1993.

Markus, R. A. *The End of Ancient Christianity*. Cambridge: Cambridge University Press, 1982.

Massignon, Louis. "Der Gnostische Kult der Fāṭima im Shiitischen Islam," "La mubāhala de Médine et l'hyperdulie de Fāṭima," "La notion du voeu et la dévotion musulmane à Fatima," "L'oratoire de Marie à l'aqca vu sous le voile de deuil de Fatima." In *Opera Minora*, vol. 1, edited by Y. Moubarac. Beirut: Dār al-Maʿārif, 1963.

————. *La Mubāhala de Medine et L'Hyperdulie de Fāṭima*. Paris: Librairie Orientale et Americaine, 1955.

Mathisen, Ralph W. "Barbarian Bishops and the Churches *'in barbaricis gentibus'* during Late Antiquity." *Speculum* 72.3 (1997): 664–97.

Matthews, Thomas. *The Clash of the Gods: A Reinterpretation of Early Christian Art*. Princeton: Princeton University Press, 1993.

McAuliffe, Jane Dammen. "Chosen of All Women: Mary and Fatima in Qur'anic Exegesis." *Islamochristiana* 7 (1981): 19–28.

McCarthy, Maria Caritas. *The Rule for Nuns of Caesarius of Arles*. Washington, D.C.: Catholic University Press, 1960.

McKitterick, Rosamond, ed. *Carolingian Culture: Emulation and Innovation*. Cambridge: Cambridge University Press, 1994.

————. "Frauen und Schriftlichkeit im Frühmittelalter." In *Weibliche Lebensgestaltung im Frühen Mittelalter*, edited by H. W. Goetz. Cologne: Böhlau, 1991.

McLaughlin, Megan. *Consorting with Saints: Prayer for the Dead in Early Medieval France*. Ithaca: Cornell University Press, 1994.

McNamara, Jo Ann. "Living Sermons: Consecrated Women and the Conversion of Gaul." In *Medieval Religious Women*. Vol. 2, *Peaceweavers*, edited by John A. Nichols and Lillian Thomas Shank. Kalamazoo, Mich.: Cistercian Publications, 1987.

————. "Muffled Voices: The Lives of Consecrated Women in the Fourth Century." In *Medieval Religious Women*. Vol. 1. *Distant Echoes*, edited by John A. Nichols and Lillian Thomas Shank. Kalamazoo, Mich.: Cistercian Publications, 1984.

————. "The Need to Give: Suffering and Female Sanctity in the Middle Ages." In *Images of Sainthood in Medieval Europe*, edited by Renate Blumenfield-Kosinski and Timea Szell. Ithaca: Cornell University Press, 1991.

McNamara, Jo Ann, and John Halborg, trans. *The Ordeal of Community*. Toronto: Peregrina, 1993.

McNamara, Jo Ann, and Suzanne Wemple. "The Power of Women through the Family in Medieval Europe, 500–1100." In *Women and Power in the Middle Ages*, edited by Mary Erler and Maryanne Kowaleski. Athens: University of Georgia Press, 1983.

Melikian-Chirvani, Assadullah Souren. "The Light of Heaven and Earth: From the Chahār-tāq to the Miḥrāb." *Bulletin of the Asia Institute* 4 (1990): 95–131.

Memarian, Gholamhossein, and Frank Edward Brown. "Climate, Culture, and Religion: Aspects of the Traditional Courtyard House in Iran." *Journal of Architectural and Planning Research* 20.3 (2003): 181–98.

Meri, Josef W. "The Etiquette of Devotion in the Islamic Cult of Saints." In *The Cult of Saints in Late Antiquity and the Middle Ages*, edited by James

Howard-Johnston and Paul Antony Hayward. Oxford: Oxford University Press, 1999.

Mernissi, Fatima. *Beyond the Veil: Male-Female Dynamics in Modern Muslim Society*. Bloomington: Indiana University Press, 1987.

———. *The Forgotten Queens of Islam*. Translated by M. J. Lakeland. Cambridge: Polity Press, 1993.

———. *The Veil and the Male Elite: A Feminist Interpretation of Women's Rights in Islam*. Translated by Mary Jo Lakeland. Reading, Mass.: Addison-Wesley, 1991.

———. *Women's Rebellion and Islamic Memory*. Atlantic Highlands, N.J.: Zed Books, 1996.

Miles, Margaret R. "Santa Maria Maggiore's Fifth-Century Mosaics: Triumphal Christianity and the Jews." *Harvard Theological Review* 86.2 (1993): 155–75.

Momen, Moojan. *An Introduction to Shi`i Islam: The History and Doctrines of Twelver Shi`ism*. New Haven: Yale University Press, 1985.

Moreira, Isabel. *Dreams, Visions, and Spiritual Authority in Merovingian Gaul*. Ithaca: Cornell University Press, 2000.

Mottahedeh, Roy. *Loyalty and Leadership in an Early Islamic Society*. Princeton: Princeton University Press, 1980.

Motzki, Harald, ed. *The Biography of Muhammad: The Issue of the Sources*. Leiden: E. J. Brill, 2000.

Murata, Sachiko. *The Tao of Islam: A Sourcebook on Gender Relationships in Islamic Thought*. Albany: State University of New York Press, 1992.

Nabhan-Warren, Kristy. *The Virgin of El Barrio: Marian Apparitions, Catholic Evangelizing, and Mexican American Activism*. New York: New York University Press, 2005.

Neff, Amy. "The Pain of *Compassio:* Mary's Labor at the Foot of the Cross." *Art Bulletin* 80.2 (1998): 254–73.

Nelson, Janet L. *The Frankish World, 750-900*. Rio Grande: Hambledon Press, 1996.

———. "Kingship and Empire in the Carolingian World." In *Carolingian Culture: Emulation and Innovation*, edited by Rosamond McKitterick. Cambridge: Cambridge University Press, 1994.

———. "Queens as Jezebels: The Careers of Brunhild and Balthild in Merovingian History." In *Medieval Women*, edited by Derek Baker. Oxford: Basil Blackwell, 1978.

———. "The Wary Widow." In *Property and Power in the Early Middle Ages*, edited by Wendy Davies and Paul Fouracre. Cambridge: Cambridge University Press, 1995.

de Nie, Giselle. "Consciousness Fecund through God: From Male Fighter to Spiritual Bride-Mother in Late Antique Female Sanctity." In *Sanctity and*

Motherhood: Essays on Holy Mothers in the Middle Ages, edited by Anneke B. Mulder-Bakker. New York: Garland, 1995.

———. *Views from a Many-Windowed Tower: Studies of Imagination in the Works of Gregory of Tours.* Amsterdam: Rodopi, 1987.

Noble, Thomas F. X., and Thomas Head, eds. *Soldiers of Christ: Saints and Saints' Lives from Late Antiquity and the Early Middle Ages.* University Park: Pennsylvania State University Press, 1995.

Nordhagen, Per Jonas. "Constantinople on the Tiber: The Byzantines in Rome and the Iconography of Their Images." In *Early Medieval Rome and the Christian West, Essays in Honour of Donald A. Bullough*, edited by Julia Smith. Leiden: E. J. Brill, 2000.

O'Dwyer, Peter. *Mary: A History of Devotion in Ireland.* Dublin: Four Courts Press, 1988.

Osborn, Eric. *The Emergence of Christian Theology.* Cambridge: Cambridge University Press, 1993.

Padel, Ruth. "Women: Model for Possession by Greek Daemons." In *Images of Women in Antiquity*, edited by Averil Cameron and Amelie Kuhrt. Detroit: Wayne State University Press, 1983.

Pagels, Elaine. *Adam, Eve, and the Serpent.* New York: Vintage Books, 1988.

Pavlides, Merope. "The Cult of Mary Compared with Ancient Mother Goddesses." In *Gender, Culture, and the Arts: Women, the Arts and Society*, edited by Ronald Dotterer and Susan Bowers. Selinsgrove, Pa.: Susquehanna University Press, 1993.

Pelikan, Jaroslav. *Mary through the Centuries: Her Place in the History of Culture.* New Haven: Yale University Press, 1996.

Pelly, Colonel Sir Lewis. *The Miracle Play of Hasan and Husain.* London: Wm. H. Allen and Co., 1879.

Peterson, Joan. *The Dialogues of Gregory the Great in Their Late Antique Cultural Background.* Toronto: Pontifical Institute of Mediaeval Studies, 1984.

Pinault, David. *The Shi`ites: Ritual and Popular Piety in a Muslim Community.* New York: St. Martin's Press, 1992.

———. "Zaynab bint `Ali and the Place of Women in the Households of the First Imams in Shi`ite Devotional Literature." In *Women in the Medieval Islamic World*, edited by Gavin R. G. Hambly. New York: St. Martin's Press, 1998.

Pohl, Walter, and Helmut Reimitz, eds. *Strategies of Distinction: The Construction of Ethnic Communities, 300–800.* Leiden: E. J. Brill, 1998.

Ragib, Yusuf. "Al-Sayyida Nafīsa, sa légende, son culte et con cimetière." *Studia Islamica* 44 (1976): 61–86.

Réal, Isabelle. *Vies de saints, vie de famille: Représentation et système de la parenté dans le Royaume mérovingien (481–751) d'après les sources hagiographiques.* Brussels: Brepols, 2001.

Rippin, Andrew, ed. *Approaches to the History of the Interpretation of the Qur'an.* Studies in Late Antiquity and Islam 5. New York: Oxford University Press, 1988.

Rizvi, Kishwar. "Gendered Patronage: Women and Benevolence during the Early Safavid Empire." In *Women, Patronage, and Self-Representation in Islamic Societies,* edited by D. Fairchild Ruggles. New York: State University of New York Press, 2000.

Robbins, Vernon K. *Tapestry of Early Christian Discourse: Rhetoric, Society, and Ideology.* New York: Routledge, 1996.

Robinson, Chase. "Prophecy and Holy Men in Early Islam." In *The Cult of the Saints in Late Antiquity and the Middle Ages,* edited by James Howard-Johnston and Paul Antony Hayward. Oxford: Oxford University Press, 1999.

Rowson, Everett K. "The Effeminates of Early Medina." *Journal of the American Oriental Society* 111 (1991): 671–93.

———. "Gender Irregularity as Entertainment: Institutionalized Transvestism at the Caliphal Court in Medieval Baghdad." In *Gender and Difference in the Middle Ages,* edited by Sharon Farmer and Carol Braun Pasternack. Minneapolis: University of Minnesota Press, 2003.

Rubin, Uri. *The Eye of the Beholder: The Life of Muhammad as Viewed by the Early Muslims, a Textual Analysis.* Studies in Late Antiquity and Islam 5. Princeton: Darwin Press, 1995.

———. "Pre-existence and Light: Aspects of the Concept of Nur Muhammad." *Israel Oriental Studies* 5 (1975): 62–117.

Ruether, Rosemary Radford, and Eleanor McLaughlin, eds. *Women of Spirit: Female Leadership in the Jewish and Christian Traditions.* New York: Simon and Schuster, 1979.

Russell, James. *The Germanization of Early Medieval Christianity: A Sociohistorical Approach to Religious Transformation.* New York: Oxford University Press, 1994.

Safwat, Nabih F. *The Art of the Pen: Calligraphy of the 14th to 20th Centuries.* London: Nour Foundation, 1996.

Savory, Roger. *Iran under the Safavids.* Cambridge: Cambridge University Press, 1980.

Schacht, Joseph. *An Introduction to Islamic Law.* Oxford: Clarendon Press, 1964.

Schäfer, Peter. *Mirror of His Beauty: Feminine Images of God from the Bible to the Early Kabbalah.* Princeton: Princeton University Press, 2002.

Schienerl, Peter W. *Schmuck und Amulett in Antike und Islam.* Aachen: Alano, 1988.

Schimmel, Annemarie. *My Soul Is a Woman: The Feminine in Islam.* Translated by Susan H. Ray. New York: Continuum, 1997.

Schlesinger, W. Beiträge zur deutschen *Verfassungsgeschichte des Mittelalters.* Tübingen, 1963.

Schubel, Vernon James. *Religious Performance in Contemporary Islam: Shi`i Devotional Rituals in South Asia.* Columbia: University of South Carolina Press, 1993.

Schulenburg, Jane Tibbetts. *Forgetful of Their Sex: Female Sanctity and Society, ca. 500–1100.* Chicago: University of Chicago Press, 1998.

———. "Strict Active Enclosure and Its Effects on the Female Monastic Experience, ca. 500–1100." In *Medieval Religious Women.* Vol. 1, *Distant Echoes,* edited by John A. Nichols and Lillian Thomas Shank. Kalamazoo, Mich.: Cistercian Publications, 1984.

———. "Women's Monastic Communities, 500–1100: Patterns of Expansion and Decline." *Signs: Journal of Women in Culture and Society* 14.2 (1989): 261–92.

Schüssler Fiorenza, Elisabeth. *In Memory of Her: A Feminist Theological Reconstruction of Christian Origins.* New York: Crossroad, 1983.

Shani, Raya. *A Monumental Manifestation of the Shi`ite Faith in Late Twelfth-Century Iran: The Case of the Gunbad-i `Alawiyān, Hamadān.* Oxford: Oxford University Press, 1996.

Shari`ati, `Ali. *Fatima Is Fatima.* Tehran: Shari`ati Foundation, 1981.

———. *Shari`ati on Shari`ati and the Muslim Woman.* Chicago: Kazi Publications, 1996.

Sharon, Moshe. *"Ahl al-Bayt:* People of the House." *Jerusalem Studies in Arabic and Islam* 8 (1986): 169–84.

———. *Black Banners from the East: The Establishment of the `Abbasid State— Incubation of a Revolt.* Leiden: Magnes Press, 1983.

Shea, George W. *The Poems of Alcimus Ecdicius Avitus.* Medieval and Renaissance Texts and Studies 172. Tempe: Arizona State University Press, 1997.

Smith, Grace Martin, ed. *Manifestations of Sainthood in Islam.* Istanbul: Isis Press, 1993.

Smith, Jane, and Yvonne Haddad. "Eve: Islamic Image of Woman." In *Women and Islam,* edited by Azīzah al-Hibri. New York: Pergamon Press, 1982.

Smith, Jonathon Z. *Drudgery Divine: On the Comparison of Early Christianities and the Religions of Late Antiquity.* Chicago: University of Chicago Press, 1990.

Smith, Julia. "The Problem of Female Sanctity in Carolingian Europe, c. 780–920." *Past and Present* 146 (1995): 3–37.

Smith, Margaret. *Rabi`a the Mystic and Her Fellow Saints in Islam.* Cambridge: University Press, 1928.

Soucek, Priscilla. "The Temple after Solomon: The Role of Maryam bint Imran and Her Mihrab." *Jewish Art* 23–24 (1997–98): 34–41.

Soufi, Denise Louise. "The Image of Fatima in Classical Muslim Thought." Ph.D. dissertation, Princeton University, 1997.

Spain, Suzanne. "'The Promised Blessing': The Iconography of the Mosaics of S. Maria Maggiore." *Art Bulletin* 61 (1979): 518–40.

Speight, R. Marston. "The Function of Hadith as Commentary on the Qur'an, as Seen in the Six Authoritative Collections." In *Approaches to the History of the Interpretation of the Qur'an,* edited by Andrew Rippin. New York: Oxford University Press, 1988.

Spellberg, Denise. *Politics, Gender, and the Islamic Past: The Legacy of 'A'isha bint Abu Bakr.* New York: Columbia University Press, 1997.

Spretnak, Charlene. *Missing Mary: The Queen of Heaven and Her Re-Emergence in the Modern World.* London: Palgrave Macmillan, 2004.

Stern, Gertrude H. *Marriage in Early Islam.* London: Royal Asiatic Society, 1939.

Stewart, Devin J. "Popular Shi'ism in Medieval Egypt: Vestiges of Islamic Sectarian Polemics in Egyptian Arabic." *Studia Islamica* 84.2 (1996) 2: 35–66.

Stowasser, Barbara. "The Mothers of the Believers in the Hadith." *Muslim World* 82 (1992): 1–36.

———. *Women in the Qur'an, Traditions, and Interpretation.* New York: Oxford University Press, 1994.

Sullivan, Richard. "The Papacy and Missionary Activity in the Early Middle Ages." In *Christian Missionary Activity in the Early Middle Ages.* Variorum Collected Studies. Aldershot: Variorum, Ashgate, 1994.

Sumption, Jonathan. *Pilgrimage: An Image of Medieval Religion.* London: Faber and Faber, 1975.

Tabbaa, Yasser. *The Transformation of Islamic Art during the Sunni Revival.* Seattle: University of Washington Press, 2001.

Thacker, Alan. "In Search of Saints: The English Church and the Cult of Roman Apostles and Martyrs in the Seventh and Eighth Centuries." In *Early Medieval Rome and the Christian West: Essays in Honour of Donald A. Bullough,* edited by Julia Smith. Leiden: E. J. Brill, 2000.

Thacker, Alan, and Richard Sharpe, eds. *Local Saints and Local Churches in the Early Medieval West.* Oxford: Oxford University Press, 2002.

Tolbert, Mary Ann. "Social, Sociological, and Anthropological Methods." In *Searching the Scriptures: A Feminist Introduction,* edited by Elisabeth Schüssler Fiorenza. New York: Crossroad, 1993.

Traini, Renato. *Sources biographiques des Zaidites.* Paris: Centre National de la Recherche Scientifique, 1977.

Van Dam, Raymond. *Leadership and Community in Late Antique Gaul.* Berkeley: University of California Press, 1985.

———. *Saints and Their Miracles in Late Antique Gaul.* Princeton: Princeton University Press, 1993.

van Uytfanghe, M. "L'Hagiographie et son publique à l'époque mérovingienne." *Studia Patristica* 16 (1985): 54–62.

———. "Modèls bibliques dans l'hagiographie." In *Le Moyen Âge et la Bible*, ed. Pierre Riché and Guy Lobrichon. Paris: Éditions Beauchesne, 1984.

Walker, Paul. *Early Philosophical Shi`ism: The Isma`ili Neoplatonism of Abu Ya`qub al-Sijistānī.* New York: Cambridge University Press, 1993.

———. *Exploring and Islamic Empire: Fatimid History and Its Sources.* New York: I. B. Tauris, 2002.

Walker, P. W. L. *Holy City, Holy Places.* Oxford: Clarendon Press, 1990.

Wallace-Hadrill, J. M. *Barbarian West, A.D. 400–1000.* New York: Harper & Row, 1962.

———. *The Fourth Book of the Chronicle of Fredegar, with Its Continuations.* London: Nelson, 1960.

———. *The Frankish Church.* Oxford: Clarendon Press, 1983.

———. *The Long-Haired Kings.* New York: Barnes & Noble, 1962.

Walsh, William Thomas. *Our Lady of Fatima.* New York: Doubleday, 1954.

Ward, Benedicta. *The Desert Christian: Sayings of the Desert Fathers, the Alphabetical Collection.* New York: Macmillan, 1975.

———. *Harlots of the Desert: A Study of Repentance in Early Monastic Sources.* Cistercian Studies 106. Kalamazoo, Mich.: Cistercian Publications, 1987.

———. *Signs and Wonders: Saints, Miracles, and Prayers from the 4th Century to the 14th.* Hampshire, U.K.: Variorum, 1992.

Warner, Marina. *Alone of All Her Sex: The Myth and the Cult of the Virgin Mary.* New York: Vintage Books, 1983.

Webster, Leslie, and Michelle Brown, eds. *Transformation of the Roman World, A.D. 400–900.* Berkeley: University of California Press, 1997.

Weig, E. "Volkstum und Volksbewusstein in Frankenreich des 7. Jahrhunderts." *Caratteri del Secolo VII in Occidente* (Spoleto: Settimane di Studio del Centro italiano di studi sull) *Alto Medioevo* 5 (1958): 587–648.

Wemple, Suzanne. *Women in Frankish Society.* Philadelphia: University of Pennsylvania Press, 1981.

Williams, Caroline. "The Cult of the `Alid Saints in the Fatimid Monument of Cairo, Part 1: The Mosque of al-Aqmar." *Muqarnas* 1 (1985): 37–52.

Wilken, Robert L. *The Land Called Holy: Palestine in Christian Literature and Thought.* New Haven: Yale University Press, 1992.

Wilson, Stephen, ed. *Saints and Their Cults: Studies in Religious Sociology, Folklore and History.* New York: Columbia University Press, 1983.

Winston-Allen, Anne. *Stories of the Rose: The Making of the Rosary in the Middle Ages.* University Park: Pennsylvania State University Press, 1997.

Wogan-Browne, Jocelyn. "Saints' Lives and the Female Reader." *Forum for Modern Language Studies* 27 (1991): 314–32.

Wood, Charles T. "The Doctors' Dilemma: Sin, Salvation, and the Menstrual Cycle in Medieval Thought." *Speculum* 56.4 (1981): 710–27.

Wood, Ian. *The Merovingian Kingdoms, 450–751*. New York: Longman, 1994.

Wright, J. W., and Everett K. Rowson. *Homoeroticism in Classical Arabic Literature*. New York: Columbia University Press, 1997.

Mary F. Thurlkill

is assistant professor of religion at the University of Mississippi.